JEWS IN AMERICAN LIFE

(from 1492 to the Space Age)

OTHER BOOKS BY TINA LEVITAN

Baolam Hechadash (Short Stories from American Jewish History, in Hebrew)

The Laureates: Jewish Winners of the Nobel Prize

Islands of Compassion: A History of the Jewish Hospitals of New York

JEWS IN AMERICAN LIFE

TINA LEVITAN

HEBREW PUBLISHING COMPANY
NEW YORK

DEDICATED TO MY FATHER
JULIUS LEVITAN
WHO ALWAYS ENCOURAGED ME
IN MY BEST EFFORTS

Permission to use the illustrations was graciously extended by the following: American Jewish Historical Society; B'nai B'rith; Congregation Shearith Israel; Frick Art Reference Library; Hadassah; Hebrew Union College; Jewish Museum; Jewish Theological Seminary; Yeshiva University; The New York Public Library; The New York Times; J. & W. Seligman & Company; Society of Friends of Touro Synagogue; James P. Warburg; Zionist Archives.

CONTENTS

PREFACE

Jews in American Life does not begin to include all the important figures of the past and present. It is limited to ninety outstanding men and women who have displayed creativity in Jewish life or who have contributed to the progress of the emerging American civilization; whose influence upon those who followed has been profound and unmistakable.

Of the ninety individuals whose stories are told, seven were women, a pleasantly surprising proportion when one remembers how sheltered and in a sense how limited a woman's life was one century and even a few generations ago.

Jews have lived in America since its discovery by Columbus. In Columbus' crew the first man to step ashore and dare to settle in the new world was of Jewish origin. And down through the history of our country Jewish immigrants have challenged the wilderness. They fought for the ramparts. They risked their lives for liberty on every battlefield. They played a leading role in our economic successes. They made notable contributions to our scientific development, to the progress of medicine and to our national life. They gave us geniuses whose mental attitudes and intellectual viewpoints introduced new elements, new temperaments and new tones in art, literature and music.

In a way the role of the Jew in the modern world has been that of pioneering. From the days of the expulsion from Spain to the days of the expulsion from Germany and thereafter, Jewish pioneers have proved influential if not dominating factors in basic situations which helped build America. Their ideas, revolutionary in thought and expression, formed the pattern of this country and made it what it is.

At the time of the signing of the Declaration of Independence, the Jewish population hardly numbered 3,000 individuals. Yet this small group made significant contributions towards winning American freedom, Their efforts were apparently appreciated and perhaps influenced the framers of the Constitution to ban any religious test for holding office.

Jewish settlers proved the point that a minority adhering faithfully to a religion abhorent to the majority yet discharging to the full all obligations of good citizenship caused no danger to the state in establishing freedom of worship—a new enlarged liberal policy of religious liberty for the first time in a modern state.

While the number of Jews coming to America tapered off during the Revolutionary period, as the immigration of Spanish and Portuguese Jews lessened, immigration of Jews from other European lands gradually increased. The poverty of the Germanic states after the Napoleonic wars, the suppression of all liberal thought after the failure of the Revolution of 1848, led German Jews to seek a more congenial haven than their fatherland. They turned to America, swelling the tiny trickle to which Jewish immigration had shrunk into a rising, youthful tide of another generation of enterprising immigrants. Many of the newcomers settled in the cities and towns of the north and south; others were caught in the great American rush westward which was then creating for our country a new empire stretching to the Pacific. Living lives of loneliness in little outposts, following rugged trails through mountain passes, tracking a path across vast prairies into new communities—they started life anew, peddled their wares on foot or with a wagon, built synagogues, established schools, founded periodicals and banded together in charitable and social organizations.

By the time the Civil War broke out the Jewish population is estimated to have risen to 150,000. Swept by the passions of the day in their newly found homes, Jews served with distinction on both sides of the conflict. In the Union forces at least ten Jews held the title of General in some form: seven were awarded the Congressional Medal of Honor. In the Confederacy cabinet of Jefferson Davis, Judah P. Benjamin was Secretary of State. In the post-Civil War period these immigrants and their children were the generation which built industrial America.

The German Jewish immigrant dominated the cultural and spiritual life of American Jewry until rivalled by East European immigrants.

From 1881 to 1920 a general total of 23,500,000 immigrants entered the United States. Of this number nearly two million were Jews who came from Russia, Poland, Rumania, Austro-Hungary and the Baltic countries. These people, like those who had preceded them earlier left their old homes because of the lack of opportunity and the intolerable persecution to which they were subjected.

They rushed to the Atlantic seaports, bringing new ghettos to our great eastern cities. The struggle for existence of vast numbers of these East European Jews, sturdy, ambitious and intelligent soon made itself felt in our economic life.

The following half-century marks the rise of American industry unprecedented anywhere. Jewish participation takes on new dimensions. The manufacture of ready-to-wear garments for men, women and children they developed from small beginnings in dingy shops to a scientific industry. To them is due the credit for making the United States the best dressed nation on earth and for fashionable style having been placed within the reach of the slenderest purse. These enterprises helped to democratize American society by eliminating the differences in dress that perpetuated class distinction from colonial days. Their competition and unbounded energy, their imaginative daring, business sagacity and merchandising ability made them important factors in cutting down the costs of merchandise distribution and in providing expanding markets for mills and factories developing the American system of mass production.

From their Yiddish-speaking ghettos came piquant phrases, expressive words, ear-tickling exotic combinations of imagery which so seized American imagination that before very long our American language incorporated these as part of the everyday speech of the land. Words and expressions like kibitzer, mazuma, kosher, blintzes, gefilte fish, it's all right by me, I should worry and innumerable others became the common currency of our language.

Within two generations Jews were entering the professions, assuming public service and joining in every phase of American life.

Hays, Jacobi and other physicians contributed to the progress of American medicine which soon attained the world's highest standards. The Schiffs, the Warburgs, the Seligmans and many others reached an eminent position in banking and finance. The theater benefited enormously through the management, direction and taste of Belasco, Frohman, the Shuberts and a host of lesser producers.

In heavy industry the Guggenheims became for a time the world's largest miners, smelters and refiners of copper and other metals. Former peddlers, Adam Gimbel, the Strauses, Altman, Filene, Bloomingdale and Stern, who made a new art of merchandise retailing opened department stores and had a tremendous influence in lowering prices and bringing a greater variety and wider range of choice in the merchandise available to the masses in the cities, towns and villages across the land. Samuel Gompers built the American Federation of Labor from meager beginnings into the largest labor union in the world. Another astonishing Jewish performance was the creation of the moving picture industry in a little more than a decade from penny arcades and nickelodeons into a vast film empire that brings entertainment to ninety-five million people weekly and provides employment for hundreds and thousands of persons.

No contribution to science has been offered the world in this century, perhaps since Galileo, than those of Albert Einstein whose theory of relativity has revolutionized all concepts of the physical universe and ushered in the atomic age and those of the Jewish physicists who played a disproportionally large role in laying its foundation.

And perhaps there is no notable contribution to the spirit of America than the inscription on the Liberty Bell taken from the Hebrew scriptures: "Proclaim liberty throughout the land unto all the inhabitants thereof."

The following chapters show, how from the beginning the Jewish influence in the building of America has been distinctive. They offer an impressive array of individual American Jews whose individual paths of life added their impact to the forging of a great democracy and to enriching life and freedom in America.

In this American history it is not difficult to select the topic of Jewish "firsts" out of the far-flung and diversified assortment which history presents. No collection of them can be but a backdrop of the cyclorama of American life showing how from the days of the founding fathers, as the years rolled on, Jews, changing and developing with their experiences on the American scene, preserving individuality and inherited characteristics, yet integrated into the surrounding life, united with their neighbors in building, upholding and cherishing a new nation.

In the preparation of this book many libraries were visited and many scholars were consulted. With unstinting generosity scholars gave of their time and their knowledge in the areas of their specialization. For their kind assistance and cooperation I am especially grateful and appreciative. I am also greatly indebted to a host of preceding historians, biographers, critics, research workers and members of the American Jewish Historical Society who freely granted me access to their valuable manuscript collection and to their published and unpublished papers.

A special debt of gratitude is due to the National Foundation for Jewish Culture who believed in this book from the start and whose fellowship encouraged and stimulated its completion.

It is hoped that this book will prove valuable for general reading and for reference and that it will further the appreciation and understanding of the impact of the Jew on American life.

Like all races and faiths which make up the United States, Jews are both a group within and a part of the nation. To know their story—their early settlers, their outstanding citizens and their special contributions to religion and industry, to science and the arts and to democracy itself—is to know the melting pot that is America better.

TINA LEVITAN

New York, N. Y.

JEWS IN AMERICAN LIFE

(from 1492 to the Space Age)

1492 § LUIS DE TORRES: Trailblazer in a New World

The history of the Jew in America starts in the year 1492. Up to that time, in Spain for hundreds of years Jews had lived in what is still remembered as the Golden Age. They had produced philosophers, scientists, scholars, musicians, and poets. They helped make Spain famous for learning and culture. But in 1492 Ferdinand, king of Spain, culminated a long succession of persecutions by ordering the Jews to renounce their religion, or leave. The inhuman Inquisition— a ruthless system of "inquiry" into the religious beliefs of the people —was set up, and many Jews, in order to conceal their identity and thus escape death, accepted Christianity and became known as Marranos. Others chose to remain Jews and went into exile.

On Friday, August 3, 1492, a little before sunrise, the day after the expulsion of the Jews from Spain, Columbus started out on his great journey. His voyage was financed by a number of Marranos. Among these were, Luis de Santangel, chancellor of the royal Spanish household, who gave Columbus his largest private contribution (17,000 ducats), and Gabriel Sanchez, chief treasurer of Aragon. He also received much information from Jewish voyagers and scientists, including Judah Cresques, "the map Jew," who headed a school of navigation; Abraham Zacuto, astronomer; and Rabbi Levi ben Gershon, inventor of nautical instruments. He took with him on his trip at least five Marranos: Rodrigo de Triana, who was the first to see land, Alonso de la Calle, Marco, the surgeon, Bernal, the fleet's physician, and Luis de Torres, the interpreter, who was to be the first to step upon American soil.

Finally, after three months of traveling, on October 12, 1492, on the Jewish festival of Hoshannah Rabbah, Columbus and his crew reached a little island in the West Indies. San Salvador, Guanahani or Watlings Island, call it what you will, was now proudly claimed by the Admiral of the Ocean Seas for their Majesties, Ferdinand and Isabella. Luis de Torres, a man of great learning, who could speak Hebrew, Arabic, and several other Asiatic languages, was sent ahead by Columbus to head the first inland expedition of any kind by white men in America. After traveling twelve leagues into the interior of the mainland, now known as Cuba, in search of the capital city of the Great Khan of Tartary, much to his amazement, he discovered a town containing fifty straw huts built in the form of tents. It was inhabited by about a thousand dark-skinned, half-naked men and women who spoke a tongue not known to the white men. However, de Torres, making himself understood by gestures and sign language, soon gained their friendship. The natives were so delighted with him that they brought cotton, ornaments and live parrots to trade.

De Torres returned to Columbus with a lively and accurate description of everything he saw and gave his account of the natives smoking tobacco. Later, he was the first white man to introduce its use into the old world. He was delighted with the magnificent, heavy-laden fruit trees, beautiful flowers, and balmy climate of the island and persuaded Columbus to allow him to settle there. He was awarded a grant of land from an Indian chieftain whose friendship he won, and with a pension from King Ferdinand built himself a house. Here he had fine gardens and meadows, and began to grow tobacco and traded with the Indians.

De Torres lost no time in inviting his coreligionists to come and join him in the new world that was free from religious persecution. In the same Hebrew letter to his old home, he gives the great American bird, the turkey, its name, calling it "tukki" from the Hebrew word for "peacock."

The first white man and the first Jew to settle in Cuba, he lived a peaceful and honorable life there, and was a symbol of the great need for freedom and security of the Spanish Jews who came to these shores and of the bold and pioneering spirit of those that followed him.

Thus Jews from the very beginning helped to discover America. In the year of exile from their happiest and most beautiful medieval abode, they helped to found the land which was to be their refuge and home in modern times.

A few scholars believe that Columbus was of Jewish origin. They say that no Spanish Jew could ever have expected aid from the king and queen of Spain, so that the discoverer claimed to be an Italian Catholic.

Luis
de Torres

§4

There were rumors about Columbus' Jewish ancestry already during his lifetime. Letters written by him to strangers have the customary X at the top to indicate the faith of the writer, but of the thirteen letters written to his son only one bears an X, and that letter was meant to be shown to the King of Spain. The others have in the place of the X a sign that looks like the Hebrew characters B and H, initials used by religious Jews meaning in Hebrew, "With the Help of God."

We find the first reference to Columbus' Jewishness in print in a diplomatic document dated fifty-eight years after the discoverer's death. The French ambassador to Spain, Burdau, writing home, refers to "Columbus the Jew." Similar references have appeared variously in extensive Columbian literature over the centuries. But in the late nineteenth century the possible Jewish origin of Columbus became a highly controversial issue between the Spanish historians and the Columbian researchers.

On the four hundredth anniversary of the discovery of America, the Spanish government invited Moritz Kayserling to investigate the origin of its discoverer. From him we learn that Cristobal Colon (who never called himself Christopher Columbus and never spoke or wrote Italian) was the son of Susanna Fontanarossa and Domingo Colon of Pontevedra, Spain, where those bearing such surnames were Jews, some of whom had been brought before the Spanish Inquisition. A royal Spanish commission was appointed to study the subject further, in order to proclaim the great discoverer of Spanish birth. Its judgment was that since the exact place or date of birth cannot be ascertained, very definite proof would be needed to contradict Columbus' claim to being an Italian Catholic.

1649 § ISAAC ABOAB DE FONSECA: Early Adventurous Author

Prior to the coming of the Jews to North America, the record is replete with cases of Jewish migration to South America, the earliest Jewish settlers going to that section which was first settled. It was not, however, until 1642 that the first organized Jewish community in America came into existence. The Dutch had captured Recife, capital of Brazil, and had driven out the Spanish rulers who brought the Inquisition with them to the New World. Many secret Jews, living there and in other parts of South America, took advantage of Holland's liberal policy by settling there and openly returning to Judaism. The settlement increased rapidly, until, with the arrival of six hundred Jews from Holland, it comprised about five thousand people.

Isaac
Aboab
de Fonseca

§6

So successful were these first Jewish settlers of Brazil as farmers, planters, and traders, that they decided to hire a professional rabbi as spiritual leader and teacher. Rabbi Isaac Aboab de Fonseca, a good talmudic scholar who was said to have been an excellent speaker, was summoned from Amsterdam. He organized the first congregation in America. It was called "Kahal Kodesh" (The Holy Congregation). Although he returned to Holland in a few years, Isaac Aboab was the earliest American rabbi. He also had the honor of being the first Hebrew author in America.

His first publication appeared in 1649, when he translated the Bible into Portuguese, and rendered into Hebrew two books dealing with mystic lore, one called, *Beth Elohim* (The House of God), and the other *Shaar Shamayim* (The Gates of Heaven). The former was published in Venice in 1576. The first edition, in its original leather binding, was acquired in 1947 by the Boston Hebrew Teachers' College from the private collection of Rabbi Emanuel Eckstein of Cleveland.

Rabbi Aboab was also author of the first Hebrew poem written on American soil, the original manuscript of which may be seen in the library of the Theological Seminary in Amsterdam. It is entitled *Zecher Rab* (The Great Remembrance) and described the sufferings of the Jews due to their loyalty to the Dutch rulers in the war with the Portuguese. Just as prosperity and freedom seemed assured and the future seemed most rosy, the Portuguese laid siege to Recife.

For nine long years the siege continued. Isaac Aboab de Fonseca went about encouraging the weary soldiers and their starving fam-

ISAAC ABOAB DE FONSECA

ilies, and leading prayers for victory. But at last, in 1654, hopelessly weakened and outnumbered, the Dutch made peace with the Portuguese. Recife and other cities surrendered.

Honorably mindful of their ally, the Dutch had requested that Portugal show mercy to the Jews. But mercy translated from Dutch to Portuguese consisted in providing sixteen ships on which Jews were ordered to embark and leave Brazil.

Quitting their homes, the fields they had planted, the mills and factories they had built, the Jews of Recife departed from the city where their Holy Congregation had known such joy.

Those who could, returned to Amsterdam. Some went to the Dutch colonies of Surinam, or Dutch Guiana and Curacao in the Dutch West Indies. Others reached the British-ruled West Indies. Twenty-three escaped to New Amsterdam to constitute the first Jewish community in North America. A few Jews nevertheless remained in Brazil to suffer continued hardships.

Thus the first work written by a Jew in America was a history of suffering related in verse.

Kayserling has described the first Hebrew author who lived in America as "an excellent Hebrew poet who left us magnificently enduring works worthy of his talents and learning."

1654 § JACOB BARSIMSON: First Jewish Settler in New Amsterdam

Although there are records of possible early Jewish settlers in other Jewish colonies, Jacob Barsimson of Holland, who came as one of a party of emigrants sent by the Dutch West India Company to help populate its colony in New Amsterdam—as the Dutch called New York—seems to have the honor of being the first Jewish settler in what is now the United States. He came to New Amsterdam directly from Holland on the ship *Peartree*, on August 22, 1654, a month ahead of a larger group of Jews.

New Amsterdam had been founded twenty-eight years before by the Dutch West India Company. It had gained a reputation as a fur trade center and for its excellent harbor.

Barsimson was allotted a weatherbeaten hut in the woods outside the settlement where Indians had bartered furs for beads and Peter Minuit had, in 1628, bought Manhattan Island for sixty guilders. As

JACOB BARSIMSON

his neighbors, he found a mixed people who were still celebrating with gay flags and bunting, the granting of a city charter. He traded with the Indians, cleared land, planted gardens and orchards, and for a period of time hired himself out as a manual laborer.

The first case in the colonies in which observance of the Jewish Sabbath was recognized by the authorities as a good reason for failure to attend court when summoned, was that of Barsimson in 1658. The record reads: "Though the defendant is absent yet no default is entered against him as he was summoned on his Sabbath." What the case related to is not noted, and no further entry appears.

In September 1654, one month after Jacob Barsimson is known to have settled in New Amsterdam, twenty-three poor but healthy Jews arrived to constitute the first Jewish settlement in North America. They came on the French bark *St. Charles* from fallen Recife, just recaptured by the Portuguese from the tolerant Dutch.

Ships headed for Holland and other points had already taken their course, but the *St. Charles* had not gone very far when a storm arose, separating it from all the others. It drifted on the high seas, only to be attacked by pirates who took the meager possessions of all those on board. After a precarious voyage it finally reached New Amsterdam.

Although it was a pleasant change from the ship, the view of New Amsterdam which greeted the little group of Jews was not that of another London or Paris, but it compared favorably with Jamestown or Plymouth or the recently founded village of Boston. Gay with red roofs and a stalwart windmill, the small community boasted a church, a fort, a storehouse of the West India Company, a pier, a crane for loading and unloading trading ships, and a city tavern, which in 1653 had been converted to the City Hall.

A considerable sum remained due the captain of the *St. Charles*, Jacques de la Motthe, for board and passage. As the principal men among them had signed an agreement whereby they had become jointly and severally liable for the whole amount, vigorous proceedings were taken against them. An auction sale was held of their goods. The newcomers being unable to discharge their indebtedness, two of the group, David Israel and Moses Ambrosius, were ordered into confinement until the amount was made up.

Peter Stuyvesant, who ruled the colony, and was angered to see the people trying to enter his little town, lost no time in making his sentiments felt. At once he wrote a letter of protest to Holland, but the newcomers wrote at the same time and were backed by Dutch Jews. A reply was sent them in April, 1655. It stated that to refuse them admission would be unreasonable and unfair, especially because of their considerable losses in defending Brazil for the Dutch, and also "because of the large amount of capital their nation has invested in the shares of this company. Therefore . . . these people may travel and trade to and in New Netherlands, and live and remain there providing the poor among them shall be no burden and be supported by their own nation." This is the charter of Jewish settlement, and the beginning of Jewish liberty in the United States. The condition laid down, to care for their poor, was kept by the original settlers, and the great Jewish community which followed never forgot this promise.

Within the ten years that Jews lived in New Amsterdam under Dutch rule, they progressed and established a firm foothold in that part of the world. They began as a small and insignificant group, but by the time of the English conquest there were a number of wealthy tradesmen among them. The economic activities of the Jews of New Amsterdam were not far-reaching, but are interesting as the first undertaken on the North American continent.

By the time the first constitution of the State of New York was adopted in 1777, Jews were put on an equality with all other citizens, New York having been the first State to grant full religious liberty.

From September 1954 to May 1955, the three hundredth anniversary of the arrival of these settlers was widely celebrated under the auspices of the American Jewish Tercentenary Committee with the active participation of all major Jewish national organizations and with the cooperation of Christian and nonsectarian groups.

On May 20, 1955, a commemorative plaque and flagpole, marking the arrival of the first Jewish settlers in 1654, was dedicated in Battery Park under the auspices of the New York Joint Legislative Committee for the American Jewish Tercentenary.

Jacob Barsimson

§10

1655 § ASSER LEVY: A Fighter for Democracy

The defense of New Amsterdam, the little Dutch settlement clustering on the tip of Manhattan Island, was in the hands of the colonists, the burghers, or citizens soldiers who had obtained such guns, pistols, and shot and powder as they could. The lurking Indians and marauding Swedes made no distinction between young and old, Jew or Christian. Following the custom established in Holland, Jews were excluded from military duty, but were required to pay a tax which amounted to a dollar thirty a month.

In the new world the early Jewish settlers had hoped to reside in a country where they could stand alongside their Christian neighbors, and with them share the hazards of defense as well as the responsibilities of peace. Accordingly on November 5, 1655, a handful of Jews under the leadership of Jacob Barsimson and Asser Levy, one of the original settlers who had come over on the *St. Charles*, demanded and secured from the Dutch authorities the right to stand guard at the stockade of New Amsterdam. (Asser Levy, whose full name was Asser Levy Van Swellen, was a Yiddish-speaking Ashkenazi). Although the request at first was refused, time and again the determined Levy mounted guard duty and passed watchful hours peering into the wilderness.

On April 21, 1657, Asser Levy won another victory in which a democratic principle was involved. Proving that he kept watch and ward like other burghers of the city, he was admitted to the burgher right, paving the way for citizenship rights for his people and other minority groups. These rights gave him tolerance rather than complete freedom; but they were far in advance of the rights given the Jews by other nations, and were one step toward the liberty embodied later in the Constitution.

ASSER
LEVY

Thanks are also due Levy and his associates for establishing the right of free trade throughout the colony. Levy, who for a while had set himself up as a trader, appealed to the authorities in Holland, who heeded his plea to keep trade open to all. Levy was also the first Jewish landowner in North America; he owned the land on which was built the first synagogue. As early as 1661 he had purchased property in Albany and acquired a plot of land on South William Street. In 1660 he was licensed as a butcher at a time when licenses were restricted to only six in the colony. His first Jewish butcher shop was located on Wall Street. The same year he built the first Jewish slaughterhouse in North America, so that "all persons should have the liberty to kill and hang therein meat."

At the time of his death in 1681, Levy was considered amongst the wealthiest inhabitants. His grounds and buildings were appraised at two hundred and eighteen pounds and the slaughterhouse, which was located outside the city gates, at eighteen hundred pounds.

No other Jew of his time seems to have had so many dealings with Christians. He was named executor in the wills of many Christian merchants. He was always ready to defend Jewish as well as non-Jewish rights. In 1671 he lent money for building the first Lutheran Church in New York.

The name of Asser Levy stands out as that of a determined and admirable character whose life work made its considerable contribution to the upbuilding of the new continent.

One of his descendants, also named Asser Levy, was an officer in the Revolutionary Army a hundred years later. An ensign in the First New Jersey Regiment, he was probably the only Jew to serve with the Jersey troops.

On February 22, 1955, during celebration of the three hundredth anniversary of Jewish settlement in the United States, *Asser Levy Place*, running from 23rd to 25th Street, between First Avenue and Franklin D. Roosevelt Drive in New York's East Side, was dedicated.

1735 § JUDAH MONIS: Hebrew at Harvard in the Early Days

The first college founded in North America was Harvard, which opened in 1636 only a few years after the first settlers came to Massachusetts. It was named for a minister, John Harvard, who left the college his library and four hundred pounds when he died.

During the first few decades after the founding of Harvard College, no course of study figured more largely than Hebrew. This was so because most of the students attending were preparing for the ministry. It was therefore required that they be able to read the Bible in its original language.

In the beginning Hebrew was taught by the president and the tutors along with the other undergraduate studies. In 1655 one of the first endowed professorships—that of Hebrew and Oriental languages—was established. Harvard students were required to spend one day each week for three years on Hebrew and allied tongues. The principal text used was the Bible. Twelve copies with the students' inscriptions upon them from the years 1651 to 1746 are extant. Another text used was Wilhelm Schickard's *Horologium Hebraeum* (The Hebrew Sun Dial), which professed to teach the elements of the language in twenty-four hours. Following the Harvard pattern other colleges such as Yale, Columbia, Brown, Princeton, Johns Hopkins, and the University of Pennsylvania, also taught Hebrew from their inception and have been teaching it to this day.

The first Hebrew grammar published in America was written in 1735 by Judah Monis. A colorful character, Monis was probably born in Italy into a family of Portuguese Marranos. He studied in Leghorn and Amsterdam before serving as a rabbi on the island of Jamaica and later in New York City. In 1720, when he was thirty-seven years old, he was awarded the degree of Master of Arts at Harvard College. He was the first Jew to receive a college degree in America as well as the only Jew to receive a Harvard degree before 1800. But he did not remain a Jew long, for in 1722—less than two years later—he was baptized in the college hall (but continued to observe Saturday as the Sabbath). The following month he was appointed instructor of Hebrew at Harvard, but it is open to question whether Monis would have obtained this position if he had not joined their congregational church. He took charge of all the Hebrew classes and began dictating his grammar, to be copied in longhand by his students, until given a grant by the college in 1735 to publish it under the title *Dickdook Leshon Gnebreet*. Type was imported from England, but arrived in an imperfect condition, and had to be supplemented by a later shipment. Monis' grammar constituted the first complete Hebrew book published in America.

The influence of Hebrew culture went far beyond the bounds of technical scholarship and professional training for theologians. In 1636, the Plymouth Colony expressly drew its charter on the template Nehemiah proposed after the return of the Jews from exile in Babylonia (Nehemiah chapters 9 and 10). When the Massachusetts Bay Colony framed its code of laws, it declared its adherence to Mosaic principles. So did the State of Connecticut when it drew up the first Constitution in the western world in the mid-1660's. The Founding Fathers knew the Bible. They were eminently capable in the exposition of all its justifications for rebellion. To them the exodus from Egypt was an inspired precedent.

In 1776, Benjamin Franklin, Thomas Jefferson and John Adams recommended for the first official seal of the United States a design whose theme was the escape of the Israelites from Egypt. Around the edges of this proposed seal ran the motto: "Rebellion to tyrants is obedience to God." This motto pleased Jefferson so much that he took it as his own and had it cut on his private seal.

It is not surprising that the committee appointed the day the Declaration of Independence was adopted should propose such a devise. The Founding Fathers drew heavily on the Bible and Hebraic tradition in laying the foundation of the new republic. The spirit of the Bible as well as Jewish history and custom were all expressed in the first Thanksgiving celebrated by the Pilgrims in the autumn of 1621. The American Revolution was cradled in the Hebraic love of freedom and liberty. Biblical influence had helped not a little in favoring and strengthening opposition to the parliamentary claim. Several decades before the Declaration of Independence, the biblical injunction taken from Leviticus 25:10: "Proclaim liberty throughout the land unto all the inhabitants thereof," was inscribed on the Liberty Bell and made the great watchword of the American people. Jewish ideals have permeated and colored the thought and feeling of this nation ever since its beginning.

Judah Monis

§14

The influence of the Hebrew language has found its way into American speech. About half the verses of the Book of Psalms have virtually become English idioms. Almost all the phrases of Proverbs, Job, Song of Songs, Ecclesiastes, and others have been domesticated by the English speaking peoples. Hebrew words have become part of the English vernacular. Cities with Hebrew names or Hebrew derivatives can be found in every part of the United States. Thus we have Sharon and Salem, Mass., New Canaan, Conn., Bethlehem, N.H., Hebron, Calif., Gilad, La., Joseph, Idaho, and Goshen, N.Y.

To this day Hebrew remains a living part of America. As a language it is taught in nearly five hundred American colleges and high schools. Its spirit is reflected in the best contemporary literature, art, and thought.

Hebrew ethics and Hebrew philosophy motivated America in its strivings for political and social justice and ideal democracy from the start.

1746 § MYER MYERS: Artist and Craftsman

Myer Myers, a silversmith, who was born in New York in 1723, is probably the first native born artist of English America—certainly the first Jew who made a contribution to American art.

The parents of Myer Myers sailed from Holland long after England changed the name of New Amsterdam to New York. After completing the legally required seven years training, the master craftsman opened his workshop. Despite the limitations imposed by time and custom, he lavished a wealth of design and detailed ornamentation on all of his work. Several of his exquisite Chanukah lamps, spice boxes, and other ceremonial objects, as well as a silver tankard showing the coat of arms of the Livingston family, still exist.

Examples of his work may be seen in museums, synagogues, churches and important private collections. All the objects carry his trade mark MM.

Myers' craftmanship and intricate workmanship produced pieces highly valued. They cover three periods of eighteenth century design —the mid-century, the classical, and the federal. Ironically, one of his pieces even found its way into the collection of the Czar of Russia.

The name of Myer Myers occurs repeatedly in the synagogue records of Congregation Shearith Israel during half a century, from earlier than 1749 when he contributed the generous sum of eight pounds to "a public and free subscription to buy wood," to his death in 1795 at the age of seventy-two. His services to the community were varied and constant, if the records refer, as they seem to, to the same man. They ranged from minor offices to that of president, from 1759 to 1770. In 1786 he was elected president of the Silversmiths' Society of New York, thus becoming North America's first Jewish member of a trade guild.

To enjoy the grace and beauty of the gifted silversmith's work, one must consult the recent book on Myer Myers by Jeanette W. Rosenbaum.

There is another early American Jewish artist who deserves mention, Joshua Cantir, of Charleston, South Carolina. Another, perhaps America's third Jewish craftsman whose name has been preserved for us, is David Lopez, also of Charleston, who was the builder and architect of the present synagogue Kahal Kodesh Beth Elohim, third oldest congregation in the United States, organized the day following Rosh Hashanah in 1750, two score years before the birth of the United States.

Solomon Nunes Carvalho, who in 1853 joined John C. Fremont's expedition to explore the Far West, is still another early Jewish artist. Carvalho made the maps which first the wagon trails, then the rails, and finally our modern highways, followed over the Rockies into California. Born in Charleston, he had in his twentieth year become a portrait painter, and had received a silver medal from the South Carolina institute for his "Moses Receiving the Tablets of the Law on Sinai," which was destroyed in 1838 when the Beth Elohim Synagogue burned down. Fortunately he had drawn a sketch of its interior, so that today we can still see the "spacious and elegant" synagogue. His best known portraits are of the eminent Reverend Isaac Leeser, leader of American Orthodox Jewry, Thomas Hunter, founder of Hunter College, and Brigham Young, governor of the Mormons.

RELIGIOUS ORNAMENTS
BY MYER MYERS,
SILVERSMITH

Carvalho made the most of his opportunities. He kept a careful record of the hardships suffered by the twenty-two men of the expedition party in which he took part in the winter cold to cross the Rockies on foot. Later he described his experiences in his book: *Incidents of Travel and Adventure in the Far West with Colonel Fremont's Last Expedition, Across the Rocky Mountains: Including Three Months' Residence in Utah, and a Perilous Trip Across the Great American Desert to the Pacific.* This work which was published in New York in 1857, is the only account of the expedition which survives and is of the greatest value to the historians of the early West.

1756 § MOSES LINDO and His Indigo Plant

Moses Lindo, a Portuguese Jew who came to Charleston, South Carolina, in 1756 after having spent several years in England, introduced the indigo industry in the thirteen colonies. On his large plantation in Charleston, he established the first indigo plant in North America and invested some two hundred thousand pounds in the business. He is said to have learned about indigo production in London where he attended the Merchant Taylors' School and there obtained practical experience in the trade. He continued a correspondence with the dyers of the London Royal Society and was continually making improvements in keeping with their findings. He even is said to have offered prizes to induce new methods of production.

The Philosophical Transactions, a publication of the Royal Society of London, contains a letter which describes his discovery of a new dye made from pouck, a native weed cooked in Bristol water.

Due to his pioneering efforts, a fabulous Carolina indigo trade developed which was responsible for the wealth of the colony, and he became its leading exporter and importer. It was his mark of inspection which qualified the Carolina grown product for acceptance in British markets. In recognition of his work in the field, he was appointed Surveyor and Inspector General of Indigo Dyes and Drugs for the Carolina provinces and had the right to use the royal coat of arms of George III over his door.

The petition to appoint him inspector was signed by the lieutenant governor, council members, members of the assembly, merchants, and planters. It stated that "because of the services rendered to this province by Moses Lindo, and as testimonial of his abilities he be made public inspector, he is the only person known to us capable of rendering this province public service in that article."

Until 1756, the annual export of indigo seldom reached 350,000 pounds. After that year Charleston exported more than one million pounds, and the amount increased until it ranked second to rice.

After serving as Inspector General for ten years, Lindo resigned because as he wrote, he could not bring himself to accept and certify inferior indigo.

Lindo was familiar with the practice of English universities in excluding Jews, and was greatly impressed by Brown University in Providence, Rhode Island, with its atmosphere of tolerance and enlightenment. He was the magnanimous donor of twenty pounds, one of the largest amounts ever given the institution to that time. Brown already had a provision excusing attendance on the Sabbath, but following acceptance of the gift we find a resolution passed by the university which reads: ". . . Voted that the children of the Jews may be admitted into this institution and enjoy the freedom of their religion, without any restraint or imposition whatsoever."

Hayman
Levy

§18

Alive to the rich potentialities of America, Jews in the early colonial days contributed their best efforts in laying the economic foundations of the country. They grew indigo in the Carolinas and furthered the whale and candle industry in New England. When the Non-Importation Resolutions of 1765 went into effect, from the very beginnings of the conflict between the colonists and the mother country, true to the teachings of their faith which is predominantly the faith of liberty, they signed the agreement and firmly abided by it. Jewish shippers then turned to the fur trade, sending their trappers, hunters, and agents as far west as the Mississippi. These traders were amongst the first pioneers and colonizers, holding the country until the land-hungry settlers could follow the trails they had blazed.

It is difficult to overestimate the part played by the firms of Joseph Simon, the Franks, and the Gratz brothers in opening up the lands that were some day to become the states of Ohio, West Virginia, Kentucky, Indiana, Illinois, and Missouri. The first breath of civilization frequently came with these fur traders and hunters who settled in the regions they had explored.

Hayman Levy, one of the greatest Jewish merchants of the period, was the head of the New York firm of Levy, Lyons, and Company and became the largest fur trader in the colonies. His was one of the principal mercantile firms in the city and had a branch in Europe known as Levy, Solomon and Company. Mr. Levy also carried on an extensive trade for many years with the Indians who brought the finest furs to his headquarters. He not only purchased all the Indians brought, but kept everything in his large establishment to supply their wants. The Indians who came to the city dealt largely with him, and at certain seasons of the year were to be seen lining the streets in the vicinity of his warehouse. There are entries in his book that show he was the first employer of John Jacob Astor, ancestor of the millionaire Astors of today, who received one dollar a day for beating furs. Nicholas Low, ancestor of Seth Low, former president of Columbia University, served as Levy's clerk for seven years, and then laid the foundation of his great fortune through a hogshead of rum purchased from his former employer, who besides rendered him substantial assistance.

The restrictive acts of Parliament and the general colonial policy pursued by the government produced a disastrous effect upon business, and Hayman Levy failed in 1768, but his assignees were enabled to discharge the whole of his indebtedness with interest. The great fire of 1776 destroyed all his property, yet he carried on his fur trade on his own account until his death in 1790.

At one time Levy was elected president of Congregation Shearith Israel in New York. But at the same meeting he was fined twenty shillings for "indecent and abusive language" uttered in the synagogue yard to the then presiding officer. He refused to serve, and was again fined for declining the office. On another occasion in 1765 he was further fined for insulting the chazzan, a Mr. Pinto. Two years later he was on the receiving end of the insult, and a different Mr. Pinto had to pay forty shillings for abusing the acting president, Hayman Levy himself.

When he died he was described in the press as a gentleman much respected by all denominations who had the pleasure of his acquaintance. *The Journal of Philadelphia* wrote of him: "His character as a merchant was without blemish; he was a true patriot, a friend of the United States, an affectionate husband, a tender father, and a sincere friend. The widow, the orphan, and the poor will lament the loss; he was benevolent and charitable to a great degree; his house was open to all strangers of good character to partake of his liberality."

1767 § AARON LOPEZ: Merchant Prince

In 1685 a group of Jews, most of them refugees from the Spanish Inquisition, landed in Newport, Rhode Island, to constitute the second Jewish settlement in North America. As time went on other Jews from Holland and the West Indies came to this haven of tolerance set up by Roger Williams. Here, Newport Jews, many of them outstanding merchants, were to become the leading business men of their day, both in wealth and pioneer projects, and were among the first to establish the soap-making and candle industry in America. They were highly responsible for the high standing which

AARON LOPEZ
(Courtesy of the American Jewish Historical Society)

Newport had as a seaport, and which it lost after the Revolution.

One of these men, Aaron Lopez, who came to Newport from Lisbon in 1752, became known as the "merchant prince of New England" and was credited in a larger degree than anyone else with the rapid commercial development which made Newport for a quarter of a century the formidable business rival of New York. Through his papers in the Newport Historical Society, we may trace his career from its modest beginnings up to the time when the entire city felt the impact of his phenomenal rise. By 1767 he owned, in whole or in part, thirty trans-atlantic ships and over one hundred coastwise vessels. They carried lumber, fish, whale oil, manufactured articles, molasses and rum to and from Newfoundland, Surinam, Madeira, the West Indies, Lisbon, Gibraltar, Cape Nicholas, Cape Francois, Amsterdam, Bristol, Curacao and the ports of the American colonies. With his father-in-law, Jacob Rodriguez Rivera, he introduced the sperm oil industry in America and began the manufacture of sperm oil and candles which greatly improved lighting. His business ventures in the whaling industry extended as far as the Falkland Islands. Yet with all the vastness of his enterprises, Lopez was a man of charm and genuine humility. Ezra Stiles, seventh president of Yale, knew him well, and wrote of him in his diary: "He was a merchant of the first eminence; for Honor and Extent of Commerce probably surpassed by no Merchant in America. He did business with the greatest of ease and exactness—always carried about with him a sweetness of behavior, a calm Urbanity, and agreeable and unaffected

Politeness of manners. Without a single Enemy and the most universally beloved by an extensive acquaintance of any man I ever knew."

Probably no man in the colonies suffered a greater financial loss in the Revolution than Lopez did. From the very start he espoused the patriot cause and donated much wealth to it, but his fleet fell into the hands of the British. When the British occupied Newport, he saw most of his wealth disappear. Part of the Jewish community followed him to Leicester, Massachusetts, where they constituted the first Jewish settlement in that state. These Jews remained in Leicester during the Revolution, conducting there certain types of business.

Strangely enough when this distinguished and useful Jewish resident petitioned the General Assembly of Rhode Island for citizenship in 1762, he received this reply: ". . . the free and quiet enjoyment of the Christian religion were the principal views with which this colony was settled."

Lopez did not appeal the decision; he made application for citizenship in Taunton where it was quickly granted. Thus was the first Jew naturalized in Massachusetts.

After Washington's victory at Yorktown secured peace, Lopez set out in 1782 with his numerous family to rebuild his commercial empire. On the road his horse suddenly bolted and threw him into treacherous quicksand. He struggled helplessly until submerged. He was buried in the Jewish cemetery in Newport. In his will he founded the Leicester Academy, and left a liberal contribution to the Redwood Library. This was a time when large philanthropic gifts were rare.

1776 § GERSHOM MENDEZ SEIXAS: Patriot Rabbi of the Revolution

The Reverend Gershom Mendez Seixas who became the minister of the first Jewish congregation in North America, Congregation Shearith Israel, and who except for a brief interval, continued in this post for more than fifty years, was the first Jewish religious leader born on American soil. Born in New York in 1745, he was related to the elite Sephardim of the congregation. His father, a Marrano in Portugal, had re-entered the covenant of Judaism and married the daughter of Moses Levy, parness and leader of the New York community of the early eighteenth century. As a young boy Gershom received his education at the congregational school established at Shearith Israel. History does not inform us how he received his later training. There was no rabbinic seminary, nor even a rabbi, in the United States. It must have been his own spirit, his constant attendance at the synagogue service, the Jewish life in his home, and what he learned from New York's chazzan, Joseph Jessurun Pinto, that qualified him by the summer of 1768, when he was twenty-three, to present himself as a candidate for the position. There were no other applicants, and the trustees elected the youthful "rabbi" enthusiastically.

Gershom Mendez Seixas

§22

Gershom Seixas did not organize a new officiant for the synagogue; but in him the chazzan-preacher found complete expression as minister and religious director. He was no scholar, but in the course of his ministry, during the few times he was called upon to cite Jewish law, he was able to refer to the *Shulhan Arukh*. His ability to write Hebrew is evidenced by a manuscript copy of a Hebrew address which he wrote for Sampson Simson when the latter was graduated from Columbia College.

The revolutionary spirit swept Seixas along in its current. Active among the Minute Men, he had reason for apprehension after General Washington's retreat from Long Island. Seixas refused to remain in New York. The English did not interfere with religious freedom, yet he took no chances. On August 4, 1776, he preached a patriotic sermon and closed the synagogue.

As an American patriot, the rabbi felt he could not live and work in a community which had lost its liberty. It was not easy for him to leave his birthplace and the friends that remained behind; he could not be sure when and where he would be able to serve another congregation. And, like every conspicuous rebel who dared defy the British king, Seixas faced imprisonment or even a traitor's death if his countrymen were defeated.

Many of the congregation agreed with their rabbi and prepared to follow him into self-imposed exile. He departed with the sacred Torah scrolls, ceremonial objects, and prayerbooks. The greater part of the congregation followed him, first to Stratford, Connecticut, and later to Philadelphia (the great refuge of patriots), where they remained until after the conflict.

In Philadelphia the members of Shearith Israel, together with other refugees, swelled the existing congregation into the largest Jewish community in North America. In 1782, the congregants carried out an old ambition to build a new synagogue. For their first minister they engaged the "patriot rabbi" of New York. Seixas assisted in organizing Mikveh Israel, the congregation that ranks high in the

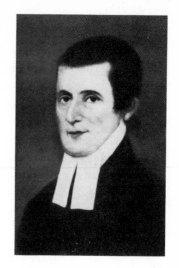

THE REV. GERSHOM MENDEZ SEIXAS

early republic. Haym Salomon, married to his cousin Rachel Franks, and Jonas Phillips, a former constituent, rallied to him and made liberal contributions to its building fund.

After the Treaty of Peace, many war refugees returned to their homes. The Reverend Seixas might have remained with Mikveh Israel but for the insistent demand that he return to New York. Before leaving, with Bernard Gratz, Haym Salomon, and two others, he petitioned the Pennsylvania authorities to amend the state constitution by removing the New Testament oath required of anyone taking public office. This was but a variant of the British oath, "on the true faith of a Christian" devised against would-be Jewish members of Parliament. No action was taken, but the petition was not drawn in vain. Four years later, the framers of the Federal Constitution assembled in Philadelphia adopted a provision that no religious test ever be required to hold office in the United States.

The Reverend Seixas returned to New York and resumed his former pulpit, and for two generations was repeatedly honored by Jews and Christians as patriot and citizen.

Gershom Seixas was the first to abandon the use of Spanish in his sermons for English and the first of his denomination to speak in the churches of America. He was also the first American cleric to institute a prayer for the government in English. A trustee of the Humane Society, he was elected by the state legislature on the first Board of Regents for the University of the State of New York. One of the incorporators of Columbia University, he served as a trustee for thirty years and rendered services on committees of this institution. As a tribute to his memory, his portrait was struck on a bronze medal issued by Columbia University and a painting of him was unveiled at the institution on its one hundred and seventy-fifth anniversary.

Gershom Mendez Seixas

Today as one enters the synagogue of Congregation Shearith Israel, he sees a bronze tablet on which is inscribed in a few words the story of the Reverend Gershom Mendez Sexias, "patriot rabbi" of the American Revolution.

§24

Not until 1845 did a rabbi ordained in Europe officiate in any pulpit of the United States. The chazzan, shochet, and mohel continued to function as religious head of many a community, until displaced in a later day by the yeshiva or seminary trained rabbi.

1776 § FRANCIS SALVADOR: An Early American Martyr

From 1776 to the present, men of the Jewish faith have been fighting and dying to preserve American independence.

Less than a month after the earnest band of patriots in Philadelphia pledged to liberty "our lives, our fortunes, and our sacred honor," Francis Salvador, colorful plantation owner of South Carolina, who won the sobriquet of "the southern Paul Revere," was killed in battle. Salvador, a brilliant young English Jew of Portuguese ancestry, had arrived in Charleston in 1773 to develop extensive family holdings there. He became famous as a soldier, legislator, and patriot. Together with Charles Pinckney and Edward Rutledge, he was among the first revolutionary characters of the state.

In 1774, although a resident of America for only a year, Salvador was elected to the General Assembly of South Carolina, the first Jew in American history and probably the first Jew in the modern world to serve as an elective officer. Because of his active part in the patriotic cause, his district made him its representative to the First and Second Provincial Congresses, which took active steps to revolt against the British. There he was named to various committees concerned with conduct of the war.

At the very beginning of the Revolution, on July 31, 1776, Salvador was killed in an Indian skirmish incited by the English. Together with his friend Major Andrew Williamson, he had set out on an expedition to round up volunteer troops to save the colonists from an Indian attack.

With a force of only forty men, the little army proceeded in the silence of the moonless night. Suddenly, a fusillade of shots poured from behind bushes, trees, and fences. The Americans had been ambushed. Major Williamson had forded the Keowee River with a detachment and Salvador was at the head of the company. With the first volley Salvador swayed heavily in his saddle. The Indians closed in on all sides, but the militia soon repulsed them. Williamson found Salvador lying in a bush, scalped but still alive. He asked whether the enemy was beaten. "Yes," was the answer. He shook Williamson's hand, said farewell, and died in his twenty-ninth year, unaware of the promulgation of the Declaration of Independence.

The whole army regretted his loss, wrote a continental journal, *The Remembrance*, . . . "as he was universally loved and esteemed by them."

In the brief period of three years, Salvador, a stranger and a Jew, sat in the representative assembly of the Provincial Congress, was listened to with unusual respect for one of his youth, and died a patriot of the American Revolution, the first Jew in America to give his life for his country. A memorial plaque dedicated in 1950 at the time of the Bicentennial Celebration of the Jewish community of Charleston reads: ". . . Born an aristocrat, he became a democrat; an Englishman, he cast his lot with America; true to his ancient faith, he gave his life for new hopes of human liberty and understanding."

1776 § HAYM SALOMON: Patriotic Financier of the Revolution

During the Revolutionary War Jews contributed their full share of patriotism off the battlefield as well as on it. When funds were needed in 1776 to support the army of Washington in the field, the names of Jews were conspicuous among the givers. When bills of credit were issued from which the element of credit was greatly lacking, Jews were conspicuous among the subscribers.

But the one who did more for the cause of the Revolution than any other Jewish civilian or soldier, was Haym Salomon of Philadelphia. He came from Poland in 1772—the first Polish Jew of whom

THE HAYM SALOMON
MONUMENT (SALOMON IS
ON THE RIGHT)

we have a record in North America—and established a business as a commission merchant in New York. Salomon prospered. Although New York was the seat of the British power in the colonies, he cast his fortunes with the patriotic Sons of Liberty. At the outbreak of the War, he was imprisoned by the English and barely escaped hanging for intercepting their supplies. When it was discovered that he could speak ten languages, he was put to work in a British prison camp as an interpreter. In this capacity he assisted American and French prisoners to escape and finally he himself escaped to Philadelphia. Had not his health been undermined by imprisonment, he might have been one of the distinguished band of Jewish patriots who fought valiantly with Washington.

Soon after his arrival in Philadelphia, Salomon opened an office in a plain little house on Front Street, "between Market and Arch." From this base of operations he was to render his magnificent services to the colonies. From the outset, Haym Salomon succeeded in Philadelphia. Most of the business of the port was with foreign markets whose trade conditions he knew intimately. His straightforward, honest methods of transacting business won him an enviable reputation.

It is significant that Haym Salomon's first official recognition as an able businessman should have come from an ally of the young republic and not the republic itself. Soon after his arrival in America, the French Minister, Chevalier de la Luzerne, appointed Salomon agent for the French government and paymaster-general for the French forces in America. In these capacities, he handled huge sums of money, but refused all commission. He considered it his patriotic duty to serve the nation that had crossed the sea to aid his adopted country. He maintained this policy in all his dealings with the government.

It is apparent from early entries in Robert Morris' diary that the new Superintendent of Finance negotiated with other brokers before he began to write that almost daily phrase, "I sent for Haym Salomon." But he was not long in learning that he needed Salomon's vision, integrity, and unselfish devotion to the cause of liberty. Salomon was regularly consulted and his sound judgment and clear thinking saved the colonists immense sums.

Salomon's official title was "Broker to the Office of Finance of the United States." That is, he was the broker through whom Robert Morris sold the securities of the weak, infant government. Morris received hides, tobacco, and agricultural products in lieu of money from the colonies. Salomon sold them for the account of the Federal Treasury. He was also called upon to act as government agent to sell captured enemy merchandise.

Handling hundreds of bills of exchange for the Superintendent of Finance was only part of Haym Salomon's contribution to the cause of freedom. He also floated loans; he endorsed notes; he contributed generously from his private means to needy soldiers and statesmen *; he equipped military units with his own money; he subscribed heavily to all government loans. At his utimely death in 1785 at the age of forty-five, it is said that he held over a third of a million dollars in paper of the new republic.

---

* James Madison, later president of the United States, who was a delegate from Virginia to the Congress sitting in Philadelphia, wrote in 1782: "I have for some time past been a pensioner on the favor of Haym Salomon, a Jew broker." So also it is recorded that had it not been for the aid "administered with equal generosity and delicacy" by Salomon to James Wilson, one of Philadelphia's most prominent patriots, he would have been forced to leave the public service.

This would seem a comfortable legacy for his wife and four children, but unfortunately the sum, badly depreciated, went with other assets to repay what he had contracted in the interests of the country. Haym Salomon died bankrupt, but without dishonor. Although Congress after Congress considered the claims of Salomon heirs, no compensation or adjustment was ever made.

Haym Salomon

§28

As an ardent Jew, Salomon was one of the founding members and a trustee of Congregation Mikveh Israel, Philadelphia's first synagogue. In 1783 he was one of the five Philadelphian Jews who in behalf of the community, petitioned the Council of Censors of Pennsylvania for removal of the Test Oath of the state which demanded that each member elected to the assembly affirm that both "the Scriptures of the Old and New Testament were given by divine inspiration."

This protest failed; but it doubtless was a contributing factor in the ultimate abolition of this test clause in 1790.

A loyal and unselfish patriot of his adopted country, the debt of gratitude the nation owes Salomon was in part paid by the erection of a statue in Chicago showing George Washington with his arms about Robert Morris and Haym Salomon. Some years ago, Warner Brothers made a short motion picture called *My Country First*, written by the celebrated actor, George Jessel, portraying some of the highlights of the life of Haym Salomon.

During the incumbency of Mayor Fiorello La Guardia of New York, a proclamation was issued setting aside "Haym Salomon Day." It was the Mayor's intent to make America conscious of the great contribution in the Revolutionary War of a young Jew who believed in liberty with all his heart, "with all his soul, and with all his might."

1778 § DAVID SALISBURY FRANKS: Soldier and Treaty Bearer

Although lovers of peace from the days of Solomon and Jeremiah, Jews have fought in all the wars of this country with distinction and honor.

On the 17th of April of '75, when Paul Revere clattered through "every Middlesex village and farm," there were about 3,000 Jews in the Thirteen Colonies—not very many, but neither was America very large or thickly populated at that time. Yet, even though they were small in numbers, Jews made their weight felt in the Revolution.

No account of Jewish participation in the Revolutionary War is complete without an account of David Salisbury Franks. He was a patriot whose spectacular career and checkered history made him the center of a controversy which took a long time to simmer down. Jefferson said of him, in a letter to James Madison: "He appears to have a good eno' heart, and understanding somewhat better than common, but too little guard over his lips."

Born apparently in Philadelphia, he moved to Montreal and when quite young served as the president of Congregation Shearith Israel (the Spanish and Portuguese Synagogue in Montreal). He continued to conduct his business in Montreal during the first months of the war. Although his neighbors were all fiercely loyal to the British crown, this Jewish merchant did all in his power to help the thirteen colonies in their desperate need. In 1775 General Montgomery led his victorious troops into Montreal, where Franks secured supplies to feed the American army and even lent his own money to pay Montgomery's men their wages. When the Americans were forced to withdraw from Canada, David Salisbury Franks prudently followed them back to the United States.

Serving as a volunteer, he rose rapidly in the ranks. Now in 1778, as it happened, it had fallen to the lot of David Salisbury Franks to receive the appointment as aide-de-camp to General Benedict Arnold. Later when Arnold turned traitor, this position of responsibility and trust brought suspicion and near disgrace to Franks. The finger of suspicion naturally pointed toward Franks as an accomplice of Arnold's treason since the Jewish patriot had been on intimate terms with the Arnold family. Wanting complete vindication he wrote to George Washington demanding a full trial in a higher court. This took place on November 2, 1780. The verdict was one of complete exoneration for Franks. When he retired from the army he held the rank of Lieutenant-Colonel.

He not only retained his rank, but was even trusted with several important diplomatic missions. In 1781 Robert Morris, United States Minister of Finance, sent him abroad with dispatches to John Jay in Madrid and Benjamin Franklin in Paris. Having acquired a taste of diplomatic life, he put himself in the way of any appointment that was likely to take him abroad. The intervention of his friends accomplished his end. "When Mr. Jefferson was going to Paris, one of the Commissioners, for making a Treaty of Peace," he took me into his family," Major Franks writes. "In the Winter of the year

David
Salisbury
Franks

§29

1784 Congress dispatched me to Europe with a Copy of the Ratification of the definitive Treaty . . . In 1785 I went to Marseilles," as Vice Consul. Franks evidently was pleased with his French appointment for Jefferson wrote to Monroe, on November 11, 1784:

"He is very anxious to be continued in it & is now there in the exercise of his office. If I have been rightly informed his services & sacrifices during the war have had their merit and I should suppose Congress would not supersede him but on good grounds."

Major Franks' narrative continues:

"In the fall of 1786, Mr. Barclay was commissioned by our ministers for making a treaty with the Emperor of Morocco & I was appointed his secretary . . . After Mr. Barclay's return from Spain . . . I was sent by him with it from Madrid to Paris & thence by Mr. Jefferson to London to get Mr. Adam's signature to it . . ."

"Thus I devoted Eleven Years of the best part of my life to the Service of my Country, in all which time, I am bold to say that I have ever been actuated by a disinterested Zeal for her Honor and Prosperity."

When Franks returned home in 1787, the new Constitution of the United States was awaiting the ratification of the Thirteen States.

Franks helped found the Society of the Cincinnati, a secret organization for the officers of the late war.

Congress voted Franks 400 acres for his war services as additional compensation under the Land Grant Law. He became involved with a real estate company in a French settlement in the Ohio Valley, the location of his land. The tactics of his associates caused him extreme dissatisfaction. Before long the Indians were on the trail and massacred all the French settlers. Meanwhile Franks had accepted an important post as assistant cashier of the Bank of the United States. His career was brought to a sudden close in 1793 either by yellow fever, or perhaps he was among the French colonists in Ohio massacred by the Indians.

His record did much to save the reputation of the Franks family, since all loyal Americans came to look down upon one of its ablest members. This was David Franks, an indifferent Jew and a Tory.

Mordecai Sheftall was the outstanding Jew of Georgia in the eighteenth century. His father, Benjamin, a German, had come to the colony in 1733, but a few months after General James Oglethorpe's arrival.

Mordecai, born in 1735, quickly achieved a considerable degree of success as a businessman. Like many other Georgians of his generation, he was active in a variety of commercial enterprises; he was a farmer, rancher, tanner, sawmill owner, shopkeeper and shipper. He was the original Jewish founding member of the Union Society in Savannah. This society, the first cooperative charity venture in America, sought to unite in its work Protestants, Catholics and Jews, in the belief that men of different faiths could work together for a common social cause. It exerted a profound influence for social betterment during the early history of Georgia. It is still in existence and continues along the lines marked out by its founders.

When the American Revolution broke out, Sheftall threw himself completely into the struggle and was made chairman of the Parochial Committee, organized by the patriots to help take care of the affairs of Georgia. Like other colonies, Georgia was divided into Whig and Tory camps, and the Parochial Committee soon became the *de facto* government. Sheftall's importance became apparent when the Royal Governor James Wright in a letter to a high British official complained that "one Sheftall, a Jew, is chairman of the Parochial Committee, as they call themselves, and this fellow issues orders to captains of vessels to depart the King's port without landing any of their cargoes legally imported."

In 1777, as the war progressed, Sheftall was appointed Commissary-General of Purchases and Issues to the Georgia Militia. In the following year the American General Robert Howe appointed him Deputy Commissary General of Purchases and Issues to the Continental troops of South Carolina and Georgia, an office which carried with it the rank of colonel. His son, Sheftall Sheftall, then only sixteen years of age was already an assistant deputy commissary of issues, serving as his father's deputy.

In the same year, 1778, the British determined to capture Savannah and to sweep north through the Carolinas, hoping thus to wipe away the shame incurred the preceding year by Burgoyne's surrender at Saratoga. Late in December, Lieutenant Colonel Archibald Campbell landed near Georgia, found a way through the swamps and routed the smaller force of defending American militiamen under General Howe. Both Mordecai Sheftall and his son were among those captured when the city fell on December 29, 1778. Mordecai might have escaped but his son could not swim. Captured with one hundred and eighty-five officers and men, he had the satisfaction of hearing the British commander refer to him as a "very great rebel." Refusing to talk, he was thrown into a guardhouse for Negroes. Ill treated by drunken soldiers and denied food for two days, his end seemed near. But German-Yiddish saved him. A Hessian officer, delighted to hear some one speak his native tongue in a foreign country, took good care of the Jewish prisoner.

Mordecai Sheftall

§32

Mordecai spent several months on a prison ship. Paroled with others, he was confined to Sunbury, a town in Georgia. He tried to escape on a brig but was recaptured by a British frigate and kept on the hot West Indian island of Antigua. Mordecai and his son were released after promising not to fight England for the duration of the war. They reached Philadelphia, and six months later the parole was cancelled when they were exchanged for other prisoners equal in rank.

While prisoners of war, Sheftall and two others continued to hold meetings of the Union Society to keep it alive. In 1825 when Lafayette laid the cornerstone of the Pulaski Monument in Savannah, a relic was deposited within it with the words: "A piece of oaktree from Sunbury County, Georgia, under which in 1779 the charter of the Union Society was preserved, and Mr. Mordecai Sheftall, then a prisoner of war, was elected president."

In 1783, following the war, Sheftall received a grant of land from the government in recognition of his services. During the struggle he had advanced monies for the maintenance of the troops. Despite appeals to Congress, these were never fully repaid.

Mordecai Sheftall was an observant Jew and took an active part in Jewish communal work. He helped organize Mikveh Israel in Philadelphia and, though financially disabled, donated three pounds for building the synagogue. He made a tiresome journey to Charleston in order to be present at the dedication of the Beth Elohim. In his own community besides donating ground for a cemetery, he furnished a room in his home for group prayer and assisted in the establishment of the Mikveh Israel Congregation of Savannah. He was also prominent as a freemason and conducted a correspondence with the leading men of his time.

1778 § JUDGE MOSES LEVY of Philadelphia

In New Amsterdam, as New York was called during the Dutch regime, there was no class of professional lawyers. Cases were tried before the court, but neither magistrates nor those who pleaded before them, had any legal education. For example, the name of Solomon Pietersen, the earliest we have on record, appears as attorney in 1654 in the court records of New Amsterdam, although he had no legal training. No name is more prominent than that of Asser Levy whose almost uniform success against Governor Stuyvesant in defending the rights of his people accounts for the fact that he appears as attorney for others also.

The colonial colleges for the most part catered to prospective clergymen and at a later date to attorneys. At that time Jews were businessmen and merchants, not ministers or lawyers. Merchants' sons who might follow in their fathers' footsteps did not receive an academic education.

Philadelphia was the seat of culture, one of the great educational centers in the new world. Not a few of the institutions of the city bore the imprint of Benjamin Franklin, who was founder of the College of Philadelphia, later to be known as the University of Pennsylvania. The preparatory school associated with the College was called the Academy. Five Jewish boys were enrolled there before 1770. One of these, Moses Levy, who was born in Philadelphia, son of a prominent merchant and signer of the Non-Importation Resolution, completed the college course and received an A.B. degree in the class of 1772. He was the only Jewish graduate of the institution in pre-Revolutionary times. After continuing his course of studies in the law school, he was admitted to the bar in 1778 to become America's first Jewish lawyer. He became a member of the Legislature, holding other public offices until 1822 when he was chosen presiding judge of the District Court of Philadelphia. In 1802 his own college elected him a trustee, a position he held for twenty-five years until the time of his death. He also appears to have been a man of property, for he sold his house on Chestnut Street for $10,000 to the Bank of North America, the first bank in the United States.

As counsel in many cases and because of his brilliant record as judge, Levy won the highest esteem of his associates of the Philadelphia bench and bar. At one time his name was mentioned in the Jefferson-Gallatin correspondence as a worthy candidate for the office of Attorney-General of the United States.

Moses
Levy

§34

President Jefferson wanted to appoint Moses Levy to the post, and on September 1, 1804, wrote the following to Gallatin, Secretary of the Treasury: "I ask the favor of you to inquire fully into the legal knowledge, judgement, and moral and social character of Levy. We must have none but a good-humored man." Gallatin replied, "As a lawyer he is superior to Dickinson, and would, I presume, do tolerably well."

After the outbreak of the Revolution, tradition has it that Moses Levy served in the Continental Army and was one of that army of picked soldiers who, on Christmas Night of 1776, at a crucial time in the battle-line of the nation crossed the Delaware with George Washington to fight in the Battles of Princeton and Trenton. Later he was for years an active member of the Pennsylvania Militia.

Today more than one-fifth of all the lawyers in the United States are Jewish. In New York City, more than three-fifths are Jewish.

At Harvard Law School, where through the 1920's Felix Frankfurter was the solitary Jewish Professor, nearly half the faculty is now Jewish and the last three deans of the Yale Law School have been Jews.

1779 § BENJAMIN NONES: Jeffersonian

Benjamin Nones, one of a group of Frenchmen who had come to America in 1777 at the same time as Marquis de Lafayette, was one of the notable Jewish officers of the Revolution. Believing heart and soul in freedom, he left a thriving wine business behind in Bordeaux and came to the assistance of the embattled Americans.

Soon after his arrival in Philadelphia, he enlisted as a volunteer in the Continental Army. He served first as a private under Pulaski, then under Baron De Kalb, and finally as major and staff officer under Lafayette and Washington. He went through the entire war, from the early campaign in the south to the final ones which ended the struggle.

Gallant conduct, especially during the siege of Savannah, brought his promotion to the rank of major. Major Nones, with those under his command at the Battle of Savannah, "shared the hardships of that sanguinary day." He became a major of a company of four hundred men composed in part of Hebrews. They were attached to Baron De Kalb's command. At the Battle of Camden, on August 16, 1780, General De Kalb, mortally wounded, was carried off the field by Major Nones and two other Jewish officers, Captain Jacob De la Motta and Captain Jacob de Leon.

Major Nones was cited by General Pulaski for valor in action, in the following letter written by a captain of the staff:

"Benjamin Nones has served as a volunteer in my company during the campaign of this year and at the siege of Savannah in Georgia, and his behavior under fire in all the bloody actions we fought have been marked by the bravery and courage which a military man is expected to show for the liberties of his country, and which acts of said Nones gained in his favor the esteem of General Pulaski as well as that of all the officers who witnessed his daring conduct."

After Yorktown fighting virtually ceased. Major Nones returned to Philadelphia and went into a partnership with Haym Salomon. But all chances of prosperity vanished in 1785 when the patriotic financier from Poland died. Nones became an official interpreter of French and Spanish for the Board of Health and for the United States government. Yet he barely earned enough to feed his steadily increasing family of fourteen children.

Feeling at home in the Sephardic ritual of Philadelphia's first synagogue, Nones joined Congregation Mikve Israel and served as its first president before and after the turn of the century.

On the national level, politics began seething with Thomas Jefferson as a candidate for the presidency. The Federalists predicted dire calamity should victory go to Jefferson the agnostic. To the Republicans, the Alien and Sedition Laws stamped the Adams administration as Bourbon despotism. Certain Federalists resorted to anti-Semitism. Such attacks might have been few. But 3,000 Jews scattered in a population of 4,000,000 in fifteen states were an inconsequential minority to attack. Some were Federalists, but in general Jews leaned toward the party of Jefferson as the more liberal, progressive and tolerant.

In one of these anti-Semitic attacks, Benjamin Nones emerges creditably. He was present at a meeting of the Philadelphia Democratic Society, the most influential in the Union. At the conclusion, the chairman asked the audience to pitch in a small sum to help defray the cost of the hall. Nones pleaded poverty for his inability to contribute. Caleb Wayne, the publisher of the *Gazette*, a Federalist organ, seized upon the incident to deride the chairman, the speakers and the audience. His reference to Citizen Nones, the Jew, intended to be funny, was derogatory.

*Benjamin
Nones*

Benjamin Nones answered with humorous defiance some of the charges that his opponent had brought against him. It appeared as an article on August 13, 1800 in the Philadelphia *Aurora*.

§36

Nones was as devoted to his religion as he was to his country. Soon after joining the army, he explained to his superior officer that he was a Jew and respectfully requested exemption from military duties on the Sabbath. The officer was much impressed by the boy's attachment to his faith and ordered that he be permitted to observe his holy day. This order, first of this kind issued in this country, is still preserved in the annals of the Revolutionary War.

It reads as follows: ". . . Benjamin Nones, being of the Jewish religion, and having signified that it is inconsistent with his Jewish religion to perform military duties on Friday nights, it is ordered he be exempted from military duties that night of the week."

Nones ran for public office. We have a most interesting campaign letter in which he tells that he is accused of being a Jew, of being a Republican, and of being poor. He proudly states that he is all three of these terrible things, but that in his opinion these make him still more worthy of election.

1784 § MOSES MICHAEL HAYS: Masonic Grand Master

For many years the ships that sailed out of America with cargoes for Europe and Asia were insured, if at all, in London. The only way the owner of a ship could insure it against the risks of shipwreck, piracy, and other ocean dangers was to take out a policy of Lloyd's of London. But by the eighteenth century sea traffic was so heavy it seemed sensible to transfer the writing of insurance to Boston. Moses Michael Hays opened a marine insurance office in Boston. Setting himself up at 68 State Street, Hays would make out a policy, describing the vessel, the voyage it was to make, the rate and amount of

MOSES MICHAEL HAYS

insurance. Boston merchants who wished to share in the risk signed their names to the policy with amounts they were willing to under-write. He did well in business and at a later date added to this "an Assurance Office for houses and household goods from loss and damage from fire, in any part of the Province." In 1784 a group of nine merchants called upon him to help make plans for a bank to serve them like the Bank of England, receiving deposits and dis-counting loans. This bank became the direct ancestor of the First National Bank of Boston, the largest in New England and one of the largest in the United States.

Born in 1739, the son of a New York merchant, Judah Hays, he had started life as a watchmaker and had been admitted a freeman in New York in 1769. Moving to Newport around 1770, he set up a modest shop as a general merchant "on the Point near Holmes Wharf." He built and freighted ships for the next two years but suffered many setbacks.

In 1776, Hays loyalty to the American cause was impugned and he was asked to sign a loyalty oath. With a courage rare for the times, when hysteria and suspicion ran wild, Hays demanded to be confronted by his accusers.

In an eloquent petition to the Rhode Island General Assembly, Hays refused to sign the oath. It was unconstitutional he held. Furthermore, he pointed out, since Jews could not vote, the oath was discriminatory. He prevailed; no one ever again doubted his loyalty.

After the Revolution, Hays settled in Boston, where he soon made his mark in business, chiefly as a maritime insurance broker. He attained wealth and a position of prominence.

He was a brother-in-law of Rabbi Isaac Touro, the first rabbi of the Newport Synagogue. It was in his household that his nephews, Judah and Abraham Touro, grew up.

To his home came many of the notables of the day, including Senator Harrison Otis and Ezra Styles, President of Yale.

He became a leading figure in Masonic circles and was responsible for the introduction into the country of the "Ancient Accepted Scottish Rite" of Masonry which comprised thirty-three degrees. In recognition of his contribution, he was elected Grand Master of the Grand Lodge at annual elections from 1788 to 1792. In 1793 he became a member of a subordinate lodge and was again elected Grand Master. Paul Revere served as a deputy grandmaster under him. His sons and grandsons constituted the only Masons in Massachusetts before 1810.

Hays was the first Jewish benefactor of Harvard College and appears on the donors list as early as 1780.

He died in Boston in 1805 and was buried in the Jewish cemetery in Newport. In his obituary, the Boston Centinel wrote: " He walked abroad fearing no man, but loving all . . . He was without guile, detesting hypocrisy as he despised meanness! Take him for all in all, he was indeed a man."

He left what was for the day a large estate, appraised at $82,000. It is interesting to note that amongst his assets, as diverse as lands in Georgia and Rhode Island, bonds and a house in Boston, were "twenty-two Hebrew books."

A portrait of Moses Michael Hays hangs today in the Masonic Temple of Boston. A copy of the Gilbert Stuart original which was lost in a fire, it shows a handsome face, firm mouth, strong chin, and dark appraising eyes.

Moses Michael Hays

§38

1786 § AARON LEVY: A Jewish Builder in Pennsylvania

The first town in America planned by and named for a Jew is Aaronsburg, Pennsylvania, which soon after its founding acquired a population of two hundred and fifty.

AARON LEVY

It happened on October 5, 1786, when the state conveyed land to Aaron Levy, an Indian trader and land speculator, whose vast real estate dealings ranged throughout the frontier of the colony and the state of Pennsylvania. Levy, who was well-known in the community, had come to America from Holland in 1760 while still in his teens to become one of the patriots of the American Revolution. With other patriots he had risked losing his life at the hands of the British by giving aid to the rebels. He was at times associated with the Gratz brothers of Philadelphia, with Robert Morris and James Wilson. Most of his life he lived on the frontier himself, in Northumberland County, where his tract of land was located. As he grew older, he apparently sought Jewish communal life, and ultimately moved back to the more settled areas, first to Lancaster and then to Philadelphia.

In June 1779, Levy purchased from a Mr. Wetzel a large tract of land, and several years later, planned the town of Aaronsburg. The town in all comprised six hundred and twelve lots, each measuring sixty by two hundred and twenty feet. Houses were laid out with taste and skill. In the naming of streets, Levy used personal names, one honoring his wife Rachel. In his vast real estate transactions he was represented by Judge Moses Levy of the Philadelphia bar.

On November 16, 1789, Levy gave the trustees of the Salem Evangelical Church two lots for the construction of a church, school and cemetery. The opening of the church as the first house of worship of the community marked one of the brightest chapters in interfaith relations in the United States. This small hamlet today has a population of three hundred and twelve. In observance of the sesquicentenninal of the opening of the church, one of the highlights of the ceremony was the presentation by the Salem Lutheran Church of a kiddush cup to Shearith Israel of New York, oldest Jewish congregation in the United States. The cup symbolized "The Return of the Gift."

Aaron Levy

§40

On the one hundred and fiftieth anniversary of the founding of the town, it was the scene of a great demonstration as thirty thousand Americans of all faiths spent a Sunday there to celebrate. The event received national publicity. Prominent figures, including Justice Felix Frankfurter of the United States Supreme Court, Dr. Ralph Bunche, United Nations diplomat and Nobel Prize winner, and the Rev. Daniel Poling, distinguished clergyman, spoke on interfaith good-will as the American way of life.

Today, there is a series of villages and towns beginning with Aaronsburg, Pennsylvania, that extend across the country along the old trails to Roseville, California; Gilman, Vermont, and Heppner, Oregon, named after hardy Jewish souls, who like Aaron Levy brought with them the first breath of civilization to hitherto untrampled territory.

1791 § BENJAMIN GOMEZ: Bookdealer and Publisher

As the years went by schools grew in numbers and people became more interested in books and learning. On July 6, 1791, the first American Jewish bookdealer and publisher opened his shop. Benjamin Gomez, the owner, was a man of intelligence and high character. He stemmed from a distinguished family of Spanish Marranos who had originated in Madrid and had established themselves in the United States at the beginning of the eighteenth century. His father Luiz Gomez, one of New York's principal merchants, was the community's recognized head for many years.

Benjamin Gomez first appeared in the New York directory of 1791 as a bookseller, when he was located at 32 Maiden Lane "near the Fly Market," where his brother Isaac Gomez, carried on business as a broker. Gomez was one of the biggest booksellers of the day and also sold stationery. A few months after he opened his shop,

Gomez ran a full page notice in a local paper to say that he had many volumes for sale including some "just imported from Dublin." Although there were no detective stories and novels in his shop, he offered a wide choice of books. All were on religious, historical, or scientific subjects, ranging from the Bible, Shakespeare, and *Arabian Nights* to books on anatomy. The following year he extended his activities to include publishing. Twenty-one of the books he published are still known to us. They include Hugh Gaines' edition of *Pilgrim's Progress* (1794), an abridged edition of *Robinson Crusoe* (1795), *Captain Cook's Third and Last Voyage* (1795), as well as *The Sorrows of Werther* (1795).

After a few years Gomez moved to new quarters at 97 Maiden Lane, and his success was sufficient to cause Naphtalie Judah of New York in 1795 to enter the trade as America's second Jewish book-seller and publisher.

Like so many members of his family, Benjamin Gomez served the Congregation Shearith Israel in various offices including that of treasurer and of president.

Gomez was also an early Jewish juror in New York City.

1792 § EPHRAIM HART: A Co-founder of the New York Stock Exchange

The first Congress of the United States under the Constitution which met during 1789-1790 in Federal Hall at the corner of Broad and Wall Streets in New York City issued $80,000,000 in stocks and bonds in order to pay the Revolutionary War debts. This action created the need for a market place for the public sale of these securities. Orders came into New York in such volume that some merchants and auctioneers began to devote most of their time to this business. By the Spring of 1792 attempts were made by these "stockbrokers" to organize and their efforts culminated in the signing of the agreement of May 17, 1792 which marks the founding of the New York Stock Exchange. It is known as the "Buttonwood Agreement" from the fact that it was signed under a large button-wood (sycamore) tree which stood in the front of the present 68 Wall Street. The twenty-four stockbrokers who signed it were the first members of the New York Stock Exchange which now has

1,336 members and whose daily transactions often exceed 10,000,000 shares.

The idea of drawing buyers and sellers to an organized central market to share in the risks and rewards of investing, generated new opportunities for investors to help develop the nation.

By 1817 the New York Stock Exchange had been formally incorporated with a set of rules which by today's standards were delightfully lax, but which did require a listing of companies whose shares were being offered for trading.

Ephraim Hart

§42

Investors bought shares which had been issued to finance the Erie Canal, the banks and insurance companies, then the railroads which opened the whole continent to trade.

By 1911 investors were buying automobile stock, one of a host of industries that helped create the kind of economy the world had never seen before.

Today more than twenty million investors are part owners of the nation's publicly held companies.

One of the orginal organizers who met in 1792 in the tiny open air market and helped found the first New York Board of Stockbrokers as it was then called was Ephraim Hart.

Mr. Hart was willing to accept the agreement which read as follows:

"We the Subscribers, and Brokers for the purchase and sale of Public Stocks, do hereby solemnly promise and pledge ourselves to each other that we will not buy or sell from this day to any person whatsoever, any kind of Public Stock at less a rate than one quarter of one per cent commission on the specie value and that we will give a preference to each other in our own negotiations."

We know from the Hart account books and correspondence that he continued to do a large and important trade.

The son of Samuel Hart, he was born in Furth, Bavaria in 1747. We do not know the exact date when he arrived in New York, but he resided in the city prior to the British occupancy of September 15, 1776. The confusion and uncertainty of war made it impossible for him to establish himself immediately. When the British took the port of New York he refused to remain under British Redcoat rule. As an American patriot, he felt he could not live and work in a community that had lost its liberty. With his friend Jonas Phillips and other New York Jews, he left New York for Philadelphia. (Later,

Phillips was to have the distinction in American history of being the only outside person to address the convention assembled in Philadelphia to formulate the Constitution of the United States).

Ephraim Hart remained in Philadelphia for several years. Gradually family after family moved to Philadelphia to join the growing Jewish community in that city. Early in 1782 a congregation was organized there under the name Mikve Israel. Hart became a member of the congregation and took part in dedicating its new synagogue.

About this time we find him a merchant, residing at 398 Third Street. In 1783 he married Frances Noah, sister of Manuel Noah, a long resident of Philadelphia and aunt of the noted Mordecai Manuel Noah of New York. Several years later, Ephraim Hart disposed of his possessions in Philadelphia, among them certain pieces of ground and returned to New York.

He started in the business of stockbroker at 52 Broad Street and later at 74 Wall Street. He was a successful businessman and made many friends, being foremost in many important enterprises. When in 1798 the Bank of Manhattan was formed by Jeffersonians as a people's bank, Ephraim Hart (with three other Jews) was among its original stockholders. He was at this period a very wealthy man and owned much valuable real estate on Wall Street which was assessed at the valuation of $11,000. He was a State Senator in 1810. At the time of his death he was a partner of John Jacob Astor, the great merchant prince of New York.

Ephraim Hart identified himself closely with the Jewish community of New York. He was a very charitable man and greatly interested in the religious affairs of New York Jewry. When the time came to reconstruct and enlarge the original Mill Street building of Congregation Shearith Israel he contributed funds and participated actively in the plan. He was one of the founders in 1802 of the Hebra Hesed ve Emet (The Fellowship of Mercy and Truth), a society for attendance upon the sick and burial of the dead, attached to Congregation Shearith Israel. It found its origin from the fact that Ephraim Hart and Naphtali Phillips, the son of Jonas Phillips, were walking on one occasion in the streets of New York and saw a funeral procession about to bury a man in Potter's Field. Upon inquiry they ascertained that the deceased was a poor and unknown Israelite. Thereupon they stopped the proceedings and had the man buried on Jewish ground. This society is supposed to be the oldest burial or mutual aid society in the United States and the oldest existing Jewish philanthropic organization in the City of New York.

Ephraim Hart lived to be a very old man, beloved and honored not only by his fellow Jews but by all his Gentile neighbors as well. He died on July 16, 1825 and was buried in the cemetery of Congregation Shearith Israel on what is now West Eleventh Street, near Sixth Avenue. The inscription on his tombstone in Hebrew states that: "He came from Furth in Germany, that he died on Sunday, 2nd day of the Hebrew month of Ab, 5585, that at the time of his death he had been a resident of the city forty years, was an exceedingly charitable man and an earnest communal worker especially in the direction of strengthening the faith of his fathers."

His daughter, Harriet Judith in 1804 met and married Benjamin Hart, son of Aaron Hart of Canada, who in 1800 was styled the wealthiest colonist in the British Empire.

Joel Hart, the only son of Ephraim Hart, was educated in England and was a graduate of the Royal College of Surgeons in London. He was one of the charter members of the Medical Society of the County of New York.

Ephraim Hart's distant kinsman, Bernard Hart, was secretary of the New York Stock Exchange from 1831 to 1853.

Ephraim Hart

§44

1812 § HARMON HENDRICKS and His Copper Rolling Mill

The great Sephardic families of New York, many of them descended from the *St. Charles* arrivals included the Hendrickses. By the beginning of the nineteenth century a number of Sephardim had become quite prosperous. Harmon Hendricks, for instance, had a copper store in Mill Street (now South William Street).

The Soho Copper Mill, the first copper rolling mill in America, was also built by Harmon Hendricks in Belleville, New Jersey in 1812. It was owned and operated by descendants of Harmon Hendricks until 1939, when the Hendricks Company went out of business and sold its plant to the Andrew Jergens Company as the site of a new factory. A stone wall and brick building near the Jergens plant are the last vestiges of this pioneer industrial enterprise which existed for many years as the oldest Jewish founded business concern in the United States.

As early as 1764, Uriah Hendricks, the father of Harmon Hendricks, established a business in metals in New York soon after his arrival from Holland. In 1776 his name appears as one of the signers

HARMON HENDRICKS

of the loyalist address of General Howe. His grandson, Uriah Hendricks II, carried on the work of the firm and in turn handed it down to his four sons. We know from the Hendricks account books and correspondence that from modest beginnings the firm reached out into all the corners of the earth for their copper supply—England, Russia, the Mediterranean, India and South America.

There was a close relationship between the Bostonian firm of Paul Revere and Son, and that of Hendricks. The Hendricks had been supplying the Reveres with material needed in their factory, some of which went into the famous warship *Constitution* and the first steamship launched successfully by Robert Fulton. In 1812 Hendricks' brother-in-law and business associate, Solomon I. Isaacs, acted as sales and financial agent for the Reveres. He carefully allocated his goods to shut off competitors and tried to consolidate his customers soundly in behalf of the Reveres. As an example of a trade monopoly the working out of this scheme holds its own in contrast with attempts to control industry by our later captains of industry.

Harmon Hendricks was active in Jewish communal affairs and in 1824 was chosen president of Congregation Shearith Israel in New York. During the War of 1812 he gave $40,000 as a government loan when the government was having difficulty with the sale of war bonds. This was one of the largest individual subscriptions for bonds ever made in the annals of American history up to that date.

He died in the 1840's, according to one report, "immensely rich, leaving over three million dollars."

In his book *The Old Merchants of New York City* published in 1863, Walter Barrett eulogized the "great copper merchant of former years" and says: ". . . No man stood higher in the community while he lived, and no man has left a memory more revered than Harmon Hendricks. When he died, the synagogue which he attended lost one of its best friends, and the rising generation of that numerous family could not have had a better example."

Henry S. Hendricks, for many years honorary president of Congregation Shearith Israel, is a direct descendant of Harmon Hendricks.

1819 § REBECCA GRATZ: Heroine of Fiction

Rebecca Gratz, the rich, beautiful, idealistic belle of Philadelphian society, daughter of the great merchant Michael Gratz, upon whom literary immortality has been conferred, is the original of the character of Rebecca in Sir Walter Scott's novel, *Ivanhoe*.

Her purity of heart, beauty of face, and loyalty to her race inspired the imagination of her friend, Washington Irving, who frequently enjoyed the hospitality of the Gratz home. In 1807, he wrote to Rebecca about the proposed visit to Philadelphia of Thomas Sully, the artist: "I think I can render him no favor of which he ought to be more grateful, than in introducing him to the notice of yourself and your connections." In the spring of 1809, Washington Irving's beloved Matilda Hoffman died of consumption and had been nursed tenderly for the last six months of her life by Rebecca, who had been her childhood friend. Going abroad to bury his grief, Irving visited and became friendly with Sir Walter Scott, then at the height of his fame and all but the acknowledged author of the Waverly Novels. For each of them it was a great meeting. It laid the foundation for a genuine friendship. "To this friendship," says Gratz Van Rensselaer, "we owe the character of Rebecca in *Ivanhoe*." For Scott was then pondering over in his mind the story of *Ivanhoe*. He told the great author about Rebecca Gratz. Scott was interested. "He immediately

REBECCA GRATZ

determined to introduce a Jewish female character and, on the strength of Irving's vivid description, he named his heroine Rebecca." When Scott finished his novel in 1819, he sent a copy to Irving with a note expressing the hope that the Rebecca of *Ivanhoe* typified all that was noble in the real Rebecca. The qualities described in *Ivanhoe* precisely fitted the original, and are those for which Scott's Rebecca has become such a popular heroine.

Rebecca Gratz read *Ivanhoe* in 1820. She wrote on the fourth of April, to her sister-in-law: "Have you received *Ivanhoe*? When you read it tell me what you think of my namesake Rebecca."

Scott's pen portrait of Rebecca might well have been written about Miss Gratz, of whom there are two excellent likenesses, the one by Sully, the other by Malbone. Sully said:

". . . that he had never seen a more striking Hebraic face. The easy pose, suggestive of perfect health, the delicately turned neck and shoulders with the firmly posed head and its profusion of dark, curling hair, large clear black eyes, the contour of the face, the fine white skin, the expressive mouth and the firmly chiseled nose, with its strength of character, left no doubt as to the race from which she had sprung. Possessed of an elegant bearing, a melodiously sympathetic voice, a simple and frank and gracious womanliness, there was about Rebecca Gratz all that a princess of the blood Royal might have coveted."

Outgrowing the romantic legend of her life, Rebecca Gratz became a leading worker for charity and education. In 1801 she became the tireless secretary of the first society organized to help the poor of Philadelphia, a non-sectarian organization known as the "Female Association for the Relief of Women and Children in Reduced Circumstances." In 1819 she organized the "Female Hebrew Benevolent Society" to care for the large number of Jewish immigrants then entering the United States. This organization was the first Jewish philanthropic agency apart from a synagogue ever established and was the inspiration for all the Jewish welfare agencies to appear later. When there were orphans to care for, Rebecca started the first Jewish orphan asylum in her city and in America; she was its secretary for forty years. After having observed how the Christians taught their children religion one day a week, she drew up the plans for the first Hebrew Sunday School in America, and was its president and supervisor for twenty-six years. This school is still in existence in Philadelphia.

Too beautiful to escape romance, she was too genuine and loyal to benefit by the love she inspired. Rebecca refused to marry outside her faith and remained a lifelong spinster, even though the man she loved was the handsome and literary son of Dr. John Ewing, noted clergyman, educator and Provost of the University of Pennsylvania.

When she died at the age of eighty-eight, she was mourned as the foremost lady in the United States and one of the noblest women in the world.

Rebecca Gratz

§48

1823 § SOLOMON JACKSON: First Jewish Newspaper Publisher

The first Jewish newspaper published in America devoted exclusively to Jewish affairs was known as *The Jew*. It was published monthly in New York, beginning March 1823, by Solomon Henry Jackson, who had a virtual monopoly of all synagogue printing. It sold for a dollar fifty a year and was delivered to New York subscribers at their dwellings and to distant subscribers through the New York post office. It ran for two years and was published primarily as a defense of Judaism against all adversaries and particularly against the insidious attacks of the *Israel Advocate* which as house organ of the American Society for the Amelioration of the Condition of the Jew, a missionary society, had set about spreading false ideas about the Jew.

In 1812 the Boston blue-stocking, Hannah Adams, of the noted presidential family, published *The History of the Jews from the Destruction of Jerusalem to the Nineteenth Century.* Hannah Adams had shown an active interest in the conversion of the Jews and was associated with America's first missionary society. Her book, with inaccurate additions was used by prominent missionary societies in England for propagating Christianity among Jews.

Jews did not dare fight back. Nor could a population of less than 6,000 scattered in all states be equipped for such a fight. Synagogues without ordained or qualified rabbis constituted the sole organization in the era when the Monroe Doctrine was formulated. Yet an individual did come forth as their champion.

Solomon Jackson, born in England and related to Mordecai Manuel Noah, had received a good Jewish and secular education. He came to America in 1787 and settled in Pike County, Pennsylvania.

Solomon Jackson operated a printing business and wrote English with style. Without outside help he began publishing the first Jewish periodical in the western hemisphere. For two years he edited *The Jew: Being the Defense of Judaism Against All Adversaries and Particularly Against the Insidious Attacks of Israel's Advocate.*

The valiant refutations of Jackson read somewhat like the public religious dialogues of the Middle Ages. His polemics contradicted the papers, pamphlets and books of the missionaries. His editorials carried on a sturdy campaign designed to keep Jews safe from the blandishments of missionaries. In short he used every weapon in his power to counteract the Society and its friends.

After 1825 *The Jew* ceased to appear. The sum total of missionary activities in the United States among Jews showed such meager results that one by one, the societies closed down. All the efforts of Dr. Peter Wilson, a Columbia University professor and authority on Josephus scarcely netted a single convert. The years of labor by the apostate Frey could not even produce one.

Solomon Jackson's activities continued chiefly in communal affairs. Almost all of the notices, tickets, constitutions, wedding certificates and similar material printed by him can be seen today in the Lyons' *Scrapbook* and in the archives of the various early synagogues. Besides serving as one-time secretary of Congregation Shearith Israel, he was active in the formation of both Congregations Anshe Chesed and Shaarey Zedek. He translated the prayerbook and published an English *Sidur* sixty years after Isaac Pinto first rendered the Spanish and Portuguese ritual in English. A decade later he printed the first American bi-lingual edition of the *Haggadah* (Passover service) in English and Hebrew.

His press was taken over by his son, J. M. Jackson in the late 1840's.

Solomon Jackson

§50

In 1837 during the worst of all American economic depressions, Solomon Jackson served as president of the Society of Zeire Hazon (the Tender Sheep). This association aimed at settling a number of recently arrived immigrants, mainly German Jews, in a cooperative group on agricultural colonies in the Far West on the fertile soil which a benign government was giving away gratis.

When Jackson's paper was discontinued, the Jews of New York had to rely on the local press for news of Jewish interest until 1843, when the Reverend Isaac Leeser, outspoken educator and opponent of slavery, founded *The Occident* in Philadelphia. By 1849, however, New York Jews began to venture into the field of Jewish periodical publication and thereafter the community never lacked organs for the dissemination of Jewish news.

1824 § MORDECAI MANUEL NOAH and his City of Refuge for the Jews

Mordecai Manuel Noah who in 1824 had declared, "We will return to Zion as we went forth, bringing the faith we carried away with us," with this statement had anticipated almost by a century the Zionism of today.

Noah's career was a varied one. He was born in Philadelphia in 1785, the son of a soldier of the Revolutionary War. The elder Noah, it was believed by some, had won the friendship of his commander, George Washington, who actually attended his wedding. During his lifetime, Manuel Noah worked at many things. He was a newspaper-man. He edited among other papers, *The New York Enquirer*, *The Evening Star*, and *The Union*. He helped James Gordon Bennett to found *The New York World*. He wrote plays and studied law. He also served as a judge, sheriff, and Surveyor of the Port of New York. But his great enthusiasm was for the history of the Jewish people.

In 1813 President Madison appointed him as American consul to

Tunis, thus making him the first Jew in America to hold a high diplomatic post in the foreign service of his country. Noah felt very sorry over the plight of the homeless Jews in the Orient and Europe, and it was here that he began to dream of a land for them. He wanted to see Palestine returned, but knowing how difficult it would be to obtain such a concession from the rulers, his thoughts turned to the great open spaces of America. It was after his return from Algiers that he sought to found an island of asylum for the oppressed Jews of the world.

Mordecai Manuel Noah

§51

In 1825 he purchased a tract of 17,000 acres on Grand Island in the Niagara River near Buffalo, as a site for Jewish settlement. Giving himself the title of "Governor and Judge of Israel," he issued a manifesto to Jews all over the world calling upon them to come and settle in the new colony which he named Ararat which was to be under the protection of the Constitution and laws of the United States.

Noah's Ararat was not intended to supplant the Zion of Holy Writ; it would become a temporary haven for the persecuted until the fulfillment of biblical prophesy. In some mysterious way the fifty square miles of Grand Island would sustain millions until the sounding of the great Shofar of Redemption.

On a bright September day in 1825, the dedication ceremonies of Ararat began with a long and imposing procession made up of Buffalo's leading citizens; prominent politicians from New York and Philadelphia; Indians gay with feathers; the militia marching smartly in orderly ranks; Mr. Noah's fellow Masons, who sometimes failed to keep step, but looked most imposing in their lodge regalia.

But soldiers and Masons and gaudy Indians were completely eclipsed by the sartorial glories of the Governor and Judge over Israel in his splendid crimson robes trimmed with ermine. Some years before he had received the honorary title of Major; although he had now grown rather portly, he still carried himself gallantly and spectators cheered him again and again.

Alas, Mordecai Noah had kept so busy preparing his speech and trying on his judge's robe that he never once considered one important detail. There were not nearly enough boats to take the yelling, pushing crowd across the river. Everybody was sadly disappointed; Mr. Noah, most of all. For, so the story goes, he had never set foot on Grand Island himself and was most anxious to see the site of his City of Refuge with his own eyes.

A hurried consultation among the authorities followed. The band began to play again; the townspeople and Indians, the Masons and

MORDECAI MANUEL NOAH
(Courtesy of the American Jewish Historical Society)

politicians and, of course, Mr. Noah marched to St. Paul's Episcopal Church. Because it was the largest building in Buffalo, the friendly rector had offered it for the dedication ceremony. The cornerstone with its carefully worded inscription was displayed; there were readings from the Prophets and Psalms, one in Hebrew, and the Benediction. Mr. Noah spoke with great eloquence—and at some length. The militia furnished a welcome ending to the celebration with a salute of twenty-four guns.

The Jews did not flock to the new refuge on the banks of the Niagara River. In fact there is no record that any Jew ever came to New York State for the purpose of settling in Ararat. Not a single building was erected. Noah returned to New York and printed his address and proclamation in the newspapers. Eventually the cornerstone commemorating the venture found its way into the Buffalo Historical Society.

But Noah did not despair when the island of his dreams remained a wilderness. Twenty years later we find him writing a pamphlet in which he advocated Jewish restoration of Zion by Jewish self-effort, demanded support of the Christian world for Jewish resettlement in Palestine, and suggested that the land be acquired through purchase. Little did he realize that fifty years thereafter another dreamer and man of action, Theodor Herzl, would call upon the Jews of the world to follow him to Palestine, and that he would receive an immediate answer.

Noah continued active in many Jewish and communal causes. His theatrical work was popular. The American scene and American history remained among his favorite subjects. Students at Columbia University staged his play, *Marion, or the Hero of Lake George*, in 1932, one hundred and ten years after it was written.

To this day in the New York Historical Society may be seen a little worn-out, paper-backed book entitled *The Wandering Boys, or the Castle of Olival—a Melo Drama in Two Acts*. It is dated 1821. It was another of the many plays Noah wrote for the American stage depicting life in America, and is sprinkled with his knowledge of the Barbary Coast and Europe.

But Noah was a great showman, even when he did not write plays. All in all, the dedication of the still-to-be-built city of Ararat had been a huge success.

1830 § PENINA MOISE: Poetess of Her People

During the greater part of Rebecca Gratz's life there was a younger woman living in Charleston, South Carolina, who resembled the Philadelphia Jewess only in her deep devotion to her religion. Miss Gratz was rich and beautiful; Penina Moise was poor and plain of face. But there must have been one good fairy who hovered over her cradle and bestowed on the child the gift denied the great lady of Philadelphia—the gift of song. The begetter of a new offspring in literature, she wrote stirring poetry full of love for her religion and her people which appeared in the leading magazines of the day and were widely read and discussed.

It is fortunate that it is not necessary to have a formal education in order to write poetry, for the girl had practically no schooling.

Shortly after the Revolutionary War the Moise family, which had emigrated from Alsace-Lorraine to the West Indies, were driven from their home on the island of San Domingo. A terrible slave uprising had not only robbed them of most of their possessions but had threatened their lives.

Abraham Moise found shelter for his family in Charleston, where Penina, one of nine children, was born. Until she was twelve she lived a happy, normal life, romping with her brothers and sisters through the rambling, comfortable house, and spending blissful hours with her favorite story books. But shortly after her twelfth birthday,

Penina's father died and uncertainty and hardship descended on the family.

Mr. Moise's death left his widow and children to face dire poverty. The older children found work and tried to support the family. Penina was now old enough to attend classes in one of the Finishing Schools for Young Ladies so popular in that day. But even if some family friend paid her tuition, the proud, shabbily dressed girl would have shrunk from associating with the daughters of the rich. And she could not be spared from her home where her frail mother expected her to share in the household duties.

Mrs. Moise's condition grew worse and she soon became helplessly paralyzed. Cleaning and cooking and helping to nurse the invalid so crowded Penina's days that often she could not escape to her cherished books until late at night. A legend has it that Penina would even study by moonlight.

While still in her teens, Penina began to write verses which at first she offered timidly for publication. To her surprised delight her poetry was accepted—and sometimes paid for—by the leading Jewish and non-Jewish papers of her day. By 1830 her poems and prose began to appear in print regularly. She was a contributor to *The Charleston Courier, The Boston Daily Times, The New Orleans Commercial Times, The Washington Union, Godey's Lady's Book and The Charleston Book,* as well as other publications.

Her family were very proud and happy, when in 1835, some of her verses were collected and published in a volume entitled, *Fancy's Sketch Book*. She became known the country over and people looked forward to her poems which now appeared as often as three times a week. Some of the most cultured leaders of Charleston read her book and offered her their friendship. They invited her to their "literary teas." Later her own home became the center of Charleston writers and scholars.

Although her work was sometimes light and humorous, her best efforts were those when as an aroused Jewess she championed her people. Her poetry on Jewish themes appeared in such publications as *The Occident.* "The Rejection of the Jew Bill in the House of Lords," "The Jews of Damascus," and "To Sir Moses Montefiore" were among her most popular works.

Her most important contribution consisted of a volume of one hundred and ninety Hebrew Hymns composed in the declining half of her lengthy life with its full measure of physical and mental pain. To this task, Penina Moise brought spiritual strivings and pious resignation, a pure heart and contrite spirit together with passionate love for Judaism. She wrote the Hymns for the use of Congregation Beth Elohim of Charleston when the Reform service was introduced. The collection was reprinted a number of times, and now there are more of her hymns in the hymnal of the Union of American Hebrew Congregations (the Reform group), than that of any other writer. They are still used in Charleston, in other American cities, and even abroad where English is spoken.

We can find space here for a few random selections. She paraphrases Psalm XXXVIII in the following verses:

> Rebuke me not nor chasten me,
> In Thy displeasure, Lord!
> But let a frail transgressor be
> To virtue's path restored.
> My heart like grass is withered up,
> Sorrow my strength destroys;
> Sin's bitter drop within my cup,
> Life's sparkling draught alloys.

And she concludes:

> For with unbroken trust will I
> In Thee, my God! confide,
> Who deigns the meek to dignify,
> The arrogant to chide.

She piously meditates on the Jewish New Year:

> Into the tomb of ages past
> Another year has now been cast;
> Shall time, unheeded, take its flight,
> Nor leave one ray of mortal light,
> That on man's pilgrimage may shine,
> And lead his soul to spheres divine?

Of "Man's Dignity" she echoes the following:

> O God! within Thy temple walls,
> Light my spirit seems, and free,
> Regardless of whose worldly calls,
> That withdraw it oft from Thee.
> Faith to the proudest whispers: Here
> Riches are but righteous deeds,
> And he who dries a human tear,
> Ne'er to mercy vainly pleads.

Penina Moise was also a teacher. She taught at Kahal Kodesh Beth Elohim's Sabbath School, which was organized only a few months after Rebecca Gratz established the first Sunday School in Philadelphia. She also conducted an exceptionally fine girl's school for many years although she became totally blind in later life.

She died in 1880 at eighty-three. Her last words were: "Lay no flowers on my grave. They are for those who live in the sun and I have always lived in the shadow."

*Penina
Moise*

§56

In 1911 the Charleston section of the Council of Jewish Women piously published a selection of Penina Moise's poetry and some of her prose.

Millions of readers have been lifted by the power of her belief and irresistible sweep of her imagination.

1832 § BENJAMIN RODRIGUEZ: Pioneer Dentist

Dentistry as an organized profession is one of the youngest in the country. Beginning with Dr. Benjamin Adolph Rodriguez of Charleston, South Carolina, we find representatives of the Jewish faith among the leaders throughout its history. A highly intellectual man and a devoted student of the arts and sciences, Dr. Rodriguez lived and worked during the period of the birth and growth of the dental profession.

After being graduated from Charleston High School and Charleston College, Rodriguez became apprenticed to Dr. V. Starr Brewster, a prominent dentist who attended the most cultured residents of the city. In 1832, upon finishing his apprenticeship, young Rodriguez received a diploma from his preceptor which qualified him to perform any operation pertaining to dentistry. Fame and fortune awaited him when Dr. Brewster departed the United States for Paris and left his extensive and prosperous practice to the young dentist.

Rodriguez's desire for knowledge was so great that after succeeding to Dr. Brewster's practice he completed the course in the Medical College of South Carolina, being graduated March 3, 1834.

Throughout his career Dr. Rodriguez was often called upon as lecturer before important dental societies. His work was quoted in standard textbooks on dental surgery, and commendations of his professional acumen appeared in lay publications.

DR. BENJAMIN RODRIGUEZ

As a dental practitioner, he directed his attention largely to the surgical phase of dental practice and to the correction of irregularities of the teeth and jaws. In 1850 he invented one of the first cleft palate obturators. He also devised many outstanding orthodontic appliances both for natural dentures and abnormalities resulting from surgical interference. For his sincere interest and effort in advancing dental science the Baltimore College of Dental Surgery conferred upon him the honorary degree of Doctor of Dental Surgery in 1850.

Thus from the start Jews have contributed to the dental profession and to the public dental health of America. They may be credited with a preponderant share of dental progress not only as specialists, educators, and scientists, but also in their organization for the advancement of the dental profession, in their development and perfection of dental appliances, in their contribution to dental literature, and in obtaining recognition for the dental profession as an ally of the purely medical profession. Old and young alike have benefited from the pioneering labors of the Jewish worker in the dental field.

*Ernestine
Rose*

§58

At the time that women in America were rebelling at their lack of independence in a changing world, Ernestine Rose, a rabbi's daughter, circulated the first petition for the property rights of women. As early as 1837 she appeared before the New York State legislature to fight for the passage of the liberalizing statute, a fight she continued for over nine years.

A practical idealist, constructive and keen minded, her development and career had been extraordinary. She was born in 1810 as Sismondi Potowski in Pyeterkow, Poland and died in London in 1892. As a child she studied the Scriptures and was observant in her practice of Judaism. But at fourteen she shocked the orthodox community of her native village by accumulating a great many doubts. Moreover, she boldly advocated equal rights for women in all spheres of communal activity.

When Sismondi Potowski was seventeen, upon her mother's death, she left home to become an apostle of humanitarianism. She traveled far and wide at her own expense and held forth on a broad range of reform topics. Alone, she visited Poland, Russia, Germany, Holland, Belgium, France, and England.

The young girl appears to have had little difficulty in associating with leaders, thinkers, and celebrities. In Berlin, Sismondi conferred with the Prussian King and castigated him for restrictions against Jews. Frederick III was impressed and she was permitted to stay as long as she liked. In Paris, she witnessed the Revolution of 1830. In The Hague, the case of a sailor's wife unjustly accused moved her girlish compassion.

Hitherto a rebel merely against social inequalities or religious tyranny, she acquired a more positive philosophy of government and society in 1832 upon coming under the influence of Robert Owen, the founder of Utopian Socialism in England. About this time Sismondi Potowski met William H. Rose, an abolitionist. They married and left England for the United States. Soon the growing country was to hear much of Ernestine Rose as a militant reformer.

Speaking with a slight and attractive foreign accent, using animated, fluent, direct, and impressive language, she advocated free public schools and called attention to the evils of the social system, wickedness of slavery, injustices to women, and the shortcomings of human character. Wherever she went, she lifted the hearts of her listeners and bound them together in the magical bond of understanding. At conventions she took a leading part as organizer, orator, parliamentarian and politician.

In 1850 she was elected delegate to the first National Women's Rights Convention in Worcester, Massachusetts. Here she met and won the respect and admiration of such liberal leaders as Lucrecia Mott, William Lloyd Garrison, Julia Ward Howe and Wendell Phillips, all advocates of women's rights, abolitionism and religious liberty. She continued as delegate to all the Women's Rights Conventions for thirty years until her health failed.

During the Civil War she joined with Elizabeth Stanton and Susan B. Anthony, Mrs. Chalkstone, a Jewess, and other anti-slavery crusaders to form the Women's National Loyal League, and was active in collecting signatures to petition President Lincoln to issue the Emancipation Proclamation.

She was the first to begin woman suffrage agitation in the West, and was largely responsible for the adoption of woman suffrage by the state of Wyoming in 1869. However, she did not live long enough to see the fruits of her labor which was finally enacted into the Nineteenth Amendment in 1920, an exploit due to her almost unaided efforts.

1842 § ADAM GIMBEL: Department Store Pioneer

Though Jews of German origin had settled in this country in the early eighteenth century, the bulk of German-Jewish immigrants migrated to the United States in the period from 1840 to 1860. These Jews were merchants, buyers, sellers and traders. They loved commerce and the clash of wits. Many of them started their lives in the new country as peddlers. Their hard work, enterprising spirit and ability to organize won for them a place of prominence in the life of the growing nation. Soon they gave up the peddler's pack and became shopkeepers.

One of this group of immigrants was a humble peddler from the province of Bavaria by the name of Adam Gimbel with whom the

ADAM GIMBEL

story of the department store movement in this country is inevitably linked.

Adam Gimbel had immigrated to New Orleans from Bavaria in 1836, when he was twenty years old, with just five dollars in his pocket and hard work on his mind. To earn money for his first stock, a peddler's pack of needles, thimbels, shoelaces and yarn, he worked on the waterfront. Adding a variety of notions and other wares to his merchandise, he travelled up and down the Mississippi Valley for seven years carrying the heavy knapsack on his back. He finally made his headquarters in Vincennes, Indiana, where he shared a dentist's office to store his merchandise. Adam made the rounds of countryside and his business grew as his reputation spread among the Indiana frontiersmen.

Adam Gimbel gave a fair price on decent merchandise. By 1842, he was able to take over the entire two-and-a-half-room frame farm building and settle down as the proprietor of a permanent trading post. The year was bad for new business. Banks were closed after the Panic of 1837 and most trading was at a halt, but Adam liked the looks of Vincennes. He opened anyway and started to build up the first Gimbel "Palace of Trade."

One by one his unusual policies went into operation. Adam Gimbel started the unheard-of custom of refunds, even on unfair complaints. To a frontiersman used to sharp trading storekeepers, the idea was revolutionary. He hung up a sign, "If anything said or done in this store looks wrong, or is wrong, we would have our customers take it for granted that we shall set it right as soon as it comes to our knowledge." He distributed a handbill, "Fairness and equality to all patrons whether they be residents of the city, plainsmen, traders or Indians." It was the "One Price House," and Adam meant it, whether you paid in money or goods." These were farsighted ideas and people eventually took to them and to Adam. Because most of his customers could not come in as often as they would have liked, Gimbel made their buying easy by stocking up with a great many varieties of goods under a single roof, thus making his place the first modern department store.

Adam Gimbel married a Philadelphia girl. The couple had a large family of seven sons. After they finished school, they all worked in their father's store. They absorbed Adam's philosophy. By 1875 the family was looking beyond their new Vincennes building. As a result the first modern Gimbels store was opened in Milwaukee in 1887. The Philadelphia store followed in 1894. At this time Adam retired from active business and his son Isaac assumed the presidency.

In Adam's time a bundle of twigs, bound firmly together beside a single broken twig adorned the director's table, whenever the seven brothers met. This was Adam's way of preaching the "solid front" of family unity and the rewards coming from it. This idea has lived on in a spectacular fashion. Half a century after Adam's death, in 1953, his grandson Bernard Gimbel became chairman of the board of directors. Bruce Gimbel is the fourth generation of the family to hold the position of president today.

By 1908 Isaac Gimbel was in New York City spearheading the Gimbels Brothers most daring venture, crashing the tautly competitive market. With his young son Bernard, Isaac began construction of the eleven story completely modern department store in Herald Square and supervised the hiring and training of a staff of 5,000 employees. The store was open to the public in 1910.

In 1923 the specialty house of Saks and Company was brought into the rapidly developing chain. One year later Gimbels introduced new fashion in women's wear with the opening of its Saks Fifth Avenue store.

The growth spiral continued with its acquisition of the Pittsburgh department store of Kaufman and Baer in 1925. After three years of physical improvements the name of the store was officially changed to Gimbel Brothers Pittsburgh, the fourth major Gimbel store.

Main store developments were followed quickly by suburban expansion. Outstanding architects and designers were engaged to create ultra-modern store designs. Construction continued at breathtaking speed and suburban Gimbels stores opened everywhere.

From a frontier trading post, Gimbels has grown to its present five hundred and eighty-nine million dollar, fifty-four store empire.

The Gimbel Corporation today is the only retail chain of its size still under the active leadership and control of its founding family. But as big as Gimbel's may be today, it all goes back to the man who first was a peddler of notions and then opened America's first department store.

Adam
Gimbel

§62   1843   §   HENRY JONES and his "Band of Brothers"

Their love of organization and the necessity of providing for the less fortunate among them caused the German Jewish settlers to lay the groundwork for important Jewish organizations.

The first national Jewish organization to be formed in the United States, and still one of the most important in its influence and work, is the Independent Order of B'nai B'rith, or Sons of the Covenant. It was started in 1843 in New York by twelve German Jews who called themselves Bundes Brüder, for the purpose of ameliorating the regrettable conditions of hatred and disunity then existing among American Jewry. The founders were all humble men; shopkeepers and artisans, of whom the acknowldged leader was Henry Jones, the efficient clerk of the Anshai Chesed Synagogue and considered the power behind the president.

This devoted member of Anshai Chesed told of bitter complaints that came to him from brethren whose applications were rejected by the Independent Order of Odd Fellows. He himself, however, an Odd Fellow and Mason could not attribute such conduct to anti-Jewish prejudice.

The suggestion was made that an all-Jewish lodge of Masons or Odd Fellows be formed, but this was opposed by the men who founded B'nai B'rith. Instead they conceived of the need for an all-Jewish fraternal order of an entirely different sort, one that would bring all the warring factions among the Jews together for good and constructive work to improve the condition of the entire community.

Henry Jones laid the philosophic foundation for the order and outlined its ideals and fundamental goals. He drafted the original ritual with the help of William Renau.

On October 13, 1843 the twelve founders met at Sinsheimer's Cafe,

HENRY JONES

on Essex Street, on New York's Lower East Side and gazing into the future envisioned a movement that while based on the teachings of Judaism, would cut across doctrinal lines and become a rallying point for Jews of varying origins, religious viewpoints and economic backgrounds.

The first lodge was not formed until a few weeks later. Meanwhile on October 21, the founders came together again and by that time had their statement of moral principles all worked out.

The Masonic Room at the corner of Oliver and Henry Streets was rented for two dollars a night and on November 12 at 8 P.M., the first meeting of the first lodge of B'nai B'rith was called to order with Henry Jones as temporary chairman. It was the birth of New York Lodge Number One which still flourishes to this day.

Although Henry Jones was the founder of B'nai B'rith, he was not the first president. Perhaps it was characteristic modesty on his part, but he accepted the post of secretary of the new group.

Unlike some other organizations which began as local clubs and then spread by chance to national proportions, B'nai B'rith was planned from the beginning as a national body with the noblest purposes. The Preamble to the B'nai B'rith Constitution is still the Preamble today:

B'nai B'rith has taken upon itself the mission of uniting Israelites in the work of promoting their highest interests and those of humanity; of developing and elevating the mental and moral character of the people of our faith; of inculcating the purest principles of philanthropy, honor, and patriotism; of supporting science and art; alleviating the wants of the poor and needy; visiting and attending the sick; coming to the rescue of victims of persecution; providing for, protecting, and assisting the widow and the orphan, on the broadest principles of humanity.

At first the order grew slowly in different parts of the country. By 1850 it had acquired 3,000 members. Although in theory any Jew was eligible for membership, in practice the first members were all German Jews and for the first seven years all club proceedings were conducted in that language. It was only later that the Order succeeded in bringing together in the same lodge the rich and the poor, the German and the Russian, the Pole and the Rumanian, the Orthodox and the Reform.

During the post-Civil War days it had acquired 20,000 members and it has been growing steadily ever since, being divided into several Grand Lodges throughout the country. Along with philanthropic work, such as the erection of orphan homes, and old people's homes for the needy, B'nai B'rith began to take steps to protect and aid the Jews everywhere. Out of this grew the Anti-Defamation League, to protect the good name of the Jew.

The B'nai B'rith spread to foreign lands in 1882, and lodges have been organized in England and Turkey, as well as Israel, with the Constitutional Grand Lodge in the United States.

In 1923 the B'nai B'rith began establishing in American universities, the B'nai B'rith Hillel Foundations for religious, educational and social activities among its Jewish students. From the time of Rabbi Benjamin Frankel, first Hillel director at the University of Illinois, to the present, Hillel Foundations have extended from the University of Alberta in the Canadian North to the University of Havana in the Caribbean South. However, the Hillel Foundations were not the first campus organizations, for as early as 1906 the Menorah Society was founded at Harvard University, coming just eight years after the first Jewish fraternity, Zeta Beta Tau.

The growth and work of B'nai B'rith after its one hundredth birthday almost doubled. During the first two years of American participation in World War II, it sold $162,000,000 worth of war bonds. In addition the order took an active part in providing blood donors and shared in the National War Fund Drive. That service brought to the B'nai B'rith the first citations made by both the Army and Navy to any civilian agency in the country.

B'nai B'rith's involvement in the birth of the State of Israel is an important part of the history of the Jewish State.

B'nai B'rith's subsidiaries, the Anti-Defamation League, the Hillel Foundations, the Youth Organization, the Adult Jewish Studies undertaking, its magazines, "The National Jewish Monthly," "Jewish Heritage," its Institutes of Judaism and a host of other activities have left their indelible mark on American and world Jewish affairs.

B'nai B'rith, now one hundred and twenty-five years old, with 500,000 members, is the oldest and largest Jewish service organization in the world. Its lodges, women's chapters and youth groups are found in forty-five countries. In Israel alone there are one hundred and fifty lodges and chapters.

Under the presidency of Philip M. Klutznick, former United States representative to the United Nations Economic and Social Council, the job of heading this organization became that of international diplomat in the complex post-Hitler world.

1847 § ISAAC HAYS: A Co-Founder of the American Medical Association

Modern medicine begins with the nineteenth century and is characterized mainly by the introduction of systematic methods and facilities for scientific research in medicine. The new teaching of medicine as a science, experimental research in adequate laboratories and organized studies of preventive medicine are the development of the nineteenth and twentieth centuries. The admission of Jews to universities, to teaching positions and to institutions for scientific research brought forth a number of brilliant collaborators who have contributed substantially to their traditional field of medicine in all of its branches.

Among the many Jewish physicians who helped in the raising of the standard of medical education in the United States, Dr. Isaac Hays of Philadelphia deserves particular mention. He was one of the most distinguished physicians of his day and one of the pioneer ophthalmologists in America. He was among the earliest practitioners to make eye diseases a specialty in this country.

He was born in Philadelphia on July 5, 1796, and received his B.A. degree in 1816 and his M.D. from the University of Pennsylvania in 1820. Within two years of graduating from medical college he was appointed to the staff of the Pennsylvania Infirmary of the Eye and Ear. He introduced some important ophthalmic instruments; among these he devised a "kneedle knife" used for operations on cataract. Hays' account of the first glasses prescribed in this country for astigmatism is still famous in medical literature.

Dr. Hays was a prolific author and able editor. Had he devoted his talents exclusively to writing and editing, he would have left a significant mark on American medical science.

In 1820, the year Dr. Hays was graduated, his teacher Professor Nathaniel Chapman, started *The Philadelphia Journal of the Medical and Physical Sciences.* Seven years later Dr. Chapman invited his former pupil on the editorial staff. Within a few months he became sole editor. Seeing the necessity of broadening its scope he changed the name to the *American Journal of the Medical Sciences*, popularly called Hays' Journal. It circulated for over half a century as the best American medical monthly. Of Hays' Journal the great physician Sir William Osler said in 1929: "It is one of the few great journals of the world and one from which it is possible to write the progress of American medicine during the past century." In 1874 Hays founded another journal *The Monthly Abstract of Medical Sciences*, the forerunner of the many abstract journals that arose subsequently. In this way he paved the way for American medical journalism, attracted the best medical writers and inspired young gifted men to attempt medico-literary work. He remained its editor for life and was succeeded by his son Isaac Minis Hays, also a prominent physician and historian.

Hays edited and enlarged upon Sir William Laurence's *Treatise on Diseases of the Eye.* This work was reprinted three times and aided substantially in advancing the knowledge of diseases of the eye. Hays' American edition of Dr. T. Wharton Jones' *Principles and Practices of Ophthalmic Medicine and Surgery* with his own original notes was considered a valuable addition to the science of medicine.

Hays' work on the eye received special recognition when he was elected president of the Ophthalmological Society of Philadelphia.

As medical science advanced in skill and prestige, the need for a permanent national organization became evident. Hays was the first to present a resolution at the New York Medical Convention in 1846 proposing a National Medical Association for the better management of standards of ethics and education. He was a founder of the American Medical Association in 1847 for which he composed a code of medical ethics for the guidance of the organization. These rules of conduct were adapted at the formation of the American Medical Association and continue today as the basis of American Medical Association principles by every state and county medical society. By these ethics Hays placed the American medical profession on the highest plane.

In recognition of his work as a founder and organizer of the American Medical Association, Hays was elected first treasurer of the organiaztion under the presidency of his former teacher, Dr. Nathaniel Chapman.

Hays' activities were as numerous as they were varied. But involved as he was with medicine and science, he still remained active in Jewish communal affairs and was a member of Mikveh Israel Congregation in Philadelphia.

He died from influenza in New York on April 12, 1879 at the advanced age of eighty-three.

1852 § SAMPSON SIMSON: Founder of Mount Sinai Hospital

One of America's great medical centers, the Mount Sinai Hospital, established as the Jews' Hospital in New York for "benevolent, charitable and scientific purposes," was founded on January 15, 1852.

The new hospital was completed at a cost of $35,000 and on June 8, 1855, took in its first patient. A four-story building with 45 beds, it stood at 138 West 28th Street, between Seventh and Eighth Avenues in Lower Manhattan, where a tomato patch once grew and where people were accustomed to build bon-fires. The hospital was founded almost single-handed by a remarkable man, an American Jew who bore the name of Sampson Simson.

A hundred years ago New York, like the rest of the country, was suffering from growing pains. Many of the new immigrants constantly pouring in from Europe had to live in crowded, unhealthy slums, and the rate of illness rose to alarming proportions. City hospitals like Bellevue existed, but for the Jewish community this was not enough. The erection of a hospital, an institution sponsored by the Jewish community itself, was a project everyone had been discussing for a long time and doing nothing about. It was then that Sampson Simson, a man of plans who had already lived a long, colorful life, came forward and with one bold stroke broke through all the difficulties.

Simson had taken a life-long interest in communal affairs, and no

SAMPSON SIMSON
(Courtesy of the American Jewish Historical Society)

cause ever appealed to him in vain. Combined with this he was an observant Jew who baked his own matzoth for Passover at home. In 1800 he had delivered an address in Hebrew on "150 Years of Jewish History in America," when he was graduated from Columbia University. He studied law in New York while working as a confidential clerk to Aaron Burr, vice-president of the United States. Then, in 1813, after being beaten up in a night attack on the streets of the city, he had retired from the growing bustle of New York to live as a country gentleman on his estate in Yonkers. Always concerned with the welfare of the Jews in Palestine, he was one of the first Americans to donate sums of money for Jerusalem charities. Finally, in 1852, at the age of seventy-two, he called upon his good friends, all leaders of the Shearith Israel Synagogue, to hear his plan for a Jews' Hospital.

The idea was very simple, but no one had ever thought of it before. Ignoring all existing societies, he wished to enroll members at five dollars a year; these members would elect trustees to guide the hospital. A group of young people had promised to run a ball and raise a thousand dollars; he himself would provide the land on which to build the hospital. The community accepted the plan wholeheartedly; incorporation papers were drawn up, and Sampson Simson was elected its first president.

By Thanksgiving Day in 1853, the cornerstone of the first Jewish institution in New York was laid. Money was raised by subscription from all sources even as far away as Judah Touro in New Orleans.

Originally a sectarian hospital, it accepted those outside the faith only in cases of accident or emergency. However, care of the Federal wounded during the Civil War, the draft riots, and the Orange Day parade riots prompted the idea of changing into a non-sectarian institution. The original consulting and attending staff were practically all gentiles, Doctors Mark Blumenthal and Israel Moses being among the exceptions.

The hospital grew with the mushrooming city itself. In 1866, to make it clear that it served the community without distinction of race or creed, it changed its name to the Mount Sinai Hospital. Four years later the hospital made the first of two moves uptown, to Lexington Avenue and 66th Street.

Sampson
Simson

§69

In the 70's, one of the first mastoid operations was performed in the hospital's newly organized eye and ear service; in 1893 a research laboratory was established; and in 1881 one of the country's pioneer schools for the training of nurses was organized. Since then 3,760 nurses have graduated from the school.

The growth of the laboratory for scientific and investigative research changed the character of the hospital from a home for the sick to a vital growing scientific institution. Antiseptic and aseptic surgery was introduced, departments separated, and specialties recognized. The Doctors Jacobi, Koplick, Janeway, Gerster, and Lilienthal were among the early leaders.

In 1904 the hospital moved from its 66th Street and Lexington Avenue address to still larger quarters at 100th Street and Fifth Avenue, now comprising 839 beds. The participation of the hospital

THE ORIGINAL MOUNT SINAI
HOSPITAL BUILDING (1855-1872)

in two World Wars, contributing a fully equipped medical unit to each; the establishment of a famous Consulting Clinic; and the gradual change of the medical staff from voluntary to more and more full-time positions, added to the repute of the institution.

Today its staff includes one thousand three hundred and fifty doctors and its facilities are the best that are known to medical science. Its twenty buildings stretch along Fifth Avenue for four crowded city blocks (from 98th to 102nd Streets) and it is still expanding. The hospital has 1,300 beds and a large clinical research center. In 1966 it cared for 25,000 patients in its private wards and aided people who made over a quarter of a million visits to its out-patient department.

On July 8, 1963, Gustave L. Levy, president of the Mount Sinai Hospital, announced plans for the establishment of a $30,000,000 medical school on its grounds.

A charter authorizing the hospital to set up the school has already been granted by the New York Board of Regents.

The medical school will embrace a Graduate School for Human Studies, a Graduate School for Biological Sciences and an Institute for Environmental Medicine, including space, radiation and behavioral medicine.

On August 2, 1967 formal affiliation ties between the City University of New York and the new Mount Sinai School of Medicine was announced to provide "a total program of medical education."

The school, scheduled to open in September, 1968, will be called the Mount Sinai School of Medicine of the City University of New York. Responsibility for its financing and operation will remain with the school's own board of trustees who will now include both the university's chancellor and the chairman of the city's Board of Higher Education.

Under the affiliation agreement, qualified students from the medical school would be able to participate in the academic programs of all units of the university, and university enrollees could take classes in the medical school . . . "to produce the competent and socially aware doctors that tomorrow's society will need."

Sampson
Simson

§70

*Judah
Touro*

§71

Judah Touro, the son of Rabbi Isaac Touro, first minister of the Newport Congregation, was the earliest and most generous of American Jewish philanthropists and civic benefactors. His wealth was largely accumulated by mercantile, shipping and other activities in New Orleans.

Arriving coincidentally with the outbreak of the American Revolution, Judah Touro was born the day before the Battle of Bunker Hill. Even his death paralleled a great historic period. He died four years after the Compromise of 1850 at the venerable age of seventy-nine.

When Judah was eight years old his father died and four years later his mother passed away. Judah and a brother and sister, Abraham and Rebecca, became the wards of an uncle, Moses Michael Hays, a wealthy Bostonian merchant. Here he learned at an early age that one could be a devout Jew and yet mingle freely with his Christian brethren, teaching them to respect his faith, while at the same time respecting theirs. After having been forbidden to marry his childhood sweetheart, Catherine Hays, his cousin, he departed for New Orleans where he is said to have been the first Jewish settler.

JUDAH TOURO

INTERIOR OF
THE TOURO SYNAGOGUE

Groomed for business, there he put into practice the theories of his twenty-eight years. With full confidence in his ability, he opened a store and dispensed "Yankee notions."

Patriotically, when the War of 1812 broke out, he enlisted in the army for active duty under General Andrew Jackson. Because he lacked military training he had been given the unskilled but dangerous job of carrying ammunition to the front lines under the guns of the British artillery forces. When struck by a cannon ball, wounded and left for dying in the Battle of New Orleans, the most decisive battle of the war, he was fortunate enough to be picked up by Rezin Davis Shepherd and treated in time. He and Shepherd became lifelong friends and business partners.

After the war, Touro returned to private life. His business expanded; he imported, exported and invested in real estate. He bought ships, grain, and goods of every kind. In a short time he became wealthy.

In 1802 when Touro arrived in New Orleans, it was a struggling Spanish-French village; at the time of his death, it had become a great city and he had played a conspicuous part in the transformation. He built the first free public library in New Orleans which was the first free public library in the world; founded the Touro Infirmary, one of the South's best hospitals; and erected the Shakespeare Alms House for the poor. The Touro Synagogue and Touro Street all perpetuate his name in New Orleans.

In his will his many bequests to institutions of all denominations all over the world continued the philanthropy which he practiced during his lifetime. He had left from two thousand to five thousand dollars to every synagogue in America then in existence. Hebrew schools, hospitals, and relief societies in America and Palestine were also left a share of his great fortune. The money which he left the Mount Sinai Hospital of New York enabled it to complete its first building. To the legislature of the State of Rhode Island he left a trust fund for the support of the rabbi of the Newport Synagogue. To carry on the charitable work of Sir Moses Montefiore in Palestine, he left the unheard of sum of $50,000. He had also donated a church building to a New Orleans Christian congregation.

Thanks to his liberal contribution of $10,000 a monument was erected at the site of the first battle of the Revolutionary War, at Bunker Hill. When this, the first public monument in America was dedicated, he was paid special homage by Daniel Webster, orator of the occasion.

Those who knew Judah Touro praised him not only for his princely gifts but his many acts of personal kindness.

Instead of waiting for an appeal to reach him, it has been said that he actually searched out the unfortunates who needed his help. The Negro slave he educated to be self-supporting and sent away to live in freedom and dignity; the aged woman who shrank from entering the almshouse; the business competitor who needed but was too proud to ask for a loan; to these and a multitude more Judah Touro extended the helping hand of brotherhood.

Truly then did he earn the epithet inscribed on his tombstone:

By righteousness and integrity he collected his wealth,
In charity and for salvation he dispensed it.
The last of his name, he inscribed it in the book of philanthropy
To be remembered forever.

Abraham Touro, brother of Judah Touro, was a great philanthropist and merchant in his own right. In addition to his business interests in Boston, he owned a shipyard in Medford and his summer home there was the town's showplace. He bequeathed $10,000 to the Massachusetts General Hospital and $15,000 to the Newport Synagogue in whose cemetery both brothers lie.

Uriah
Phillips
Levy

§74

Uriah Phillips Levy, who was born in 1792 in Philadelphia, was one of the most colorful figures in American naval history. Although his biography sounds like fiction, it is the true story of an apprentice sailor who rose from the ranks to become a commodore in the United States Navy.

Grandson of Jonas Phillips of Revolutionary fame and cousin of Mordecai Manuel Noah, the ten-year-old Uriah first sailed the seas as a cabin boy. Apprenticed at fourteen to a ship master for four years, he then studied seamanship in the Naval School in Philadelphia. A second mate at eighteen, he commanded two years later the schooner *George Washington* of which he owned a third. At twenty-one he experienced the first real adventure of a life crammed with exciting triumphs and defeats; his crew mutinied, seized the vessel and left him stranded and penniless on a remote island. But Levy managed to get home, accuse the mutineers, and have them all brought back to the United States and convicted.

When the War of 1812 broke out, he immediately volunteered for service and was commissioned as Sailing Master in the United States Navy. Until 1813 he served on the ship *Alert*. Then he went on the brig *Argus* which captured several prizes. Levy was placed in command of one, but finally was himself captured by the British and kept as a prisoner for over a year until the end of the war.

After his release, although he rose rapidly in rank, his years in the navy were far from untroubled. Some of his friends believed that Uriah's frequent quarrels with his brother officers were due entirely to their jealousy of one who had served as a cabin boy while they received their training at Annapolis. Others declared Levy's troubles grew out of his own impatient temper. But Levy insisted that his troubles were due, neither to his humble beginnings nor to his fiery temper, but solely to his loyalty to the faith of Israel.

He used his phylacteries daily and spent the Sabbath at rest in his cabin, except during battle or when duties were extremely pressing.

Proud of his Hebraic ancestry, Levy was once forced into a duel because of anti-Semitic name-calling. He made every effort to avoid his adversary by not aiming at any vital area. After several shots had

COMMODORE URIAH PHILLIPS LEVY

been exchanged, Levy realized that his opponent meant to kill him. He was thus forced to aim and killed the slanderer.

There were many other unpleasant episodes in store for him. In Paris he heard a French officer and a civilian hiss the name of President Jackson, so he promptly challenged them, extracting apologies both to himself and to his nation.

The opposition of his fellow-officers in the Navy grew more and more bitter as Levy was promoted from the ranks.

He was tried six times by court-martial and repeatedly degraded in rank. At one of these times he happened to be in Brazil and was offered a high position in the Brazilian Navy by the Emperor himself. But he proudly declined, saying that the humblest position in his country's service was preferable to royal favors. He insisted on a chance to vindicate himself, had a special commission of inquiry appointed by Congress and was reinstated as Captain. In 1860 his complete loyalty and efficiency as an officer was proved and he was promoted to the rank of Commodore, the highest rank in the United States Navy at that time. He was one of the first individuals to fight against the barbarous practice of flogging on the high seas which due to his efforts finally culminated in the passing of a law abolishing forever corporal punishment in the United States Navy.

Levy was so ardent an admirer of Thomas Jefferson that he donated a statue of the President which now stands in Statuary Hall in the Capitol in Washington. For many years he was the owner of and preserved Jefferson's beautiful home in Monticello which stands on a magnificent hill just above the University of Virginia and established it as a memorial to the democratic president. His home later became a national shrine.

Uriah Phillips Levy

Uriah Phillips Levy, valiant and determined, died in New York in 1862, shortly before the outbreak of the Civil War. He offered his entire fortune to President Lincoln for his country's use proving that he was as humane as he was brave.

He is buried in Cypress Hills Cemetery, Long Island.

§76

On March 28, 1943, the U.S.S. Levy, a destroyer-escort, was named in his honor and launched at Port Newark, New Jersey.

Commodore Levy's name was further memorialized when the Jewish chapel at the Norfolk Naval Base was named the "Commodore Levy Chapel." The ceremonies held in 1959 in conjunction with the naming of the chapel—the Navy's first permanent Jewish chapel —were sponsored by the National Jewish Welfare Board's Armed Services Committee and the Norfolk Jewish Community Council.

1862 § ABRAHAM JACOBI: Savior of Children

Today spread all over the country there are hundreds of pediatric clinics that treat thousands of children. Doctors learn, practice, and teach in them. But it was not until 1862 that the first pediatric clinic in this country was established. In that year Dr. Abraham Jacobi, a Jewish physician, opened the parent clinic.

Dr. Jacobi was born in Hartum, Westphalia in 1830 and came to the United States in 1853. In the manner of European students of that day, he had gone from one University to another, from Griefswald to Göttingen and from there to the University of Bonn, from which he graduated in 1851. He first studied Oriental languages, but soon was attracted to medicine through his interest in anatomy and physiology. Meanwhile the Revolution of 1848 broke out, and the young student was drawn into the struggle. When he went to Berlin to appear for his examinations, he was seized by the Prussian authorities and imprisoned for a year and a half in the fortress at Cologne. Finally, acquitted of the charge of treason, he made his escape to Hamburg where he boarded a ship for England. From

DR. ABRAHAM JACOBI

England he embarked on a forty-three day voyage to the United States, landed in Boston and from there made his way to New York. He set up offices at 20 Howard Street and in the first year of practice earned nine hundred and seventy-three dollars. A year later he attracted the attention of the medical profession with the invention of the laryngoscope. From then on, for over a period of forty-two years, he was connected with numerous hospitals in New York and taught pediatrics in the New York medical schools. He made many significant contributions to the field of infant feeding and inaugurated the first medical bedside instruction in America.

When Columbia University's College of Physicians and Surgeons appointed Jacobi professor of infant pathology and therapeutics in 1860, the first systemized instruction in that field began. It was upon this appointment that the clinical and scientific aspects of pediatrics in this country had their starting point. Here, two years later, he established a pediatric clinic—the first in the country.

Dr. Jacobi was the first doctor in America to recognize the importance of boiling cow's milk for infant feeding, and persistently recommended it as early as 1877. When diphtheria antitoxin was discovered, he was one of the first physicians in America to apply it in practice.

The respect and admiration in which he was held by his colleagues was demonstrated by the honors they showered upon him. He was the first immigrant elected to the presidency of many medical societies including the American Medical Association; and he received honorary degrees from Harvard, Yale, Columbia, and Michigan.

At the age of seventy-five this passionate democrat told the graduating class at Yale: "The greatest gift America has given to the world is not the realization of a republican government—ancient culture exhibited it before and allowed it to perish by political short-sightedness, lust of conquest and undemocratic jealousy. It is anesthesia!"

Abraham Jacobi

§78

Thus for the first time the monster pain was put in its proper perspective.

Dr. Jacobi died at the advanced age of eighty-nine after a stirring life as practitioner, teacher, author, and outstanding figure in American medical circles. Four days before the end his prescription restored a babe to health. His chief work is the *Collectanea Jacobi* which was published in 1909.

One of the hospital buildings of the new $200,000,000 Bronx Municipal Hospital Center, a teaching center of the Albert Einstein College of Medicine of Yeshiva University, bears Dr. Jacobi's name as does the medical library of the Mount Sinai Hospital.

1862 § ARNOLD FISCHEL: First Jewish Chaplain in the United States Army

Thousands upon thousands of Jewish refugees had crossed the Atlantic to help build a life of freedom for all. Now in America, they found a nation in chains. They rallied behind Lincoln to help make America the land of the free, for white men and black men alike.

As soon as the Civil War broke out, Congress passed, on July 22, 1861, the act establishing the national defense; and it was provided that each regiment should have a chaplain, as had been the custom heretofore, "to be appointed by the commander on a vote of the field officers of the company." It further provided that "the chaplain so appointed must be a regular ordained minister of the Christian denomination."

This gave rise to widespread comment and agitation which was taken up by the newspapers and many public patriotic societies. The then recently organized Board of Delegates of American Israelites

THE REVEREND ARNOLD FISCHEL

presented to President Lincoln, and to the Senate and House of Representatives, a memorial setting forth the facts that the Acts of Congress "be formally amended, so that there shall be no discrimination as against professors of the Jewish faith, in the several laws affecting the appointment of Chaplains in the service of the United States."

Reverend Arnold Fischel of Congregation Shearith Israel of New York, backed by the authority of the Board, went to Washington to point out the need to President Lincoln and was instrumental in bringing about the change in the law. In the meantime, without official recognition, he took upon himself the duty of visiting camps and hospitals, ministering to the needs of Jewish soldiers.

On May 20, 1862, the law was changed to include rabbis, and thereupon President Lincoln appointed Rabbi Jacob Frankel of Philadelphia as the first Jewish chaplain. This appointment was followed by that of two others—Rabbi B. H. Gotthelf of Louisville and Rabbi Ferdinand Sarner of New York—who immediately entered upon discharge of their duties. No Jewish regimental chaplains, however, were appointed during the war.

In the Spanish-American War the question of chaplains did not arise, as the war was comparatively short.

During World War I President Wilson appointed six Jewish chaplains and for the first time was authorized to appoint a regimental chaplain. He selected Rabbi Elkan C. Voorsanger. Since Rabbi Voorsanger was already abroad as a volunteer with a hospital unit, he received his commission there, on November 24, 1917. He held the first Passover services in the war zone, at St. Nazaire, in 1918—the first Jewish holiday celebration officially conducted by an officer of the United States Army.

Ultimately twelve rabbis saw active service as regimental chaplains, ten of them abroad. Thirteen others were commissioned First Lieutenant Chaplains and served in camps and cantonments with the army in the United States.

Arnold Fischel

The first rabbi appointed a Navy Chaplain was David Goldberg, of Corsicana, Texas, who entered the service in October 1917.

§80

During World War I, the Jewish Welfare Board was organized to represent and be of assistance to the men and women who served in the armed forces of the United States. With the consent and under the supervision of the Secretary of War and the military authorities, the Board helped in securing Jewish chaplains who conducted religious services for the Jewish personnel in the armed services, as well as providing recreational activities and being of service wherever needed.

The Jewish Welfare Board's Commission on Jewish Chaplaincy continued its work during World War II under the direction of Rabbi Aryeh Lev, often going to endless pains to fly chaplains to remote areas for Passover celebrations and other Jewish holidays. The number of Jewish chaplains reached three hundred and eighty-four.

One of the most inspiring stories of heroism and devotion to come out of World War II was that of the four chaplains who perished aboard the *Dorchester* in the North Atlantic on February 3, 1943, because they chose to give up their lifebelts to helpless GIs rather than save themselves. So epic was the event, with its message of ultimate consecration, that the picture of the four chaplains—a Jew, a Catholic, and two Protestants—linked arm in arm on the deck of the sinking ship and praying aloud, each in his own way, has become firmly etched upon the memory of America.

The Chaplains were Rabbi Alexander Goode, Father John Washington, Rev. George Fox and Rev. Clark Poling.

In the Fall of 1950, soon after the fighting began in Korea, the three major rabbinical associations (the Reform Central Conference of American Rabbis, the Conservative Rabbinical Assembly and the Orthodox Rabbinical Council) set up a unique voluntary draft system through which all rabbis upon ordination become subject to at least two years of chaplaincy duty. This program has now become a permanent system for providing a continuous flow of Jewish chaplains into all branches of the armed forces. Since its inception a quarter of a century ago, nearly nine hundred rabbis have been endorsed and served as chaplains by the Commission on Jewish Chaplaincy.

In 1967 alone the total number of full-time military and Veterans Administration Jewish chaplains on active duty reached seventy-four. There were also more than two hundred and fifty civilian rabbis serving as part-time chaplains.

On August 21, 1967, a twenty-three-year-old Orthodox rabbi, Chicago-born Chaplain (Captain) Franklin Charles Breslau, who has a degree in electrical engineering and who was ordained a rabbi by the Hebrew Theological College in Skokie, Illinois, became the first Jewish chaplain to complete airborne training and win the United States Army's parachutist badge.

Chaplain Breslau was joined in the first of his five qualifying jumps by Protestant Chaplain Charles Brinkmeyer and Catholic Chaplain John McCullagh. This became the first tri-faith jump in the history of the Army.

1864   §   JUDAH P. BENJAMIN: Confederate Statesman

Although sympathies of the Jewish population as a whole was with the North when the seething ferment between the North and South burst into the flame of the Civil War, Jews also gave signal service to the Confederacy. Judah Philip Benjamin was the outstanding Jew in the South's struggle and held three successive posts in the Confederate Cabinet of Jefferson Davis, who found him indispensable. His loyalty to the system of slavery surprised Jews and Christians alike. A Northern Senator, Benjamin F. Wade, who knew the devotion of the Jews to freedom and justice, called Mr. Benjamin "an Israelite with an Egyptian heart."

Judah Philip Benjamin was born in 1811 of an old Sephardic family in the British West Indies. His parents migrated to Charleston, South Carolina, shortly after the War of 1812 where young Benjamin received an early education. At the age of fourteen he entered Yale University where he is accounted one of her distinguished students although he never graduated. Early in 1828 he moved to New Orleans, there obtained work in a business concern, and began studying law at night. At the age of twenty-one he was admitted to

JUDAH PHILIP BENJAMIN

the Louisiana Bar and in a short time won a high reputation in the legal field.

A passionate Southerner, he ran for the Louisana State Assembly, and was elected. Subsequently, in 1845, he was elected member of the convention held to revise the constitution of his state. His ability as a jurist became recognized both nationally and internationally, and President Pierce tendered him the position of Associate Justice of the Supreme Court of the United States. He preferred politics, however, and in 1852 went on to the United States Senate, and he was reelected six years later.

With the slavery issue in the forefront, Benjamin upheld the issue as well as the principle of state sovereignty. Like many Southerners, he long resisted secession, but when the step was taken, he cast his lot with the Confederacy. His former colleague in the Senate, Jefferson Davis, appointed him Attorney-General, then Secretary of War, and finally Secretary of State. Benjamin was the President's most trusted adviser and was often referred to as "the brains of the Confederacy."

When the Confederate forces suffered one crushing defeat after another, Benjamin was made the scapegoat. At the end of the war, penniless and over fifty, he found his way to London. Here he was befriended by Disraeli and Gladstone. He once again resumed the practice of law, and began writing books which brought him a fortune. His book on *Sales* is still recognized as authoritative in law schools. He made an income of $100,000 a year; acknowledged one of the leading barristers of England, he became the first American Jew to hold the title of King's Councillor. (The second American to hold this title was Arthur Goodheart, dean of the law faculty of Oxford University and nephew of Herbert Lehman, former United States Senator and Governor of New York).

The first dinner ever given in honor of an American by the Bar of England was tendered to Benjamin upon his retirement. Graced by the Lord Chancellor, the Lord Chief Justice, high officials of the Empire and the most eminent members of the profession, Benjamin was toasted and eulogized as the only man "of whom it can be said that he held conspicuous leadership at the Bars of two countries."

When he died in 1884 a contemporary newspaper said in a leading article: "His life was as varied as an eastern tale, and he carved out for himself by his own unaided exertions, not one, but three histories of great and well earned distinction. Inherent in him was the elastic resistance to evil fortune which preserved his ancestors through a succession of exiles and plunderings . . . "

Such was the acclaim with which this strange career came to an end.

1864 § FREDERICK KNEFLER and Other Union Generals

Hundreds of Jewish soldiers gave their lives for the cause of Negro emancipation in the war between the states. Many led campaigns against the Southern forces. Three foreign-born Jews—August Bondin, Jacob Benjamin, and Theodore Wiener—joined John Brown, and later all three enlisted in the Union Army. The Seligman brothers of New York raised two hundred million dollars to help carry on the war. For centuries the Jew had fought for his own freedom. He was happy now to protect others against oppression.

Ten Jews held the title of general in some form in the Union Army. The highest military rank was attained by Frederick Knefler of Indianapolis, an immigrant Jew born in Hungary who volunteered as a private in his home town of Indianapolis and rose to be colonel of the 79th Indiana regiment. He took part in the battle of the Army of the Cumberland and saw much service under Generals Rosecrans, Thomas and Grant. He rode with General Sherman on his historic March to the Sea in 1864. His highest actual rank was Brigadier

General, to which the temporary rank of Brevet Major General was later added for heroic conduct in the battle of Chicamauga. After the war Knefler received the appointment of United States Pension Agent with headquarters at Indianapolis.

Three other Jews were also full colonels and brevetted brigadier generals. Edward S. Solomon, who later became Governor of Washington Territory on the Pacific coast, left Germany at eighteen and settled in Chicago in 1854. When the Civil War broke out he joined the 24th Illinois Infantry as Second Lieutenant. General proficiency and gallant conduct raised him to the rank of major. Disagreement in the regiment caused Major Solomon to resign. With others he organized the 82nd Illinois Infantry which he later commanded. He took part in the fighting at Chancellorsville and his behavior during the three-day Battle of Gettysburg was such that Major General Carl Schurtz in a dispatch to General Howard, commander of the 11th Corps, mentions "Lieutenant Colonel Solomon of the 82nd Illinois Infantry who displayed the highest order of coolness and determination under very trying circumstances." On June 15, 1865, the Secretary of War Edward M. Stanton advised Brevet Brigadier General Edward S. Solomon that his rank had been raised.

Leopold Blumberg, who saw service in the Prussian-Danish War, was one of the first Jewish soldiers who received promotion to first lieutenant in the German Army. After the failure of the 1848 Revolution Blumberg refused to remain in his native land where the reactionary authorities reimposed ancient restrictions on Jews. He left Germany in 1854 and settled in Baltimore.

After the bombardment of Fort Sumter he abandoned a successful business to help preserve the Federal Union. Fortunate enough to escape hanging by the pro-Southern mob, he assisted in organizing the 5th Maryland Regiment, of which he became acting colonel. For a time he served near Hampton Roads and was then attached to the Mansfield Corps throughout the Peninsular campaign. Under his command as Major, the 5th Maryland Regiment took part in the fierce fighting at Antietam. His horse shot under him, the major received a severe wound in the thigh. Confined to bed for months, and although continuing to live a dozen years longer, he never fully recovered. Lincoln appointed him provost marshal of the Third Maryland District, and President Andrew Johnson ordered him elevated to the rank of brevet brigadier general of the United States Volunteers. Blumberg was a leading member of the Har Sinai Congregation and several other Jewish organizations, upon his return to civilan life.

Philip J. Joachimson of New York as district attorney had secured the first conviction for the inhuman traffic in slaves. It was only in character for Judge Joachimson to resign his post in order to assist in the war effort. His help in organizing the 59th New York Volunteers brought him the appointment of colonel. The regiment was stationed in Fortress Monroe and he was made U. S. Paymaster. Later he was transferred to New Orleans and placed under the command of the notorious General Benjamin F. Butler. Severely hurt in a fall from his horse, Colonel Joachimson became disqualified for military duty. His services were considered of sufficient importance for Governor Fenton to honor him with the rank and title of Brevet Brigadier General of the New York State Militia. He remained active in Jewish communal activities until his death in 1890.

Frederick Knefler

§85

On July 12, 1864, Congress authorized the award of the Congressional Medal of Honor, the highest that can be given to an American soldier and the most difficult to obtain. Seven Jews won the Congressional Medal of Honor, the first one going to Sgt. Leopold Karpeles.

Karpeles, who was born in Prague in 1838, had come to the United States at the age of twelve. Soon after his arrival, he joined his brother in Texas whose business was conveying caravans across the Mexican border. When the Civil War broke out, he enlisted in the army in Springfield, Massachusetts. He was awarded the Congressional Medal of Honor for his act in rallying the men of the 57th Massachusetts Volunteers around the flag and turning a retreat into a victory. The official citation read: "At the Battle of the Wilderness, May 6, 1864, while color bearer of his regiment, he rallied the retreating troops and induced them to check the advance of the enemy."

Much later, during World War I, this distinction was continued among Jewish soldiers. Nine governments heaped awards upon Sgt. Benjamin Kaufman, who fought so valiantly at Argonne, and his own country gave him its highest award. For many years he served as national commander of the Jewish War Veterans in the United States.

While the lives of these Jewish soldiers were more spectacular than that of most youths of their time, it is typical of what Jews, in their loyalty to the land of their adoption, have accomplished in many fields of American adventure.

Moses
Ezekiel

§86

In the nineteenth century, America was still a fairly young country in which forests had to be cleared, houses erected, railroads built and rivers spanned. It was hardly an era propitious for the development of the fine arts. Nevertheless, there lived at that time a Jewish sculptor of international renown, Moses Jacob Ezekiel, who not only made pretty statues, but perpetuated in bronze, marble, and clay the beauty and noble aspirations of mankind as well as its ugliness and vicissitudes. His unusually distinguished career as artist included several international medals, and the honor of knighthood both from the king of Italy and the emperor of Germany. In 1872 the highest honor was bestowed upon him, when he had the privilege of being accepted as a full-fledged member in the world-famous Imperial Academy of Arts in Rome. He was the first American and the first Jew to receive such a distinction.

Ezekiel was born in Richmond, Virginia, in 1844. As a young boy he attended the Virginia Military Academy and showed great talent in drawing. When the Civil War broke out, he volunteered in the Confederate Army and served throughout the war. He then went abroad to study sculpture, won a prize which took him to Rome for further study, and lived there most of his life in a luxurious modern studio which he installed in the ancient Tower of Belisarius. To his studio came the leading notbles of the world—including Garibaldi, D'Annunzio, even the King and Queen of Italy. Among his friends were Robert E. Lee and Franz Liszt.

His works were exhibited in art salons of many European cities. For one of his earlier works, his bas relief "Israel," he was awarded the Michel Beer Prize of Rome. American history was another of his favorite subjects. It was in recognition of his colossal bust of George Washington that the Imperial Academy accepted him into their fold. His best known work from the Jewish point of view is his heroic statue, "Religious Liberty." It was commissioned by the B'nai B'rith as a gift to the people of the United States on the centennial of American independence. It stands in Fairmount Park, Philadelphia.

Among Ezekiel's other subjects into which he chiseled the Judaic spirit, are "Adam and Eve," "Cain," or the "Offering of the Rejected,"

MOSES EZEKIEL

"David and Queen Esther," and "Eve," which stood in the palace of the San Souci before the Russians took over East Berlin; the torso of "Judith" and the monument to Massarani in the Jewish cemetery in Rome. The memorial to the international banker Jesse Seligman, ten feet high, stands at the entrance hall of the Hebrew Orphan Asylum.

Ezekiel died in Rome in 1917, but because of the war his body was not returned to the United States until four years later when he was given the unusual honor of a burial in the National Cemetery at Arlington. Rabbi David Philipson officiated at the service which was held at the Arlington Memorial Amphitheater on March 30, 1921. This was the first public exercise held in the famous structure where the grave of the Unknown Soldier is located.

Rarely have there been more fluctuating estimates of a man's work than the varied appraisals to which Sir Moses Ezekiel was subjected. After Ezekiel's first efforts were scorned, he was recognized as a pioneer. There followed a period in which he was alternately honored and assailed. For a while his creations, regarded with faint approval, were largely neglected. Then, a few years later, Ezekiel was rediscovered and ranked as one of the most outstanding sculptors of the nineteenth century.

*David
Lubin*

§88

Jews have taken part in making American business synonymous with enterprise and achievement. Such a Jew was David Lubin, a dreamer and enthusiast who forgot himself in one great cause after the other.

Born of Orthodox parents in Klodowa, Poland, in 1849, Lubin was brought to America as a child and settled in New York's East Side. At the age of twelve, he left school and went to work. The adventurous youngster was a strong supporter of Lincoln, who represented his own ideals and hopes. When the Civil War broke out he ran away to sea and tried to join the army. From that time on he shifted for himself, making a trip across the continent to San Francisco. Joining a prospecting expedition to Arizona, he was lost two days in the desert without food or water. After being rescued he returned east to his family. In 1874 when he was twenty-five years old, he made a trip across the continent again and landed in Sacramento, which at the time, although the state capital of California, was still a rough mining camp.

Above a basement saloon, Lubin started a little store under a sign D. LUBIN—ONE PRICE STORE. Here, he established the principle of selling merchandise at retail with fixed prices marked in plain figures on each item. In a short while he won everyone's respect for his honesty and fair dealing, and the Mechanic's Store, as it came to be called, became a Sacramento institution. By 1874 he had established and advertised several business principles which today represent fundamental precepts of retailing but which then were startlingly new: (1) to sell at one price only; (2) to mark all merchandise with the selling price in plain figures; (3) never to misrepresent merchandise; (4) to buy or manufacture goods at the lowest price possible; (5) to figure out at how low a profit the goods could be sold. The enterprise became not only the largest retail store in Sacramento but later added a San Francisco store. He thus founded one of the first chain of stores in America.

As his business grew and people from far and near came to buy from him, he solved the broader problem of transportation by establishing for the first time in America the mail order house. The de-

DAVID LUBIN

velopment of the mail order house from that time on, is the saga of modernization of rural life.

In 1884 Lubin made a journey to Palestine. He always considered it the climax of his career. Upon his return to America, his interest in business shifted to farming. He began to study soils and methods by which California farmers could best raise products for the market, a study he felt could apply to the rebirth of Palestine. He soon became owner of the largest fruit-packing company in the state and founder of California's Fruit Growers' Exchange. At this time he was also one of the early sponsors of cheap parcel post.

Convinced that the consumer could buy food more cheaply and farmers could get more by-products through cooperation on a world-wide basis, he founded the International Institute for Agriculture. Nation after nation saw the feasibility of his plan and forty-five countries joined on May 25, 1905, to form what was the first permanent international cooperative in the world, the precursor of the League of Nations.

Lubin was appointed first United States representative to the Institute and continued in this post for ten years. The King of Italy, Victor Emanuel III, gave a splendid building for its use. Nations sent their official representatives and technical experts to cooperate with Lubin, who worked equally for the American farmer and the common man the world over.

Emphasis upon his Jewishness was an outstanding characteristic of Lubin. Samuel Gompers, in his autobiography, *Seventy Years of*

Life and Labor, calls attention to this: " . . . Lubin insisted upon forcing upon all with whom he came in contact his pride in his Jewish ancestry. He stated upon any and all occasions that it was his greatest glory that he was a Jew."

On January 1, 1919, David Lubin died in Rome at the age of seventy, overflowing to the last with fiery enthusiasm, never ceasing his untiring labors for his cause.

David Lubin

§90   1875 § ISAAC M. WISE: Organizer of Reform Judaism in America

As the eighteenth century progressed a change came about with the *Enlightenment*. The Age of Reason began to supersede the Era of Faith. Freedom of thought, tolerance in religion and equal protection of the law began to receive the approval of the most brilliant minds. These explosive ideals stimulated the French Revolution which declared war upon the divine institution of kingship as well as on the totalitarian monolithic church. The rallying cry of "Liberty, Equality, Fraternity" led to the demolition of the ghetto walls and the liberation of its captive dwellers.

Progressive spirits were now pondering the status of Judaism in a changing world. Would the ancient doctrines and worship be suited for the century of progress? The majority were content with the practices and ceremonies of orthodoxy that had bound their forefathers. But a minority strove to reform the ritual, beautify its services with organ music and mixed choirs, admit women as equal participants, shorten the service and use the vernacular for prayer and sermon. Such was the religious climate of 1819 when Isaac Mayer Wise was born in Bohemia.

Typical of his day and age, the boy gathered Hebrew learning at *heder*, the religious elementary school and also from his father and grandfather. When young Isaac left home for more advanced courses in the *yeshiva*, he depended on the kindness of families who followed the old Jewish custom of regularly inviting *yeshiva* students to share their meals. Determined to become a rabbi, he went on to study in the famous rabbinical schools of Prague and Vienna. A government decree, intended more to restrict than to benefit, required secular academic knowledge of rabbis. For two years Isaac Mayer studied at the university. He then became rabbi at Radnitz in Bohemia. The Austro-Hungarian Empire, still guided by Holy Alliance principles, interfered with the internal life of Jews. The young rabbi, filled with the revolutionary fervor then in the air, resented bureaucratic control of private rights, emigrated in 1846 to America.

After a short stay in New York, he became rabbi of Albany's Orthodox Congregation Beth-El. Although the congregation was made up of German immigrants, Rabbi Wise insisted upon preaching in English. In his sermons and articles he soon began to write for one of America's earliest Jewish papers, the "Occident," the rabbi fearlessly defended Reform Judaism. The suggestions that he made for changes which would make it easier for Jews to fit into American life brought a storm of criticism and accusations. Many of the Albany Jews considered Isaac M. Wise far too radical to be their rabbi.

So in 1854 Isaac M. Wise answered the call to serve Bene Yeshurun Congregation in Cincinnati, the third largest Jewish community in the nation; then the Queen city of the West.

The Ohio city, which in years to come was to be known as the Cradle of Reform Judaism in America, had welcomed its first Jew in 1817. Jonathan Jonas, brother of President Lincoln's early friend, was an English Jew. At first Jewish settlers in Cincinnati were almost exclusively English; but by 1830 Jewish immigrants from Germany began to outnumber them. These German Jews warmly welcomed the changes Rabbi Wise instituted; they stood behind him in his many efforts to build and strengthen Reform Judaism. There he remained for the next fifty years, changing, altering and revising ritual and custom until they took on the form they have today. An Orthodox congregation to begin with, Bene Yeshurun became a Reform congregation. Rabbi Wise introduced the idea of worship without covering the head. He installed an organ. He put in a mixed choir. He instituted Friday night services for the first time in America. He introduced family pews so that men and women could worship together. He started Confirmation of both boys and girls in place of the Bar Mitzvah ceremony.

The Civil War held up Rabbi Wise, but the expanding West and the completion of the transcontinental railroad in 1869 aided him in his task as religious reformer.

The surprising growth of American Reform Judaism was largely due to the energy, leadership and organizing ability of Isaac M. Wise.

Dedicating his whole life to the cause of Reform Judaism in "the spirit of the age," Isaac Mayer Wise never intended to divide the Jewish community into different groups. He was convinced that

ISAAC MAYER WISE

Judaism in the free atmosphere of America must develop along lines which he favored. Wishing to include all Jews in his early plans at union, he emphasized that he was not in favor of radical change. For a conference he called in Cleveland in 1855 he prepared a special statement to show that he did not intend to cast aside the great tradition of the Talmud. He wrote: "The Bible as delivered to us by our fathers and as now in our possession is of immediate divine origin and the standard of our religion. The Talmud contains the tradition, legal and logical exposition of the Biblical laws which must be expounded and practiced according to the comments of the Talmud."

Rabbi Wise hoped to include Orthodox Jews in setting up a committee to decide on changes in Jewish observance. The Orthodox did not wish to join with him. The strongest attacks against him came, however, from other Reform rabbis. Rabbi David Einhorn was a leader of a group of radical Reformers in the east who did not wish to consider Talmudic law in any way binding. They saw no need to bow to old traditions. All the laws were outmoded, they said, except the "eternal truths" of Jewish ethics. Rabbi Einhorn did not share the desire of Rabbi Wise to develop a progressive Judaism which would include Jews with traditional loyalties. Finally in 1885, Dr. Kaufmann Kohler of New York, a member of the Einhorn wing of Reform Judaism and far more radical than Rabbi Wise, called a conference of Reform rabbis only, which met in Pittsburgh and formulated a platform of the beliefs of Reform Judaism.

Toward the end of the century and the end of his life, Rabbi Wise realized that the Jews of the United States seemed determined to follow different roads.

To the Orthodox Jew, Reform Judaism was not only distasteful but shocking. Convinced that it would spell the downfall of Judaism, the Orthodox leaders, all East European Jews, carried on a bitter and relentless fight against Reform.

As the conflict sharpened, it was inevitable that a third group should develop along the middle road. These were Jews who believed that Reform was right in some respects and Orthodoxy in others. The Conservatives, as they were to be called, believed that some changes ought to be made, but that beyond that Judaism required no further modernization.

Meanwhile for two decades Rabbi Wise was agitating for the establishment of a theological school to furnish competent rabbis for Reform congregations. To establish this school firmly, Rabbi Wise had to organize the Union of American Hebrew Congregations as its sponsor. As a result of his many years of labor in October of 1875 the Hebrew Union College received its first group of students. Classes met in two synagogues in Cincinnati and fourteen books made up its first library. Rabbi Wise became the professor of history of the small but dedicated faculty of the new seminary. Founder, president, director and dean as well, he became personal adviser to every student, welcoming every class, inviting the entire student body to his Passover Seder each year. Even when he was a very old man Rabbi Wise continued to serve the college as president and instructor. Out of this modest beginning grew one of the great institutions of Jewish learning. Today its seven buildings stand on twenty acres in a fashionable Cincinnati neighborhood. Many scholars of high reputation have served on its faculty.

When he was seventy-one he formed the third enterprise on which he had set his heart, and which required an even longer and harder struggle, the Central Conference of American rabbis. His aim was to create a central religious authority, or synod, for Reform Judaism. Beginning with the first in 1855, Wise took the lead in convening a number of rabbinical gatherings, most of which suffered from dissensions which did more to retard his objective than advance it. Finally, in 1889, the Central Conference of American Rabbis was organized for the reform rabbis of the country. It became a permanent body that commands respect and obedience without the power to coerce or impose sanctions. It adopted the Union Prayer Book which became standard for Reform worship in 1894. (Not until 1967 was it to undergo any revision.)

In addition to his preaching, lecturing and furthering Reform Judaism throughout the land, Rabbi Wise led a busy life editing and publishing two papers which he founded, *The American Israelite* in English and *Die Deborah* in German. He also wrote ten books on theology, two histories, a dozen novels, some of them in German, and two plays.

Isaac M.
Wise

§94

When he died in 1900, Rabbi Wise could feel gratified in all that he had done, for the sixty-one graduates of his Hebrew Union College were the rabbis of the leading Reform congregations of America and the body that speaks the mind of Reform, or Liberal Judaism, as it now calls itself, was steadily growing.

Within the past decade Reform congregations have increased from three hundred to six hundred and sixty-five.

1876 § MORRIS ROSENFELD: Poet of the Sweatshop

The first stage of idealization of America by immigrants was generally followed by a second stage, disillusionment. The golden dreams of America as a veritable heaven on earth are dissipated when the immigrant finds himself face to face with the practical problems of earning his bread. The necessity of working from dawn to sunset and even far into the night in a sweatshop left the newly arrived person little leisure to enjoy the vaunted freedom of America.

It is not surprising then that the first authentic Yiddish literature to emerge from the American scene was a literature of protest against the rigors of the needle trades. The four most gifted Yiddish poets of the time, Morris Rosenfeld, Morris Winchevsky, David Edelstadt and Yossef Bovshover, all were united by the single purpose of fighting the wretchedness of the sweatshop. Their poems, particularly those of Rosenfeld, bemoaned the harshness of life in the garment district, and described the pale overworked wives and emaciated children in the most graphic and piteous terms. Rosenfeld, the "Dante of the Sweatshop" was acclaimed by William Dean Howells as one of America's most notable poets. His moving poem,

"Machine", authentically conjures up the image of those early days in the garment industry:

"Here's existence without thought or feeling;
This drudgery, soul crushing and bitter, has drained
The deepest, the highest, the richest, the noblest
Which struggling man through progress attained.
The seconds, the minutes, the hours, speed by
Fleeting, they vanish like chaff in a gale
As if to o'ertake them, I drive the machine
Furiously, but without hope, sense or avail.

"At times when I listen, I hear the clock ticking
Saying such things as never had meaning before.
The pendulum prods me, lashes me, goads me
To labor faster, produce more and even more.
The clock and machine are in league with the Boss
The cold stare and pointing hands reveal my foe
The striking, the ticking, the humming, the roaring
All in chorus unite and proclaim "Sew!"

*Morris
Rosenfeld*

§95

A poet of the masses and himself a product and a victim of the sweatshop, Rosenfeld is revolutionary in the theme and tenor of his

MORRIS ROSENFELD

song. Reared in the spirit of traditional Judaism, he draws much of his inspiration from the old literary sources, but for form and versification he is indebted to the English and German masters, especially Schiller and Heine. At the same time he is original in treatment of his subjects and in the pathos and imagery with which his writings abound. His collection *Liederbuch* (New York, 1897) was the sensation of the day in Yiddish literary circles and its translation into English by Professor Leo Wiener of Harvard (*Songs from the Ghetto*, Boston, 1899), introduced him to the more prominent American universities, where he was invited to give readings of his poems, and to the larger non-Jewish world. Rosenfeld probably did more than any other Yiddish writer to bring home to the American reading world the economic tragedy as well as the spiritual beauty of the lowly and dingy ghetto and the yoke of serfdom brought about by the Industrial Revolution.

Dozens of his poems haunt the mind, and many of them will live as long as the language.

Morris Rosenfeld

§96

1877 § EMILE BERLINER: Genius With Sound

To some of us the most wonderful of all marvelous inventions, of which we have so many in these days, is the talking machine or phonograph, no matter by what name we call it. That a black flat disc with tiny lines should be able to give us the golden voice of Melba or Caruso, the wonderful tones of a violin in the hands of a master, the full crash of a brass band or the winged words of a great orator, seems impossible to believe. Yet we know that it is true.

Scientists had known for a long time that it was possible to make a record of the vibrations of sound; but the first practical instrument to do this was patented by Thomas Edison in 1877. By simply reversing this machine, it was found that you could "make it talk." However, the first successful talking machine record and the one most of us know today was patented by a German-born Jew named Emile Berliner who lived in Washington, D.C., in the first decade after the Civil War.

For several years the Edison Company was selling phonographs which reproduced on soft wax cylinders the human voice in a mechanical nasal twang.

EMILE BERLINER

Discarding the cumbersome cylinder as impractical, Berliner invented the flat disc, which propelled the reproducing stylus or needle in a groove of even depth and varying direction. This disc of hardened rubber material could be produced in large quantities and sold cheaply. The movable reproducer was a great improvement over Edison's fixed machine. The Berliner gramophone developed into the Victor Talking Machine with its masterhead of a dog listening to "His Master's Voice," the primitive forerunner of today's complex stereo systems. Victor records became a medium of culture and pleasure the world over.

This won Berliner fame and wealth when he was quite a young man and he spent his entire life in study in various fields, often leading to new inventions.

For his development of the so-called "lateral-cut-method" of recording the human voice, which became the heritage of radio broadcasting, Berliner was awarded the Elliot and Cresson Gold Medal by the Franklin Institute of Philadelphia.

Yet strange as it may seem, Berliner knew little or nothing of science and electricity, his formal education having ended in high school. He had read, however, a book or two on physics and even found time to enroll in evening courses at famed Cooper Union College in New York.

In the same way much of the glory that goes to Bell for having invented the telephone should go to Berliner, for it was he who really made it a practical instrument. Bell's invention lacked a practical transmitter, since it used magnetic induction and the human voice produced only weak undulating currents. Berliner's invention patented in 1877 as a telephone receiver permitted a clear sound of greater volume and resulted in the increase in distance of communications. The Bell Telephone Company soon bought the rights to the Berliner transmitter; and he was engaged for three years as chief instrument inspector. Berliner continued to make improvements in telephony and was the first to use an induction coil in connection with transmitters. This transmitter is used in all our telephones today. Without Berliner's contribution the commercial telephone would be inconceivable.

His tinkering with the telephone led Berliner to invent another acoustical device: the microphone. The value of this invention becomes apparent when you realize that the radio, television and recording industries would be silenced without it. The original Berliner microphone now occupies a place of honor in the Smithsonian Institute in Washington.

Berliner's inventive genius reached out and noticeably affected the domains of many other inventions. He discovered methods of improving the acoustics of buildings; made the motion picture projector possible; added further devices to the telephone, and invented the air-cooled engine with revolving cylinder now used extensively in airplanes.

The helicopter was the last practical invention to engage his mind. In 1919 his son Henry, a graduate of Cornell and M.I.T., actually flew the first workable flying machine of this type. While it has been said that every American war has been marked by some new invention, even the Vietnam War had not revealed the full measure of change that may be wrought by the helicopter.

Having had little formal education himself, Berliner ensured education for others by contributing to the Hebrew University in Jerusalem. Berliner also showed great interest in the rebuilding of a Jewish state in Palestine. He favored the Jewish pursuit of agriculture and assisted the National Agricultural School in Doylestown, Pennsylvania.

President Herbert Hoover, in speaking of him, said: "The German immigrant boy, Emile Berliner, has become one of America's most useful citizens."

Active to the end, Emile Berliner died in Washington on August 3, 1928.

His novel inventions may not have enlarged man's spiritual stature, but it made his world more enjoyable, more communicative, and more colorful than it had ever been before.

In 1867 Joseph Seligman passed up the best bargain since Peter Minuit's original purchase of Manhattan Island from the Indians. He rejected an offer to buy all the land north of Sixtieth Street and west of Broadway—up to 121st Street, where Grant's Tomb now stands, including most of what is now West End Avenue and Riverside Drive—for $450,000, a fraction of what a single city block would cost now. Had he decided differently, the Seligmans would today easily be the richest family in the world.

Joseph Seligman

§99

To educate his five sons, Joseph Seligman employed Horatio Alger, the future writer, as tutor. One can easily surmise how Horatio Alger hit upon his pattern from rags to riches through pluck and perseverance.

For many years the Seligmans set the tone of German Jewish society in New York City and were conspicuous as heroes of the American success story.

Joseph Seligman was born in Baiersdorf, Bavaria in 1819. During a period of reaction and denial of rights he managed to graduate from the Gymnasium of Erlangen and acquire what was equivalent to half a college education. He studied literature and the classics and after two years delivered the valedictory oration to the University in Greek. The poverty of the Germanic states after the Napoleonic wars and the suppression of all liberal thought prompted him to seek the land of opportunity.

He came to the United States during the great depression of 1837, yet found a job in one of the Pennsylvania stores owned by Asa Packer. Joseph explained that he was good at figures and the future millionaire and founder of Lehigh University hired him as a cashier-clerk. The salary of $400 a year might have satisfied many a native son, but 18-year-old Joseph sensed a better future in business. He turned his savings into merchandise—small jewelry, some watches, rings and knives—and was perfectly willing to set out on foot from village to farm in Pennsylvania, carrying a 100 to 200 pound pack on his back, at the same time reciting the passages of the Greek classics he had acquired at Erlangen.

Shrewdness riveted in honesty, when driven by ambition and

energy and held steady by thrift, simply could not miss. A store in Lancaster was the reward for peddling. The store gave Joseph a warehouse for his goods. He could expand his line into heavier, larger and more general merchandise—boots and overshoes, brooms, bustles, hardware and bags of feed. He was evolving from a foot peddler to a small-town merchant. As he prospered he brought his seven brothers to this country.

The plantations of the South held greater promise for business than the small farms in Quaker Pennsylvania. His stock of merchandise was transported from Lancaster to Selma, Alabama, where with the two eldest brothers he established three dry goods shops. The other brothers branched out in various towns, but under the direction of Joseph, increased their resources and experience. By 1848, the Seligmans, now adult and Americanized, moved to New York City.

In New York, Joseph and James started an importing business; William opened a clothing establishment in St. Louis, Missouri; while Jesse and Henry operated a store in Watertown. Ulysses S. Grant, a young lieutenant stationed at Sackett's Harbor on Lake Erie, came to buy and began a lifelong friendship with Jesse that extended to Joseph and the other Seligmans.

In 1849, the gold-rush to California swept across the nation. Leaving their brother Henry to manage the store in Watertown, Jesse and Leopold decided to try their luck in the mad scramble for the Pacific coast. Here the Seligmans added to their far-flung chain of stores one in gold-rush San Francisco, where it was the only general store to survive the Fire of 1851. With the subsequent profits, the Seligmans' chief business became the import of California gold. They were the first of the German Jews to go into banking. They learned banking fundamentals so well that the firm of J. & W. Seligman & Company, was the only New York commercial bank not closed by the Panic of 1857.

The Seligman brothers had prospered and were more than ready to weather the financial hurricane. The example of the Rothschilds pointed to the advantage of concentration and expansion within the family circle. With Joseph at the helm, they started banking but prudently held on to the profitable clothing business. This precaution proved fortunate, for shortly afterward, when the Civil War broke out, President Lincoln called for volunteers. Soon the largest mass of recruits ever yet enrolled in the American Army were under arms. The Seligmans were equipped to furnish the armed forces with uniforms on a large scale. They received huge contracts and after the

JOSEPH SELIGMAN
(Courtesy of J. & W. Seligman & Co.)

war demonstrated their patriotism by carrying the million dollar debt owed by the Navy for an additional year—an extension highly appreciated by the harassed War Department.

Joseph Seligman had virtually invented international banking in America. He expanded the scope of his New York institution until the Seligmans became an international organization with foreign branches in England, France and Germany. It is said that, when the Federal Government's credit needed support in financing the Civil War, the Seligmans succeeded in selling $200,000,000 of government bonds to European investors. This was a service in the opinion of the historian W. E. Dodd as helpful toward winning the war as the Battle of Gettysburg.

In 1871 the firm of J. & W. Seligman & Company was appointed one of the fiscal agents of the United States to secure the conversion of its wartime loan, the "5-20s," into new 5 per cent bonds.

In the years following the Civil War, the mergers, bankruptcies, organizations and reorganizations of American railroads were creating an enormous field for stock and bond speculation. By 1869 Joseph and his brothers had already acquired a working capital of over $6,000,000, and their firm became the first German Jewish banking concern to enter the railroad-securities field. Joseph Seligman undertook to sell the South Pacific's first bond issue. Meanwhile he was also helping to finance the Atlantic and Pacific Railroad. In the years to come his investments escalated from three railroads to over a hundred. At times, he himself seemed to be confused by his activities.

In 1873 Joseph wrote: "I am disgusted with all railroads, and shall never again be tempted to undertake the sale of a railroad bond. I am daily engaged in two or three railroad meetings and therefore, cannot attend to office business as much as I want to."

His distaste for tying up money in anything that could not be sold quickly showed up again and again in his distrust of real estate.

The services of the Seligmans enhanced their prestige in Washington. Joseph, already politically prominent, was among those who urged President Lincoln to appoint Ulysses S. Grant commander-in-chief of the Union Armies. At Grant's inauguration as president of the United States, Joseph stood near him on the platform as he took his oath of office. That evening, Joseph showed up at the Inaugural Ball and waltzed with Julia Grant. Later in 1874, Joseph Seligman respectfully declined the office of Secretary of the Treasury in Grant's cabinet.

In 1877 Joseph Seligman was at the height of his career. Moreover he had been one of a committee which rescued the city of New York from the corruption of the Tweed Ring. Financially successful, socially recognized, politically powerful, he ranged among the nation's great. But neither character, prestige, nor patriotic service could ward off the vicious attack of anti-Semitism.

Joseph Seligman's barring from the Grand Union hotel in Saratoga, where he applied for accommodations, became a national controversy. Henry Hilton, the hotel's manager, had been a local New York politician connected with the notorious Tweed machine.

The Reverend Henry Ward Beecher, outstanding and acknowledged champion of the Jews, then America's leading clergyman, brother of the author of *Uncle Tom's Cabin* and the most popular and respected preacher of his day, made the Hilton-Seligman Affair the subject of a widely publicized sermon entitled "Gentile and Jew." It was repeatedly reprinted, until it became a sort of American classic. His potent voice formulated for many ardent followers their attitudes towards Jews.

Months passed and the affair continued to dominate the news as other clergymen, following Beecher's example, had their say.

The Hilton-Seligman Affair was the first publicized case of anti-Semitism in America.

Joseph tried to forget it. In the months that followed, he refused to speak of it.

Joseph Seligman remained a leader in Jewish communal affairs until his death in 1880. One of the founders of the Hebrew Orphan Asylum, he was also president of the German Hebrew Benevolent Society, formed to assist the oppressed German Jews. Loyalty to Judaism did not preclude his interests in the teachings of Felix Adler. Always the intellectual concerned with ideas, he became the first president of the Ethical Culture Society. He also served as a member of the Board of Education of the City of New York and presided over the first Rapid Transit Commission.

Shortly after his passing, among the many items in the paper was the note that the village of Roller's Ridge, Missouri, through which one of Joseph's railroads passed, had voted to change its name and would thereafter be known as Seligman, Missouri, in tribute to the great man's life.

1879 § ADOLPH SUTRO: Pathfinder in the Far West

Almost as soon as it happened, no dwelling place of man was too remote to learn the news that gold had been discovered in California. Adventure beckoned to the Pacific coast, the El Dorado, where gold was lying about in quantities enough to make the finder wealthy overnight.

By 1851 the heyday was over, but people on the eastern seaboard did not realize it. Adolph Sutro, a Jewish adventurer who turned his face to the West, was born in Rhenish Prussia and had come to the United States in the great German migration of 1848. The family first settled in Baltimore, but lured by the stories of the gold rush, the twenty year old youth boarded a ship that sailed to Colon. He then crossed the Isthmus on a wagon drawn by a scrawny horse. Another boat at Panama carried him to the Golden Gate.

The San Francisco which he first beheld that winter day of 1851 had already outgrown the insignificant cluster of Mexican huts which had been the original settlement. Prospectors went out with pans, shovels and pickaxes to dig into the earth. Few returned with pay dirt. The most promising plots of ground were either staked out or held for the original claim owners. The city was crowded with

ADOLPH SUTRO

people of all sorts and conditions: the vicious and the respectable, the dissipated ruffians and evangelists, the gambler and the criminal. But thousands of decent, law-abiding newcomers were either in legitimate business or looking for locations in which to make a start. Sutro opened a tobacco shop on the ocean front.

For nine years he piddled along with small business, but got nowhere. Then came the sensational news of the bonanza strike in the Sierra Nevada by the discovery of the Comstock Lode in Mount Davidson. He crossed the state line but could not connect with the mining enterprises. Yet the change proved beneficial when he started a mill to extract and reduce quartz in Dayton, Nevada. Soon he developed a new process of amalgamating and was equipped to work on the tailings from other mills.

While Sutro was successfully operating his mill, he watched with deep interest the problems baffling the miners in the Comstock Lode. The fabulous rich output of the mines was seriously threatened by floods from underground sources. There perhaps lay an opportunity to utilize his knowledge of mining engineering. Adolph Sutro pondered long and earnestly on some method by which the mines could be saved.

After intensive calculation, Sutro devised a project that, he was sure, would overcome all difficulties. He planned a tunnel, ten feet high, twelve feet wide and almost five miles long, running parallel with the mines sixteen hundred feet beneath the surface and leading from the Carson River to the Comstock Lode. For ventilation, four air shafts would bore into the tunnel, which would drain off the accumulated water into the river. The tunnel plan also involved putting railroad tracks through it.

The vision of the completed tunnel obsessed Sutro. Construction would run into at least $5,000,000, he estimated. But once completed it could produce as much as $6,000,000 a year in revenue with a minimum of upkeep. The tunnel became his day and night dream for fourteen years. Fortunately the quartz mill could pay the initial cost of setting the project in motion. To induce the banks to finance the construction, a scientific blueprint and a survey together with a prospectus, were essential. He had to employ civil engineers to examine the terrain and estimate the lines, geologists to report on the mineral character of the Comstock and surrounding rock, and journalists to explain and advertise the advantages of the tunnel.

After initial opposition, it dawned upon him to appeal for loans to the people most vitally concerned, the Nevada miners. And they responded generously. The completion of the Sutro Tunnel became possible when unexpectedly an English bank supplied the additional capital needed.

The construction of the tunnel was started on October 19, 1869 at the village of Sutro and was completed after ten years of intermittent toil at a cost of $6,500,000. In 1879 it was hailed as a miracle of engineering. But once completed the project held no further interest for its promoter. When offered $5,000,000 he sold his share in the tunnel and conveyed all his stock in the Sutro Trust Company.

Adolph Sutro returned to San Francisco a famous man and a millionaire. He believed in the growth of the city and invested his capital in real estate.

As a bibliophile Sutro attained distinction when he asssembled over 200,000 volumes. His collection, the largest private library then in existence, consisted of ancient classics that had been stowed away in monasteries, and Hebrew manuscripts obtained in Jerusalem. Unfortunately the great bulk was destroyed in the 1906 earthquake followed by the fire. About 70,000 volumes saved from the catastrophe were donated to the City and today are housed in the Sutro branch of the California State Library.

Sutro loved gardens and took great delight in the vast grounds of his estate. First he built a dignified white mansion which crowned a high flower-covered cliff beside the Pacific. Next he designed a garden in which he tried to combine Greek beauty and European folk lore with the luxurious growth of California. For along some of the garden walks reproductions of classic statues gleamed whitely through shrubs, heavy with blossoms, while here and there peeped out brightly colored plaster gnomes which must have reminded the owner of the fairy tales of his German boyhood.

Adolph Sutro

Adolph Sutro owned a tenth of the city's land; he felt he must share his good fortune with San Francisco's citizens. He gave them not only Sutro Park (his estate) but added a museum and an aquarium to his gift. Although in 1894 San Francisco was not yet one of the large centers of Jewish population, the citizenry showed their esteem when they elected Adolph Sutro as mayor.

§106

1881 § ADOLPHUS S. SOLOMONS: Co-Founder of the American Red Cross

While the Civil War was being fought, the foundations for a great humanitarian movement were being formed in Geneva, Switzerland. In 1863 a congress of delegates met to found the International Red Cross. The United States at first remained aloof, partly because of the sympathy of the European nations toward the Confederate cause. During the later 1870s, however, private meetings were held in the homes of Washington citizens in anticipation of American adherence to the Red Cross convention.

One of the principal meeting places was the home of Adolphus Simeon Solomons, a New York-born Jewish publisher who had become prominent in Washington's communal affairs and its philanthropic organizations.

Born in 1826 of English parents, his father was a journalist who wrote editorials for New York papers. He attended the University of the City of New York for his general education. Already in the state militia at fourteen, he was made sergeant five years later and was honorably discharged in 1847. He went to work for a concern that imported stationery and fancy goods and was sent on a business mission to Europe when Secretary of State, Daniel Webster, appointed him "Special Bearer of Dispatches to Berlin."

Later he moved the publishing plant of Philip and Solomons to Washington and for a number of years obtained from the Government its printing contracts. His influence in high places is evident by his friendship with most of the presidents of his time.

ADOLPHUS S. SOLOMONS
(Courtesy of the American Red Cross)

In his book *Reminiscences of Abraham Lincoln,* Adolphus Solomons tells of asking Lincoln to sit for a new picture in the photograph department of his publishing house at 911 Pennsylvania Avenue. When the President came he wore a troubled expression. The negative did not show up well and Lincoln caught the disappointment on Adolphus' face. He agreed to pose again saying "Solomons, tell me one of your funny stories, and we will see if I can't do better." This was his last picture. Five days later the assassin's bullet ended the life of Abraham Lincoln.

Even while living in New York, Solomons participated in philanthropy, serving as a member of various social and welfare agencies.

Perhaps the most significant of his humanitarian efforts were those he donated to the American Red Cross.

In spite of the paucity of information we find him a signatory on the Articles of Incorporation of the Red Cross, dated October 11, 1881. It was in his home in Washington that the decision was reached to form the national organization. He was one of its two vice presidents and the first treasurer. President Chester A. Arthur appointed Clara Barton, Judge Joseph Sheldon and Adolphus S. Solomons to represent the United States Government at the International Congress of the Red Cross held in Geneva. Solomons was elected vice-president of that Congress. One of the original five members of the New York executive of the Red Cross Relief Committee, he served during the Spanish-American War when the board was enlarged to twenty-five members.

In all Solomons remained an active member of the organization for seventeen years and made significant contributions to it during its early formative years.

The American Red Cross, as originally organized, planned not only to relieve suffering in war but from any national or international catastrophe. As later described by Clara Barton it was a movement in the interest of humanity, for the relief of suffering from war, pestilence, famine, flood, fires, and national calamities.

Numerous handwritten letters from Clara Barton to Mr. Solomons relating to eyewitness disaster reports, her problems with the early organization of the Red Cross and her continued efforts to raise funds for the organization are now in the possession of the American Jewish Historical Society. The reports, telegrams and letters prove conclusively her dependence upon Mr. Solomons.

Many of the documents recall tragic events in the United States where the Red Cross played an important part in saving both lives and property. Among the most famous catastrophes covered in the correspondence are the Ohio River flood of 1884 and the Johnstown, Pennsylvania, flood of 1889. In a report of the flood conditions in the Cincinnati area dated February 18, 1884, Clara Barton reported to Mr. Solomons: "I have been out all the p.m. on a relief boat where the food was drawn up in baskets from the boat to the second and third story windows—poor frightened prisoners in the sweep of the flood . . . under one toppled brick block lie seven bodies still, only to be reached when the water leaves."

In another letter Miss Barton asked the advice of Mr. Solomons: "So my good vice-president and kind counselor I send out these hasty thoughts to you, and your clear judgement will at once see if there is anything in them, and will call me at once."

Solomons' whole-hearted benevolence attracted notice at home and abroad.

The feelings of contemporaries towards Adolphus S. Solomons are summed up in the tribute of the American Jewish leader, Louis Marshall: "He believed in the sacred duty of personal service, and he performed that duty as a religious act, with cheerful heart, serious mind and willing hand, thoroughly and not perfunctorily. . . . When he died, on March 18, 1910, in his eighty-fourth year, he was gathered to his fathers, a faithful custodian of the noble traditions of his people, and a saintly champion of the deathless mission of Judaism."

During the Spanish-American War, with Solomons still a member of the executive board, the American Red Cross was to render important service in ministering to the needs of American soldiers. In subsequent war and domestic disaster relief, it assumed a role that has made it an almost indispensable organization in American life.

In 1917 when the Red Cross adopted a nurses' hospital uniform, it turned to Henry A. Dix, a Russian Jewish immigrant, to design it. Then the Dix Red Cross uniform took its place as international insignia, and became recognized in whatever corner of the earth called for the ministrations of that noble institution.

In May 1965, at the eighty-fourth anniversary of the founding of the American Red Cross, it was reported that since its inception it had given $329,600,000 worth of aid for assistance to victims of domestic disasters. This figure did not include the expenditures for services to the armed forces and veterans which during World War I was $40,900,000. During World War II the Red Cross responded with funds totaling $502,100,000. The conflict in Korea required a new upsurge in Red Cross Programs for the armed forces, veterans and their families. During these years the Red Cross spent an additional $111,000,000 for relief and rehabilitation.

At the present time the American Red Cross gains its support and gives its services through some 3,600 chapters, serving fifty states and the United possessions. Two million volunteers are helping to carry out its programs. Its annual membership exceeds forty-five million, including nearly nineteen million Junior and Senior High School Red Cross members.

1881 § MEYER GUGGENHEIM: Copper King

Early in 1848, Simon Guggenheim, who had wearied of the cruel conduct and economic oppression of his Gentile townsmen, left his native Switzerland with his family of fourteen souls and set off for America. Their ship took the customary two months to cross the Atlantic, entered the mouth of the Delaware River, and deposited them all in Philadelphia. Simon was then fifty-six; his oldest son Meyer was twenty. Father and son set off peddling into the anthracite country. Half a century later the Swiss economy of watches and cheese would seem small alongside the Guggenheim empire in copper, lead, tin, nitrates and other minerals.

What may have been the greatest single fortune in America, outweighed only by that of John D. Rockefeller, began very modestly.

After a few years of incredible hardships before these later developments, father Simon Guggenheim plodded the streets of Philadelphia offering shoelaces, ribbons, needles and such articles as were not usually obtained in the small shops off the main business section. Adding the much-used polish for iron stoves, Meyer trudged the open highways from hamlets to farms carrying the heavy knapsack on his back.

Meyer
Guggenheim

§110

Profits enabled Meyer to attempt other lines of business. During the Civil War all kinds of goods were in demand. The United States Army gladly bought his essence of chicory and coffee beans roasted, ground, boiled and bottled which was relished by the soldiers.

Meyer Guggenheim's business acumen constantly perceived new frontiers of opportunity and sources of revenue. He dealt in pepper, condiments and spices from the West Indies brought by clipper ships from Amsterdam. The Pennsylvania Salt Company enjoyed a monopoly in lye used by families in the making of soap out of the fat saved from food. Meyer picked up an option on English caustic which when melted was equivalent to lye and sold much cheaper. The Guggenheim product proved such competition that the salt company bought the lye business and paid a heavy profit. Meyer loaned extra cash to friends and received mortgages secured by real estate. He had also done some speculating in the stock market.

One day Meyer Guggenheim received a consignment of embroideries from his wife's uncle in Switzerland. A letter explained that Uncle Myers had started a factory that would embroider lace cheaply by machine, a process hitherto done expensively by hand. He had produced more than he could sell in Europe and believed that the lace would go well in America. His price was but a small coverage on cost.

The alert Guggenheim sensed the new possibilities immediately. The lace came at the right time. Meyer had been wondering what to do with his older sons who showed no disposition for school but keen interest in business. He formed a partnership, Guggenheim and Pulaski, with offices in Switzerland, later in New York. Daniel Guggenheim, only seventeen, but the shrewdest of the boys, went with Morris Pulaski to Switzerland to finish his education and learn the lace embroidery business. While the business prospered there intervened an incident which ultimately brought the Guggenheims, for a time at least, into the category of the Rockefellers, the Morgans, the Fords and the DuPonts.

MEYER GUGGENHEIM

Losing money after the Civil War, Charles Graham, a dignified Quaker from Germantown, attempting to retrieve his fortune by investing his remaining two thousand dollars in some Leadville, Colorado silver-lead mines, applied to Meyer Guggenheim for a loan. The map of the gulch and the Quaker's promotional enthusiasm forced Meyer to declare "if the mine is as good as all that I won't lend you a penny. I will take a partnership." The partners traveled to Leadville, but all Meyer could see on the hill was a deep shaft filled with water. The manager seemed confident of a big strike if he had the necessary machinery for pumping out the water and enough funds to continue digging.

Meyer returned to Philadelphia not over confident. During the next few months more and more of Meyer's money was needed to keep the pumps going. Nervous irritation increased with each telegram asking for another $1,000. One day a messenger brought in a telegram from Leadville which read: "Rich strike—mine yielding fifteen ounces silver, sixty per cent lead-Harsh." Excited, he grabbed a pencil and computed that fifty tons a day would produce $1000 in silver. He was indeed a millionaire. From that day in 1881, the spice business and even the profitable lace-embroidery firm seemed a mere trifle. Mining meant big business worthy of smart men's efforts.

He would set up a smelting plant that would refine his own metal and serve others. The embroidery firm was sold and his three older sons went wholeheartedly into mining and smelting. By 1882 Meyer's holdings were large enough, according to his biographer, to "enlist and hold the attention of all of his sons," who had been working for him all along. Meyer formed M. Guggenheim's Sons for this purchase, in which each of his seven boys was an equal partner. Meyer began lending his sons money to go out and buy and build smelters. In 1888 the boys bought their first smelter in Pueblo, Colorado, for $500,000, and soon they had another in Mexico. The profits they divided were enough to hold anyone's attention. In 1890 one mine alone was worth $14,556,000. A year later, the Guggenheims had made so much money that they decided to form a trust of their own, consolidating about a dozen of their refining operations under the name of the Colorado Smelting and Refining Company.

Meyer Guggenheim

§112

In the rise of trust building, H. H. Rogers and the Rockefellers formed the American Smelting and Refining Company which monopolized the smelters' industry. They invited the Guggenheims to enter on attractive terms.

At a critical time the Guggenheims endeared themselves to labor, to miners and to the general public by complying with the Colorado eight-hour law, by paying a better price for gold and silver ore, by advancing loans to hardpressed miners and by keeping open during the shut-down ordered by the Smelters' Trust. In 1901 the Trust capitulated on the terms of the victor and the Guggenheims took over the Smelters' Trust. The family received $45,000,000 in stock and became the majority stockholders of the American Smelting and Refining Company, perhaps the most remarkable deal in Wall Street history.

Within a generation the Guggenheims stood out as the world's copper kings. They refined silver and extracted lead and zinc. They developed tin mines in Bolivia and dug gold in the region of the frozen Yukon. The Guggenheim Exploitation Company sent forth engineers to roam throughout the world searching for profitable mines and ores, minerals and metals. At the invitation of the Belgian King Leopold II they became partners in the diamond fields of Angola and the Congo. They extracted nitrate in Chile and drew rubber out of plantations in the Belgian Congo. They monopolized the mining industry of Mexico and controlled the Smelters' Trust through the American Smelting and Refining Company. They initiated and launched such gigantic enterprises as Kennecott Copper Corporation, Nevada Consolidated, the Esperanza Gold Mine in

Mexico and the Chile Copper Company. There were years when the Guggenheims produced more than one-half of the world's copper.

The highest point in Guggenheim wealth and power came with the First World War. No one was better prepared for the role of purveying essential metals, first to the Allies and later to his own country, than Daniel Guggenheim. The Guggenheim corporations were geared to their top efficiency in production and distribution. In fact it is difficult to envision an Allied victory without their resourceful organizations. All the sons threw their energies into the war effort. The younger generation enlisted in the armed forces and their fathers worked selling Liberty Bonds, helping the American Red Cross and serving on war boards that directed phases of the conflict.

Meyer Guggenheim and his sons distinguished themselves by their benefactions to philanthropic and humanitarian causes. For six years Simon Guggenheim represented Colorado in the United States Senate. The John Simon Guggenheim Memorial Foundation, which he established in memory of his first-born son, dispenses thousands of fellowships to artists, scientists and scholars without regard to race or creed.

On New York's Fifth Avenue between 88th and 89th Streets stands the Solomon Guggenheim Museum that houses old masters, as well as twentieth century foreign and American painting, sculpture and non-objective art. The Murray and Leonie Guggenheim Dental Clinic cared for the needs of thousands of school children free of charge on East 72nd Street in New York City for a period of thirty-six years before it closed in the Spring of 1967, having been supplanted by Federal and State legislation.

Several years before Lindbergh startled the world with his solo flight across the Atlantic, Daniel Guggenheim, instigated by his son Harry, subseqently ambassador to Cuba, began contributing funds to various universities for research in the study and promotion of aviation as a safe and useful means of transportation when the then new-art of flying was in the doldrums of the 1920's. He then set up the Daniel Guggenheim Fund for the Promotion of Aeronautics with an initial $2,500,000 for loans to commercial companies for landing fields, beacon lights and air markings. By taking up where he left off, and following the methods he established, the Daniel and Florence Guggenheim Foundation has been able to aid materially in bringing about greater safety, reliability, speed and range in air transportation and to help speed the progress of flight into space.

Other matters of lifelong interest to Daniel and Florence Guggenheim have also been favored by the Foundation. Among these have been many projects in music, medicine, health and religion.

Meyer Guggenheim

1882 § HENRIETTA SZOLD: Gallant, Indomitable Crusader

§114

The lot of the Jew in Czarist Russia was not a happy one. In 1881 there began a hideous nightmare of oppression, rioting, and bloodshed, as dreadful as the orgies of the Spanish Inquisition. Pogroms broke out wherever there were Jews. Jews were persecuted or expelled and thousands of them fled in the wildest exodus in Jewish history, to Germany, Austria, France, England, and Palestine. Between 1881 and 1910, 1,562,800 Russian and Polish Jews came to the United States. The same harsh treatment befell the Jews in Galicia, Rumania, and Austro-Hungary, and from these countries as well came hundreds of thousands of refugees.

The problem of the Jewish community arising from the influx of these refugees in the early 80's became intense because of the lack of existing societies capable of coping with the situation. In 1882 the Young Men's Hebrew Association of New York established a downtown branch, the first Jewish neighborhood center for immigrant groups. The rooms were located at 244 East Broadway, but within a year the Y moved to 206 East Broadway, where a new building had been erected for the Hebrew Free School Association. The activities conducted here included, for the first time, Americanization classes, English for foreigners, and related subjects. One of the teachers was Emma Lazarus, the famous poetess, whose immortal words are inscribed on the base of the Statue of Liberty. The work conducted for the immigrants inspired Jacob Shiff to refer to the "noble missionary work among the Russians conducted by the YMHA."

Baltimore, Maryland, also received many of the refugees. The home of Rabbi Benjamin Szold, one of its prominent spiritual leaders, was constantly filled with haggard men and women asking for advice. To help the newcomers, his daughter, Henrietta Szold, organized classes to teach the immigrants English and the ideals of democracy, patterning her curriculum after the earlier New York one. In 1898 she rented a room above a store in the cheaper section of town and began classes with thirty pupils. During the first semester more than fifty heads, young and old, often father and son, touched each other over the primer, together learning their A B C. The heart throb of it warmed Henrietta's body and soul on the cold wintry nights in the long rides of the horse-cars from the Baltimore slums to her father's home. Soon others learned about the school and came to join. The superintendent of schools saw that the movement was the answer to a great problem and the public school system throughout the country incorporated the program.

The immigrants made an adaption to their environment. Their children, now grown into adults, differed from their fellow Americans only in the traditionally acceptable American differences which leaves to each man free exercise of his religious convictions.

Fifty years after Henrietta Szold began her Americanization classes, Mayor La Guardia conferred upon her the "Freedom of the City of New York" and said that it was Americanization work such as hers and that of the YMHA that made possible his own ascent to the mayoralty and had saved America from a new slavery.

From Baltimore where Henrietta Szold was born on December 21, 1860, to Jerusalem where she died on February 13, 1945, the life of this gallant, indomitable crusader was filled with service for her people. As one of the pioneer builders of Jewish culture in America she is gratefully remembered as editorial secretary of the Jewish Publication Society and translator of a number of Hebrew books including Graetz's monumental *History of the Jews,* Slouschz's *Hebrew Renaissance* and Lazarus' *Ethics of Judaism.*

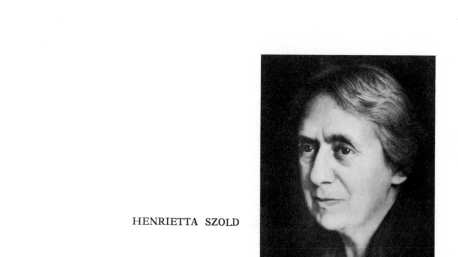

HENRIETTA SZOLD

Nevertheless, her real monument was her work in Zionism, for Hadassah, the women's Zionist organization of which she was the founder, and for Youth Aliyah (immigation), through which she saved many young Jewish lives from the inferno of Nazi Germany and other lands of danger.

Henrietta Szold had been a Zionist for years. It seemed a natural part of her love for Judaism and her concern for the Jewish people. "I became converted to Zionism," she wrote, "the very moment I realized that it supplied my bruised, torn and bloody nation with an ideal—an ideal that is balm to the self-inflicted wounds and to the wounds inflicted by others."

Henrietta Szold

§116

When she left for her first trip to Palestine, friends told her that seeing actual conditions in the Holy Land might make her lose her faith in Zionism. On the contrary, she came back "more than ever convinced that our only salvation lies that way."

In 1909—she had then almost reached fifty years of age—she went for a visit to Palestine. Here she found hard conditions in public health. Here she saw for the first time the appalling prevalence of trachoma, the dreaded eye disease that led to so much blindness among children and adults. Determined to do something about the health of the people in the Holy Land, she conceived the idea of district nursing. Upon her return to America, through her enterprise and exertion was founded the American Zionist medical unit which eventually led her to the founding of Hadassah, the women's Zionist organization.

In New York City, on March 3, 1912, a dozen women met with Miss Szold in Temple Emanu-El and formed the first chapter of Hadassah. The charter members chose the Hebrew name of Queen Esther for their group as they had organized on the Feast of Purim. The quotation from Jeremiah on their seal expressed their purpose: "For the Healing of the Daughter of My People."

After the First World War Henrietta Szold went to the Land of Israel for the second time and lived in Jerusalem. She helped establish needed hospitals, clinics and health services all over the land. When she was seventy-two she wanted to return to her relatives, but then began the frightful era: Hitler rose to power.

Henrietta Szold, who felt the coming tragedy, left immediately for London and Berlin to lead the Youth Aliyah project. She mobilized the Yishuv and Jews in the Diaspora to participate in the rescue of youth from the inferno of Nazi Germany, British White Paper restrictions and Moslem oppression and to bring them to Palestine.

Their problem of adjustment, their health, their education, all were her concern.

In the years 1933 to 1945 that Henrietta Szold was head of Youth Aliyah, 30,000 orphans and unaccompanied children who otherwise would have been killed in concentration camps were saved. Altogether Youth Aliyah had rescued and rehabilitated more than 50,000 youngsters in the Palestine that is now Israel. She who had no children of her own and who never married had indeed become a mother to her people.

Two stamps honoring Henrietta Szold were issued on December 14, 1960, the centenary of her birth. The first, issued by the State of Israel, was one of several commemorations scheduled to mark "Henrietta Szold Year." The second was issued by the United States Post Office. The Szold stamp shows the first president of Hadassah and the Hadassah-Hebrew University Medical Center in the background.

To pay further tribute to the memory of Henrietta Szold the New York City Board of Education dedicated a Lower East Side public school in her name. This was the first time that a public school was named for a Zionist leader.

Today, twenty-two years after her death, Hadassah, the women's Zionist organization which Henrietta Szold founded and the institutions it created stand like giants on the health and welfare landscape of the new Jewish state. As for decisiveness in the affairs of men, Hadassah, with 318,000 members, more than 1,350 chapters and groups in fifty states, and a current annual budget of over ten million dollars—wields as much financial and political power in American Zionist deliberations and as much influence on fundamental social patterns in Israel, as any cluster of Biblical heroines of antiquity, with the possible exception of Eve.

1882 § DAVID BELASCO: Theater Innovator

A man of eccentric manner both in dress and demeanor, David Belasco was nonetheless one of the greatest influences in the American theater. When he first appeared in New York as a young director and playwright, the theater was relatively cheap and tawdry, as well

DAVID BELASCO

as unnatural and unrealistic. Belasco breathed new life into an old art and brought naturalism and the modern touch to the stage.

At the same time, Belasco was contributing many significant features to the theater itself. He was the first to introduce electric lighting to the stage in the 1880s, the new invention of Thomas Edison. What he did to the style and manner of the performer was practically a revolution in the art of acting. No one could ever mistake a Belasco production since it was indelibly stamped with his own inimitable touch and genius.

David Belasco, son of a leading English comic actor, was born in San Francisco in 1853. His father, an orthodox Jew, had gone there to prospect for gold. At sixteen, young David was through with school and trying his hand with show business. For several years he trouped from town to town as actor, manager and playwright.

Since his short stature and high-pitched voice were handicaps in his acting, Belasco soon turned exclusively to directing, producing and writing for the stage. When work out West ran low, he came East to tackle the New York stage. Soon he became famous as a director. In that role, he was noted as harsh, dictatorial, autocratic, but above all imaginative. Until Belasco began to produce plays, audiences were satisfied to see a library represented by rows of books painted on the scenery; when Belasco showed a doctor's office on the stage, he not only used real volumes but chose the very medical books a doctor would need. He surprised audiences by bringing on the stage a genuine switchboard. For one production he constructed a complete Childs' Restaurant on the stage and actually fried eggs. The first play he produced, Bronson Howard's *Young Mrs. Winthrop* (1882) ran for nearly two hundred performances and made a tremendous impression. Belasco's own *May Blossom* which followed was performed a thousand times in the Madison Square Theater and drove speculator's tickets up to five dollars each. His original play of western life, *The Girl of the Golden West*, was made into one of the first operas with an American setting. Its premiere was held at the Metropolitan with Toscanini conducting and Caruso and Amato in the chief roles. Shakespeare's *Merchant of Venice* had in Belasco's staging the longest run ever remembered on Broadway.

In the modern theater Belasco holds his high place not only as a playwright, as an original worker especially in the field of stage lighting, but also as the man who discovered and trained a number of our leading actors. Mary Pickford graduated from his school to become America's sweetheart. Another, David Warfield, became one of the most prominent Jewish actors of his day. His starring of Fannie Brice in the play *Fanny* lured her into her first and only dramatic role.

In all Belasco produced four hundred plays ranging from minstrel shows to high tragedy, from fairy tale to musical comedy, from melodrama to pageantry. The works of some one hundred and twenty-five different authors, they included one hundred and fifty dramas of his own.

Today David Belasco's influence is still plain to see in almost every play shown. The American theater can truly thank him for raising it to an artistic level as high as any in the world.

1882 § SAMUEL GOMPERS: Labor Statesman

Labor Day, observed on the first Monday in September, has come to be one of the most generally celebrated holidays in the United States, ranking along with Washington's Birthday, Independence Day and Thanksgiving. A large share of the credit for the enactment of the law establishing Labor Day as a national holiday is given to Samuel Gompers, one of the most distinguished leaders of American labor of the last century. It was first celebrated in New York on September 5, 1882, with parades held by the Knights of Labor.

Gompers, an English-born Jew who came to America during the Civil War period, was one of the founders and for almost forty years president of the American Federation of Labor.

As a small boy in England, Samuel was sent to a Jewish free school and to a night school where he studied Hebrew and the Bible. At the age of ten, he went to work, apprenticed to a shoemaker, at six cents a week wages. He soon changed to cigarmaking at an increased wage of twelve cents a week. With the assistance of the Cigarmakers' Society (Union) of England, which had established an emigration fund to relieve unemployment by ridding England of superfluous cigarmakers, the family came to America in 1863. They established their home in Houston and Attorney Streets in New York's East Side, and father and son began making cigars at home. Samuel managed to pick up some odds and ends of an education at Cooper Union. At sixteen he went to work in a cigar factory.

Through the years of deprivation, Gompers learned how important it was for workingmen to act together and how much power they had when they did. In 1873 he became a member of a cigarmakers' union and a year later was made president of Local 144 which was to make labor history. In 1877 Gompers and his friends, Adolph Strasser and Ferdinand Laurell, led a cigarmakers' strike in protest against unsanitary working conditions. From that beginning, Gom-

Samuel Gompers

§120

SAMUEL GOMPERS

pers went on to develop his ideas about the relationship between workers and employees until he had clearly in his mind the objective to which he was to devote the rest of his life—a united labor front.

At the age of thirty-one, in 1881, in Pittsburgh, at the first national meeting of labor he attended, he was elected a vice-president of the Federation of Trades and Labor Unions.

In Columbus, Ohio, in 1886, he then formed the nucleus of what was to become the American Federation of Labor out of the remnants of a federation of organized trades and labor unions. He was chosen president of the new group at an annual salary of $1,000. As the American Federation of Labor grew stronger and bigger, Gompers came to be acknowledged everywhere as the spokesman of the American worker and labor's most famous champion.

Samuel
Gompers

§121

The first great campaign of the American Federation of Labor was the struggle for an eight hour day. This was eventually won, but more improvements were sought. Gompers then proceeded to arouse the country's consciousness for decent wages for workers, clean shops, and successful arbitration machinery, all of which he felt could best be achieved through the organization of unions.

As a result of Gompers' activity as founder of the American Federation of Labor, the garment and clothing industry, through techniques of mass production and distribution, has made the people of the United States the best dressed nation on the earth. The American worker was lifted from the slough of human despair and hunger to human dignity and hope.

During World War I, Gompers mobilized labor behind the American war effort. In 1918, President Wilson appointed him to the Commission for International Labor Legislation which was founded to make new and better labor laws for all the governments of the world.

When Gompers died in 1924 the American Federation of Labor had grown to a membership of 5,000,000, and he had lived to see his dream of organized labor come true in the land of the free.

In 1933 national tribute was paid to the great labor leader when President Franklin D. Roosevelt dedicated the Gompers Monument in Washington. Of bronze and marble, it shows Gompers seated in front of the three allegorical figures representing Unionism, Fraternity, and Brotherhood.

In January 1950, on the occasion of the one hundredth anniversary of the birth of Samuel Gompers, one of the first stamps carrying the picture of a Jew, the Gompers stamp, was issued by the United States Post Office.

Other Jewish leaders in the American labor movement who came to these shores as poverty-striken immigrants, then rose to prominence in the nation's labor history, include Meyer London, the first Socialist leader to be elected to the United States Congress, Sidney Hillman, David Dubinsky, president of the International Ladies' Garment Workers' Union, and Jacob S. Potofsky, president of the Amalgamated Clothing Workers.

Samuel Gompers

§122

1883 § EMMA LAZARUS: The Voice of Liberty

The most treasured historic documents of our American heritage were assembled in a special collection following World War II and placed aboard the famous New York State's Freedom Train exhibition that travelled throughout the Empire State.

The most significant piece of paper to become an emblem of American humanity toward all refugees from persecution was included among New York State's Freedom Train's exhibition. Borrowed from its shrine in the archives of the American Jewish Historical Society, from the original manuscript autograph notebook of the poems of Emma Lazarus, "The New Colossus" was placed on display in New York State. Thousands of its citizens gazed in reverence on the original document, in ink that has faded eighty-five years, but in words that never dim:

> "Not like the brazen giant of Greek fame,
> With conquering limbs astride from land to land,
> Here at our sea-washed, sunset gates shall stand
> A mighty woman with a torch, whose flame
> Is the imprisoned lightening, and her name
> Mother of Exiles. From her beacon-hand
> Glows world-wide welcome; her mild eyes command
> The air-bridged harbor that twin-cities frame.

> "Keep, ancient lands, your storied pomp!" Cries she,
> With silent lips. "Give me your tired, your poor,
> Your huddled masses yearning to breathe free,

The wretched refuse of your teeming shore,
Send these, the homeless, tempest-tost to me.
I lift my lamp beside the golden door!"

Had she written nothing but these fourteen burning lines, this woman's name would always be remembered for her noble soul and humane heart. These words will live when many other poems are forgotten. They will tell the world the story of Emma Lazarus, who returned to her people.

*Emma
Lazarus*

§123

A hundred years ago a little dark-eyed girl was growing up in the comfortable home of her Sephardic parents in New York City. Though her private tutors taught little Emma classic literature and modern language, none acquainted the gifted child with the glorious past and present of her people. As she matured, he friend, Ralph Waldo Emerson, highly praised Emma's early poems about Greek legends. Basking in the glow of his praise, Emma continued to pursue her "calm hellenistic" ideals of beauty. In 1879 she was brought to a rude awakening of her Jewish soul. The papers blazed the awful tidings of Russian persecutions. A great wave of immigrants was hurled at the shores of the New World. Emma Lazarus saw them in Ellis Island; she saw their poverty and distress, but also their pride and devotion to their ancient faith. From then on she seemed to be reborn for the rest of her all too short life, and belonged, as one of her heroines termed it, "wholly to her people." She learned Hebrew and translated into English some of the finest medieval poets, Ibn Gabirol, Judah Halevi, and Benjamin of Tudela. She began to study the history and religion of her people. She thrilled at the heroism of the Maccabees and wrote "The Banner of the Jew," which is still recited in our religious schools. She read how a whole Jewish community in the fifteenth century faced the choice of conversion or death at the stake. For them there could be only one choice: men, women and children danced into the flames while they sang the praises of God. Miss Lazarus put this glorious tragedy into a poetic play entitled "The Dance to Death." Even more powerful is her poem, "Crowing of the Red Cock," in which she speaks of later martyrs in Russia. Long before Zionism became a contemporary force, she was the first to appeal for funds to colonize the Jews in Palestine and dreamed and wrote of the Return of the Exiles. Full of sympathy for the persecuted, she rose to attack the dark forces of persecution and found the words that were to create for her a niche for all time among American immortals.

Her most famous poem, "The New Colossus," was created under

EMMA LAZARUS

very interesting circumstances. The French sculptor Frederic Auguste Bartholdi had designed the Statue of Liberty which was intended as a gift of the people of France to the United States to commemorate the one hundredth anniversary of the Declaration of Independence. Money was still needed for the huge pedestal on which the statue was to rest. One day in the year of 1883, a Mrs. Constance Harrison, particularly inspired by Joseph Pulitzer's editorials in *The New York World*, undertook the publication of a folder of poetry and sketches by famous authors and artists to be sold for the benefit of the pedestal fund. When she approached Emma Lazarus, the poetess replied that she could not write verse on order. But, said, Mrs. Harrison, "think of the Russian refugees."

The reminder proved successful. Two days later Emma Lazarus handed the fund "The New Colossus," a poem that depicts America as the hope of the oppressed. Its benefit sale brought an unheard-of amount for a short piece of poetry: $1,500. The verses went from mouth to mouth, from continent to continent, and in 1903 they were inscribed in the bronze tablet which first was placed on the interior wall of the pedestal and later, for better visibility over the entrance to the Statue of Liberty which stands in New York Harbor where it welcomed immigrants to the New World. Emma Lazarus was thirty-four years old when she wrote the poem that expressed her faith in America and the principles for which America stands. As the authoress of the famous oft-quoted sonnet she was universally acclaimed as the champion of American liberty and democracy, just as the statue itself has become the symbol of our liberty.

At the height of her fame, sorrow struck her. She fell seriously ill and then seemed to recover. Her father, whom she loved dearly, died. She sought consolation in travel and toured England, France and Italy. But she became so deathly sick that only her great desire to return to her beloved America enabled her to do so.

"A great princess is fallen in Israel," wrote the poet Stedman when she died at the age of thirty-eight. All the synagogues of New York held services for her, an immortal American and a prophetic champion of Israel who had sung:

"The spirit is not dead, proclaim the word,
  Where lay dead bones, a host of armed men stand!
  I ope the graves, my people, says the Lord
  And shall place you in your promised land."

In 1949 the centenary of Emma Lazarus' birth attained world-wide attention.

Her tombstone stands in a Long Island graveyard, and a public memorial to her was put up in her native New York City.

1889 § LOUIS BORGENICHT: He Started a New Industry

Before the American advent of the German Jew and his progress here from peddler to storekeeper, to merchant, to merchandise jobber, and finally to manufacturer, there was such wide differences between the dress and living standards of the rich oligarchy of aristocrats and the American proletariat that class distinction made itself apparent wherever people assembled. The genius of the German Jew as garment manufacturer and distributor of merchandise helped make democracy work in the United States. These Jews abolished that class distinction in dress which from colonial days had always enabled the haves and the have-nots to be told apart. Their garment factories, replacing in large measure what had originally been a handicraft producing made-to-order clothing, developed into one of the early mass production systems in the country.

As the cycle swung and Jews from Eastern Europe—largely Russian Jews—toward the last quarter of the nineteenth century dominated American Jewry, they took over the clothing and garment

LOUIS BORGENICHT

trade where the German Jews had left off. Soon the fashions of the minute were almost instantaneously available equally within the purse of the shopgirl as well as that of the society queen; and the clerk was apt to set the pace for the boss in the latest styles for men.

Children's clothing made by machine also became a permanent fixture in the American home, and constitutes big business. Yet until comparatively recently, even while clothing manufacturers were developing the art of ready-made suits for men, and dresses and cloaks for women, little attention was given to anything of the kind for children. It was still thought that every mother with a needle and thread could laboriously put together a garment. The situation did not undergo change until a poverty-stricken Jewish immigrant, Louis Borgenicht, coming to America from a small Galician village and beginning as a peddler in the New York ghetto, saw his opportunity in 1889 and had the foresight to start a new American industry.

His story was at first the ordinary account of the poor alien struggling for a foothold amid his new surroundings. Prompted to push-cart merchandising, he sold pots, pans, socks, and stockings. Then he noticed that no one in the whole city of New York was making children's aprons. Without capital, but with the aid of his wife and a few second-hand machines, he began to manufacture aprons which he peddled from house to house.

From the making of aprons he turned to children's dresses. He came to the conclusion that ready-made clothes would save mothers endless work, the material and sewing would be better than home-made, and the prices would be lower than that of similar mother-made garments.

Now for the first time designing clothes for children was not a question of fashioning down or taking grown-up fashions and scaling them to fit the youngsters, but a matter of original thought. Clothing for children was based on utility as well as appearance.

Although when Borgenicht started there were three other New York manufacturers making children's dresses in a limited way, one, an East Side tailor who sewed them to order, and two other enterprises that turned out expensive special garments, his creative energy made him by far the pioneering leader.

With a leap and a bound, American became clothes conscious in those days of the ending decade of the century. Soon there were countless competitors. As Borgenicht kept ahead of the rest, he soon became known as "King of the Children's Dress Trade," and his business grew into many millions. Ready-made children's clothing appeared from Maine to California. He had created a modern miracle business—an American industry designed to make American home life easier, more colorful, and more dramatic—and exceeding eighty million dollars a year.

1888 § JACOB JOSEPH: Chief Rabbi of New York

In 1886, eighteen Jewish congregations in New York City led by Congregation Beth Hamidrash Hagadol of Norfolk Street united to secure a prominent Russian rabbi for the newly created office of Chief Rabbi of the Orthodox community with a view of introducing order and discipline into their religious life. Two years later, a man who had great faith in the tremendous possibilities of Jewish life in America, stepped off a vessel in New York harbor. This man was Rabbi Jacob Joseph, the first and only Chief Rabbi America was ever to have.

Rabbi Joseph, who was born in Kovno, Russia, in 1848, studied at the world famous Yeshiva of Volozhin. He gained considerable renown as a student of Talmud and became famous as a preacher. He was rabbi of several lesser Jewish communities when, in 1883, he was appointed maggid or preacher of the Jewish community of Vilna. In 1888 he published *Lebeth Yaakov*, a collection of homilies and notes to his rabbinic writings, of which a new Warsaw edition appeared in 1900. Even he, however, was unable to unite the people.

On July 7, 1888, at his first sermon in the Beth Hamidrash Hagadol (the oldest and largest synagogue of East European Jewry in New York) on Sabbath Nachamu, when the prophetic portion from Isaiah, "Comfort ye, comfort ye, my people" is read, the audience overflowed onto the street where a large crowd was waiting to catch a glimpse of the new Chief Rabbi. The sermon impressed everyone with its stress on loving-kindness, for understanding among his followers, for the recognition to be sought by the practice of virtue, moral living and deeds of charity. The Yiddish was clear and distinct without gestures or undue emphasis. Those who came to scoff remained to praise. The general press, the Yiddish and Anglo-Jewish publications, reported favorably. His adherents were jubilant as respect for the Chief Rabbi grew and spread uptown among the Reform Jews. Everything seemed to augur well for Rabbi Joseph when a misstep upset the era of good feeling and brought a tragic end to the experiment.

The kosher system of slaughter and preparation of meat for consumption has an importance in traditional Judaism altogether incomprehensible to non-Jews or even to non-observant Jews. Its significance to the devout is linked with the preservation of Jews and Judaism. The preparation becomes an intricate ritual, requiring organized supervision. Thus when the elated leaders of the Orthodox Jewish community saw the respect their Rabbi evoked, they concluded that such veneration should succeed in bringing about the enforcement of kashruth. They aimed to reorganize the system and place kashruth under strict surveillance of an association. But all organizations involve expense. So the leaders decided to impose a penny tax on every fowl slaughtered by the *shohet* and to instruct housewives not to buy a slaughtered chicken unless it had attached a tag with the imprint: *Rav ha-Kolel* Jacob Joseph. The income from the one cent tags would be used to pay the cost of supervision. Rabbi Joseph objected to the procedure, but was overruled by the practical businessmen who maintained that it was the approved American practice of meeting overhead.

Immediately a storm broke forth. Opponents of the Chief Rabbi joined forces. Prominent among the dissenters were those rabbis who had not been consulted about setting up a Chief Rabbinate in New York. The butchers opposed to supervision organized as the "Hebrew Poultry Butchers Association." They were joined by radical

Jacob Joseph

§128

elements, the socialists and anarchists, who seized any occasion to expose the "gouging methods of clerical exploitation."

When Rabbi Joseph's six year contract expired it was not renewed. The butchers who accepted his supervision were induced to pay his salary. He still held the title of Chief Rabbi, but bore the humiliation of his decline and neglect with stoic dignity. But inwardly the wounds were festering. Soon confined to bed, he spent his remaining six years as an invalid. Nor did financial distress help to ease his pain. He died July 28, 1902, at the age of fifty-four.

Rabbi Joseph's funeral was attended by 100,000 Jews who turned out to pay their last tribute of respect, the respect denied him when he was alive in their midst. As the procession was passing the printing press factory of R. Hoe and Company, on East Broadway and Grand Street, some anti-Semitic workmen and apprentices began jeering and throwing bolts and nuts from the upper windows. This precipitated a riot in which many of the mourners were injured or mistreated by the police.

Rabbi Jacob Joseph's grandson, former State Senator Lazarus Joseph, later served as comptroller of the City of New York.

Former comptroller Joseph's son, the great-grandson and namesake of Rabbi Joseph enlisted in the United States Marines in 1938 after graduating from Columbia University and became a captain in the Solomon Islands, the scene of furious fighting, probably the youngest officer of that rank in the Marine Corps. He was killed in action June 1942, the very day his father was leaving home for an

RABBI JACOB JOSEPH

appointment in Washington with Lieutenant General Thomas Holcomb, Commander of the United States Marine Corps, to discuss joining the service himself.

Jacob Joseph

§130

The Rabbi Jacob Joseph Yeshiva at 165 Henry Street, New York City, bears Rabbi Joseph's name. Originally established in 1901 by Rabbi Jacob L. Andron and his father, Rabbi Samuel L. Andron, it was then known as the Beth Sefer Tifereth Yerushalaim. Many notables graduated from the school, among them Judge Simon H. Rifkind, Dr. Alexander Sachs (who was sent as Albert Einstein's personal envoy to persuade President Roosevelt to undertake the development and production of the atomic bomb), and Professor Oscar I. Janowsky. Today it has a student population of 1,000 and has grown to include a Mesifta for the ordination of Orthodox rabbis.

A playground facing the Rabbi Jacob Joseph Yeshiva bears Captain Joseph's name.

1890 § ABRAHAM GOLDFADDEN: Father of the Yiddish Theater

For many years America had the best Yiddish theaters in the world, which produced plays under the best directors and evoked much popular interest. Its growth had been especially interesting for it was strictly an American deevlopment, going far beyond anything ever done in that language in Europe. Sometimes likened in its field to Dublin's Abbey Theater and to the Moscow Art Theatre, rising costs and dwindling audiences led to its disbandment in 1950. Today it is being reactivated as a subsidized venture.

The founder of the Yiddish theater and also of theater music was Abraham Goldfadden, who wrote both the libretto and lyric and also provided the music. Since there was no body of drama written in the common language, he had to start from scratch writing plays, musicals, training actors, directing and stage managing and choosing costumes. With no models to follow he had to create his own forms and techniques appropriate to a culture which had hardly progressed since the seventeenth century.

Jewish audiences responded immediately.

Goldfadden turned to the glories of the past for material and composed operettas that would foster the spirit of self-respect and opposition to tyranny.

When he came to New York in 1883, he found his fellow immigrants slaving at low wages and living in squalid poverty, unable to escape the dreary monotony of their lives. Lost to the language and mores of the Broadway stage, they embraced Goldfadden's ideas with delight and the Yiddish Theater blossomed.

Like Irving Berlin of today, Goldfadden, who was not a trained musician, was able to create songs that will remain in the repertoire of the Jewish people for generations to come. The greater portions of his melodies were borrowed largely from the liturgy of the orthodox synagogue. Goldfadden also adapted well-known melodies from Italian and Russian operas, as well as from French and German musical comedies. He majorized or minorized the melodies, imparted a Jewish flavor to them, a Jewish atmosphere and idiom, set lyrics to them, and introduced them on the stage. His lullaby, "Rozhinkes un Mandlen," was sung in many languages by singers of the popular idiom. His famous opera *Shulamith*, first produced in 1890, is still often played today.

Since most of the actors of Goldfadden's generation were recruited from the choruses of synagogues, a new era began with Boris Thomashefsky who imported actors to America who were suitable for the Yiddish stage. With a small group, mostly amateurs, Thomashefsky formed a troop and began giving two performances a week. The first theater was in a small stage rented in the old Bowery Garden. Not long afterwards, a far superior group of actors arrived from London and forced the others to disband. In 1890 with the arrival of Jacob Adler many successful years followed. The Jews flocked to see one of the greatest actors of the day who played every kind of role imaginable. Its outstanding writer for many years was Jacob Gordin, who wrote seventy plays, some original, and some translations. For some years the Yiddish theater produced more vaudeville than drama, but finally there came a revival.

In 1918 Maurice Schwartz and Jacob Ben Ami, talented Yiddish actors and directors, leased the Irving Place Theater, a former playhouse, and introduced art into the Yiddish theater. With *Dos Verforfen Vinkel*, they scored a great success and moved into the Yiddish Art Theater on Second Avenue, once the site of Peter Stuyvesant's estate. This theater has since produced original plays by excellent writers, and the movement has spread to other leading American cities.

The Yiddish theater has not confined itself, but has brought to its crowded houses Shakespeare and Moliere, Oscar Wilde, George Bernard Shaw and Feuchtwanger. But the main strength of the

Yiddish theater has always been derived from authors whose genius is rooted in the phenomena of Jewish life. Its leading spirits have been: Sholom Aleichem, who gave the theater *Tevye, the Dairyman, Hard to Be a Jew, Wandering Stars,* and *Stempenyu*; I. L. Peretz, who wrote *Der Golom, Der Nier Nigun,* and others; and I. J. Singer, whose *Yoshe Kalb* is an extraordinary landscape of movement and form, and who is responsible for those great epic chronicles, *The Family Carnovsky* and *The Brothers Ashkenazi.* Its most famous composers include Achron, Chernyavsky, Olshanetsky, Rumshinsky and Sholom Secunda.

In 1951 the New York City Opera Company decided to produce *The Dybbuk,* one of the most famous of Yiddish plays. This play held the highest box-office attendance of Yiddish theaters in the country.

By 1966 the number of Yiddish theaters in New York City had dwindled to two—one in Manhattan and one in Brooklyn—and membership in the Hebrew Actors' Union had decreased from 1,500 in the 1920's and 30's to 240.

Abraham Goldfadden

§132

1892 § NATHAN STRAUS: Safe Milk for All

One hundred years ago a growing lad in Georgia was dreaming how wonderful it would be to save a human life. That boy, Nathan Straus, grew up to be a man whom untold multitudes of men and women living today owe their lives.

An immigrant boy, he was born in Bavaria on January, 31, 1848, the son of Lazarus Straus. One son, Isidor, is remembered as one of the founders and later president of the Educational Alliance of New York, an institution which did much for the Americanization of the immigrant. Another son, Oscar, was three times Minister to Turkey and Secretary of Commerce and Labor, the first American Jew to serve as a member of a president's cabinet. Nathan Straus, the youngest son, was to make a famous family even more famous!

Lazarus Straus, the father, a Rhine Bavarian, who often had spent some time as an itinerant vendor of general merchandise on the plantations of Georgia, had settled in 1853 in that state, at Talbotton, as the keeper of the general store when Nathan was six years old. There he remained till the end of the Civil War, when he moved north. In 1866 the father took the family to New York City and

NATHAN STRAUS

started a business in crockery and glassware, while Nathan, now in early manhood, was sent to business college. He later joined his father's firm and proved an extraordinary salesman. Under his management the business prospered.

One day in 1874 Nathan called on the firm of R. H. Macy and Company with two porcelain plates under his arm. The clever salesman interested Mr. Macy so successfully that he arranged for the firm of Lazarus Straus to rent the basement of the Macy store for a crockery department.

In the same year when Nathan Straus was twenty-six, he and his brother Isidor became partners in the Macy firm, and in 1887, they were the sole owners of the business. With their investments and joint partnership a new era in Macy's history began and the department store retail trade began growing to its present size. By 1893 they had crossed over to Brooklyn and bought an interest in the store now known as Abraham and Straus.

Nathan Straus became one of the wealthiest merchants in the world but seemed glad to retire that he might devote all his time to his hobby—philanthropy. The most famous of his many philanthropies, which saved the lives of many thousands of babies and has helped to preserve the health of children in our own day, was the

Straus Milk Fund. The story of its origin has been told many times, but it is well worth repeating.

In 1892 dairies lacked adequate milk inspection. Milk often became infected and brought sickness and even death to those who drank it. Nathan Straus lived with his family on his country estate; he prided himself on his fine herd of cattle. One day his livestock manager explained that his family could no longer have milk from their own cows because one had died of tuberculosis. Mr. Straus then began to think of what danger his family had been in and what danger there was present everywhere from the milk that people drank. He believed that the milk of a tubercular cow might transmit the disease to human beings unless the milk were treated in some way that would kill the germs of the disease.

Thousands of American babies were dying each year, but no one knew why. Straus began an investigation of the dairies of New York. Many of them were very dirty. He found them breeding places for sick cows. Soon he became convinced that impure milk was the leading cause of fatality in children.

In 1892 Straus attended a congress of physicians and scientists in Brussels where the great French scientist, Louis Pasteur demonstrated that the germs in milk become absolutely harmless when treated by the Pasteur method. He returned to America determined to educate the country in the advantages of purifying milk by pasteurization as the process was called.

At his own cost he set up pasteurization laboratories where milk could be treated and made safe to drink. He then established the Straus Milk Fund which distributed pasteurized milk at Straus' own milk depots at less than cost to needy people and in the hot summer months without charge to poor babies. In the first year alone over 34,000 bottles were given out. As a result of Straus' activities thousands of babies were saved from illness and the death rate was cut in half.

Meanwhile Mr. Straus began his great campaign for adequate milk inspection by the state. He withstood the attacks and ridicule of many business men who sold milk and did not believe in the process he had installed. Straus would not give up the battle and triumphed in the end. Twenty years passed and at last he was able to close his private pasteurization laboratories, for in every state in the union pasteurization finally became a law.

Straus' ardent desire to do the greatest good in the most direct way carried him further into social welfare work. During the long, cold winter following the depression and unemployment brought about by the Panic of 1892, he distributed over a million and a half baskets of coal for five cents each to the New York poor. The next year, he distributed over a million tickets for fuel, lodging and food. His benefactions and gifts to humanity earned him the name of "the great giver."

In 1923 the people of New York acclaimed him their greatest benefactor in the field of social welfare. President Taft said of him: "Nathan Straus is a great Jew and the greatest Christian of us all."

Nathan Straus was a devoted Zionist and carried his benefactions to Palestine where he founded a Pasteur Institute and two beautiful health centers in Jerusalem and Tel Aviv, for all the needy, Jew and Arab alike. He gave funds for soup kitchens and many other charitable activities in the Holy Land. He established a factory there for the making of buttons from mother of pearl. Nathan Straus had in the early days provided funds to pay for the passage of the first two Hadassah nurses who brought hope and healing to Palestine. He and his equally generous wife, Lina Straus, who had sold her jewels to aid the cause believing that the work must go on.

On his eightieth birthday, on January 31, 1928, Natanyah, a colony established in B'nai Benjamin in Palestine was named in his honor.

Nathan Straus, who invested not only money, but time, energy and skill in the services of mankind, died on January 12, 1931, at the age of eighty-three. The death of the Grand Old Man of American Jewry called forth tributes from high and low, from far and near.

He had given large sums for the relief of those who suffered from the ravages of the First World War. His death spared him the knowledge of the horrors of the Hitler persecutions and of another conflict even more terrible.

1893   §   LILLIAN WALD: The Angel on Henry Street

Sixty-four years ago, a frightened, tearful child stood in the doorway of a tenement room on New York's Lower East Side and sobbed to the nurse inside who was conducting a class on home care for the sick, "My mamma's sick. Please, won't you come home with me?"

Instantly the nurse dismissed the class and hurried with the child to where the mother lay.

Lillian Wald, trained nurse, opened a new chapter in humanitarian service when she answered that little girl's call. Stemming from the famous Henry Street settlement which she founded and which became the "heart" of her activities, this chapter is filled with stories of improved health conditions, cleaner, safer homes, and the saving of many lives.

Lillian
Wald

§136

Lillian Wald was born to Max and Minnie Wald in Cincinnati, Ohio on March 10, 1867. The family soon moved to Rochester, New York. Here the young girl was reared in luxury, but instead of the social life she might have had, she chose to take a nurse's training course in a New York City hospital and dedicate herself to the service of others.

After her graduation from the Women's Medical College of the New York Infirmary in 1891, she instituted classes to teach folks how to care for sickness in the home. She had seen through kind, sympathetic eyes how sickness frightened people and made them helpless, and she was the first to plan some method of overcoming this fear.

Together with her friend Mary Brewster, who was also a nurse, she went to live in New York's Lower East Side where the people needed her help the most, and began a nurses' service, the first visiting nurses in the world. Little did she realize that less than fifty years later there would be an army of more than twenty thousand visiting nurses in the United States. This service grew and ultimately became the Visiting Nurses' Service which continues to furnish assistance to the needy and sick in their homes today.

Soon after her nursing service began, Miss Wald saw that her quarters were not nearly large enough to care for the throngs who came for her help. Therefore, she moved to Henry Street, to the settlement that became so important that one little boy said he thought "God must live there."

When Miss Wald saw the noisy and littered streets which served as the only playground the East Side children knew, she turned the backyard of the settlement into a little park where children and grownups might play and rest in the fresh air and sunlight. Thanks to the fine example set by her, city playgrounds have been established all over the United States.

In 1902 Miss Wald organized the first city school nursing work in the world and the United States became the first country to start regular medical care for school children. She also started the first "bedside school" for handicapped children, which proved the pattern for many such schools in all parts of the country.

Sickness and tragedy received another blow when she urged

authorities to organize a Federal Children's Bureau, which was established by Congress in 1912.

During the depression of the early 1930's, before public relief was taken over by the Federal Government, the Henry Street Settlement issued thousands of food tickets, gave aid, and directed relief.

Known during her lifetime as "the Angel of Henry Street," Lillian Wald retired in 1933. She died at her home in Westport, Connecticut on September 1, 1940.

The substantial and dignified headquarters administration building of the Visiting Nurses' Service of New York in fashionable Murray Hill today is a far cry from its humble beginnings in the East Side at the turn of the century. How this and other pioneering social welfare projects and agencies were initiated by a selfless, imaginative, and creative American Jewish woman, is vividly and dramatically unfolded in Beryl Williams book entitled *Lillian Wald: Angel of Henry Street*.

1896   §   HENRY DIX: An American Business Adventure

The history of the Jew in nineteenth century America is marked by his development of the clothing industry. Starting in the eighteen-thirties, with factories that produced crude, cheaply made clothing, he developed the industry so well that by the end of the century dresses for women and suits for men, of good quality and cut, were being produced in such quantities that their price was within the reach of most people. These enterprisers eliminated the differences in dress that perpetuated class distinction from colonial days; in this they helped to democratize American society.

Into this picture fits Henry A. Dix, who came to America in 1892 from a small, poverty-stricken village in the Ukraine, and had the foresight to start a new branch in women's wear—the manufacture of uniforms.

Soon after his arrival in America, Dix and his wife, attracted by the cheerful little village of Millville, New Jersey, decided to capitalize on their experience as shopkeepers in Russia by opening a dry goods store there. They supplemented their shopkeeping by peddling through the countryside, selling the rural population "Mother Hubbard" wrappers for everyday wear and "tea gowns" of flowered

HENRY DIX

sateens for Sunday wear, produced in the New York sweatshops. One day they came to the conclusion that if they themselves could produce something which was better-looking and cost no more, women would prefer to buy such garments.

With no knowledge of manufacturing, and with no acquaintance with dressmaking or tailoring, husband and wife designed and made their first gowns. They found a youth who had worked in a Philadelphia dressmaking shop and hired him for twelve dollars a week as a mechanic and designer. The village girls were hired as operators. Their garments grew steadily better, and before long they were turning out something which was far ahead of anything else at the price on the market.

From the very first, Dix insisted that every garment should be marked "Made by Henry A. Dix" and that it should be simple in style, of good material, and carefully stitched. In competition with "job lot" cheap wrappers and house dresses, he emphasized quality —"not how cheap, but how good" his merchandise could be for the price.

In 1896 there came a development in his business—a change to the making of uniforms for working girls, so that help in hotels, waitresses in restaurants, maids in households, and saleswomen in shops might have simple, neat costumes. Up to that time the working girl on her job had made use of any old second-best dress.

The same Dix standard of quality, taste, workmanship, simplicity, and fair prices applied to the "Dix Uniforms." They became a popular success from coast to coast. A new branch of the women's wear industry was created.

In 1917 during World War I, when the Red Cross adopted a nurse's hospital uniform, it turned to Dix to design it. The Dix Red Cross uniform took its place as an international insignia and became recognized in whatever corner of the earth required the ministrations of that noble institution. Soon thereafter the United States Government appointed Dix to supply army and navy nurses' uniforms.

In 1922, looking back over his seventy-two years, long years of struggle with never an idle day, Henry A. Dix, essentially a man of simple taste grown rich, faced the problem of the future. As the year drew to a close, he turned his business over to his employees. Newspapers acclaimed the first incident of its kind in American history:

Man Who Gave Workers $1,000,000 Business Calls It Merely Justice . . . Dix never had a strike in a quarter of a century. Has made all he wants—declined big price for plant so his employees could have a chance.

The Dix Story ends in 1938, the year in which he died at the age of eighty-eight; but after him lives the institution he founded and his ideas, so typically American.

1896 § ADOLPH OCHS: "All The News That's Fit To Print"

More than a century ago a small group of men started a new morning paper in New York City. They called it "The New York Daily Times." The first edition, printed on September 18, 1851, had only four pages and sold for one cent.

Henry J. Raymond, its founder, thought that a newspaper that printed more straight news about important events all over the world might attract more readers than those that printed scandal and the details of their owners' personal quarrels.

Raymond lived up to his promise and gave New Yorkers a serious newspaper with more important news than any other. Within a year it had done so well that it went from four pages to eight, and as it doubled in size it doubled in price. It sold in increasing numbers.

George Jones stepped into Raymond's place after Raymond died in 1869. By that time the newspaper had prospered. It had outgrown its first home in three years, its second within another three years, and in 1857 had build the biggest newspaper building of its time at 41 Park Row, opposite New York's City Hall.

In 1891, three years after he added several more floors to the building at 41 Park Row, George Jones died. The men who took over in his place tried to keep "The New York Times" going the same way he had, but somehow they couldn't.

Hard times forced the paper to decline. It lost much of its advertising and as it took in less money its staff grew smaller and could not give as much news as it had while Jones lived. Five years after Jone's death, it seemed that "The New York Times" might go out of existence.

It would have, too, if someone had not stepped in just in time to save it.

The man who saved "The New York Times" was a Southerner named Adolph Simon Ochs. He was the son of Captain Julius Ochs of Knoxville, Tennessee, who had been a Union Army officer and a teacher and merchant before that.

The family was poor when Adolph Ochs was born on March 12, 1858. Its home was then in Cincinnati. Adolph started his newspaper career in 1872, at the age of fourteen. That year he took a twenty-five cent a day job sweeping floors and running errands for his hometown newspaper, "The Knoxville Chronicle."

Five years later, young Ochs purchased the almost bankrupt "Chattanooga Times" with a borrowed $800. Within a relatively few years, the young newspaper publisher made that moribund newspaper one of the most influential in the South.

In 1896 Ochs was invited to reorganize "The New York Times" which was steadily moving toward bankruptcy. Just three years later, Ochs became owner of "The Times" which he purchased for $75,000 and put it on the road of becoming a great newspaper.

Because he was a printer, he was able to make it look better. He knew just how to arrange headlines and bold type. He was a good businessman, too, and immediately improved the business and financial sections.

He had several new ideas that had never been tried before. He thought that a newspaper might well print once a week, a whole section of news and reviews of the latest books. The idea caught on with readers and book publishers and became highly successful.

Then Ochs thought that a new kind of newspaper magazine might attract more readers. Most newspapers didn't bother in those days to keep their magazine sections built around fresh news; they ran articles that were meant to be entertaining but were not directly related to what was happening in the world.

"The New York Times Sunday Magazine Section," as Ochs developed it, was as successful as the weekly book section. Both brought more readers and more advertising.

Schools and colleges—both teachers and students—began to read "The New York Times" for they found that they could learn more from the news sections and from its special book and magazine sections than they could from almost any other newspaper.

Adolph Ochs

Adolph Ochs got up a slogan for "The New York Times" that still appears on its editorial page every day and tells its chief aim: "All the News That's Fit to Print."

§141

Once Ochs had restored that aim on "The New York Times," the newspaper grew to greater heights than it had ever before known.

New York, the entire world, for that matter, had undergone great changes between Raymond's time and Ochs'. The telegraph was in use everywhere, the cables brought news across the ocean swifter than lightning, telephones were being used for swifter relaying of news stories.

New York had almost 4,000,000 people in it a few years after Ochs saved "The New York Times," so the newspaper had many times the number of readers that Raymond's or Jones' newspaper had. And it was easier to distribute because the railroads were faster and reached many more places.

ADOLPH OCHS   ARTHUR HAYS SULZBERGER

The newspaper took advantage of all the quicker ways to get news and deliver it. It sent men to every corner of the earth to watch for important news. It had more reporters in the United States and in far-off countries than any other newspaper.

Eight years after Ochs brought "The New York Times" back to its feet, he needed much more room for his staff, for additional presses and for his big advertising force. He spent millions to build the Times Building that Stanford White patterned after Giotto's Florentine tower. Longacre Square was named "Times Square" after his building, which was one of the city's first skyscrapers, when it was finished in 1905. "The New York Times" became so popular that even the skyscraper tower was not big enough.

Ochs did not try to keep for himself all the millions of dollars "The New York Times" kept earning. He spent two-thirds of its earnings for better news coverage and newer equipment. He spent large sums for the best stories of modern explorations, for the best accounts of pioneer flights of aviation, for complete news about advances in science, in invention and in medicine.

Whenever governments or great statesmen or famous explorers, doctors, inventors or educators had anything important to tell the world they came to know that "The New York Times" would give them more space for their statements than any other newspaper.

Married to the daughter of Rabbi Isaac Wise, Ochs was one of the prominent leaders of Reform Judaism. He also headed the fund-raising campaign for the Hebrew Union College. The Adolph Ochs Chair in Jewish History bears his name.

Recognition came to Ochs from many other quarters. Medals were awarded by foundations and honorary degrees were conferred by universities. The decorations of foreign governments were offered but Ochs accepted only the Honor of Chevalier and later, Commander of France's Legion of Honor.

When Ochs died on April 25, 1935, "The New York Times" ranked with the greatest newspapers on earth.

Ochs grandchildren, the son and three daughters of his daughter, Mrs. Arthur Hays Sulzberger and her husband, inherited the newspaper. Adolph Ochs designated his son-in-law, Arthur Hays Sulzberger, as successor in his will.

As publisher, Sulzberger has largely left the day-to-day operations of "The Times" to its managing editor, Turner Catledge and his huge staff (close to 100 foreign correspondents, more than 500 domestic correspondents—30 in Washington, D. C.,—and some 275 New York City reporters).

However, on big, far-reaching policies, with regard both to news and editorial opinion, Sulzberger has made the final decisions.

Under him, "The New York Times" has published more news and more significant news "firsts" than any other newspaper. It has also won more journalistic awards, as of 1966, it garnered thirty-four Pulitzer Prizes as well as awards for public service and contributions to education, for helping to create better understanding among nations, for wide-ranging articles to broaden public knowledge and for consistently maintaining a high quality of reporting that has helped to strengthen Democracy.

1901 § SOLOMON SCHECHTER: Builder of an Institution and of An Idea

Solomon Schechter, one of the founders of the Conservative Movement in American Judaism, was a noted Hebrew scholar, mystic and philosopher. By his discovery and interpretation of the treasure of ancient Hebrew manuscripts in Cairo, he added more than any man in modern times to our knowledge of Hebrew literature in antiquity and the middle ages. As president of the Jewish Theological Seminary of America where he spent the last thirteen years of his life, he laid the foundation and set the tone for that outstanding institution which for decades after his death has been known as "Schechter's Seminary."

Schechter was born in the little Rumanian town of Focsani in 1848. His ancestors belonged to a sect of the *Chassidim* who stressed the joy of the Torah and the virtue of study and learning. His early youth was spent in *heder* and *yeshiva*, where he acquired an extensive and profound knowledge of Bible, Talmud and the later rabbinic literature. Upon reaching the age of sixteen he entered the famous rabbinical school in Lemberg (Lvov) to study under one of the greatest Talmudical authorities of his day. He continued his studies at the rabbinic schools and the Universities of Vienna and Berlin where he mastered the techniques of modern Jewish scholarship and historiography. He admired the work of Leopold Zunz, and hoped, as Zunz had, to spend his life in research into Judaism.

In 1882 Schechter was called to England as tutor of Claude G. Montefiore, a member of England's aristocratic family of wealth and culture.

SOLOMON SCHECHTER

Besides guiding Montefiore's studies, Schechter taught at Jews' College in London. But most of his energies went into research at the British Museum and the Bodleian Library among the old Hebrew manuscripts that had been gathering dust. This work led to the publication of a volume that placed him in the top rank of Jewish scholarship. With the most painstaking labor Schechter edited, corrected and compiled a tractate of the Babylonian Talmud, *Aboth de Rabbi Nathan,* that existed only in a mutilated text due to errors made by copyists. The keenness of his perception and scholarly intuition are also shown in his two volume work on the *Jewish Sectaries* in which he sheds new light on the period between the completion of the Hebrew Scriptures and the rise of Christianity.

Schechter's reputation grew and Cambridge University in 1890 appointed him Lecturer and later Reader (Associate Professor) in Rabbinics and Keeper of the Hebrew manuscripts at the University Library.

Among his friends were two learned Christian women in Cambridge, Mrs. Agnes Lewis and Mrs. Margaret Gibson, enthusiastic collectors of Hebrew and other Oriental manuscripts, who had picked up a bundle of Hebrew fragments in Cairo. They consulted Schechter for an explanation of the writing on these scraps of parchment.

From the century-dimmed words Schechter recognized one of the fragments as part of the lost Hebrew original of the *Book of Ecclesiasticus* or *Wisdom of Ben Sira* belonging to the Apocrypha written in Palestine about 200 B.C.E. which had been known only in Greek translation. These findings confirmed Schechter's suspicion that the common source for all such fragments was the archives of an ancient synagogue in old Cairo where for over a thousand years, worn-out manuscripts of the Jewish community had been deposited. This was known as the "Genizah," meaning the buried archives of the Jewish community, a cemetery of books and documents which were no longer used.

Subsequently in the Fall of 1896 Schechter journeyed to Egypt, found the Cairo depository and acquired for the University of Cambridge about 100,000 pieces of ancient manuscripts, some of them complete books, others only torn bits of pages. Schechter using a device to protect his nose and throat and wearing a dust coat spent six years in a room in the University library sifting the fragments and classifying them according to subject matter. Much of his later work was based on the deciphering and the application of these manuscripts, and the discovery through them of unknown works of Jewish history and literature. And much of the work still remains to be done by later scholars. The prizes Schechter found, he stated: "I would not change for all of Wall Street."

Nearly the whole of the Hebrew text of the *Book of Ben Sira* was recovered in different manuscripts. Schechter published an edition of it that marked a revolution in the knowledge of Hebrew of the earliest post-Biblical age because it was the only Hebrew writing which had come down from the Persian period in Jewish history. The discovery of the "Genizah" was as epoch-making for the study of the Bible and Jewish history from the time of the destruction of the Jewish state to the medieval period as the discovery of the Dead Sea Scrolls in our own day. Schechter might have spent the rest of his life studying the manuscripts and discussing their contents in scholarly books, but when he received the call to become the president of the recently organized Jewish Theological Seminary of America, on the decline since the death of Sabato Morais, its founder, he felt it his duty to come to America. He accepted the position on November 24, 1901.

On coming to America, Schechter's objective was in his own words: "to take charge of the Seminary . . . to establish a training school for Rabbis which adopting what is best in modern thought but at the same time teaching traditional Judaism in such a manner as to awaken fresh interest in our glorious past, should create a Conservative School removed alike from both extremes of Radical Reform and Hyper-Orthodoxy." This was virtually the original purpose envisioned by Sabato Morais and his group when forming the Seminary.

In his inaugural address delivered in 1902 before an assembly of all sections of American Jewry, rabbis and laymen, Schechter insisted at the outset on the catholic purpose of the institution. The community of America was drawn from all parts of the globe. Each wave of arriving immigrants brought its own rituals and dogmatisms all struggling for perpetuation. It was to be one of the aims of the Seminary to bring unity into that diverse mass. He envisioned the Seminary as a center of traditional yet scientific Jewish scholarship. He made it clear that the Seminary could not ignore the revolutions in human thought brought about by the eighteenth and nineteenth centuries. "The Seminary must employ every tool of research and criticism in its devotion to truth. Yet it must adhere faithfully to Torah." "The religion in which the Jewish ministry should be trained," Doctor Schechter stated, "must be specifically and purely Jewish, without any alloy or adulteration. . . . We must make an end to these constant amputations if we do not wish to see the body of Israel bled to death before our very eyes. We must leave off talking about occidentalizing our religion as if the Occident has ever shown the least genius for religion. . . . There is no other Jewish religion but that taught by the Torah and confirmed by history and tradition, and sunk into the conscience of catholic Israel. . . . Any attempt to place the center of gravity outside the Torah must end in disaster."

He was most concerned about the unity of Judaism in America. The unity of Israel, in his view, was a union of doctrines, precepts and promises.

These were to be the main features of the cumulative ideology of Conservative Judaism: the belief that *Klal Yisrael* is the historic basis for the unity of the people; the avowal that the traditional mitzvot (commandments) are necessary for the establishment of a Jewish way of life; that "Judaism can be adapted to the changing conditions according to Biblical and Talmudic teachings in all the development of the tradition in all ages."

Schechter set about gathering a faculty of distinguished scholars who could train and inspire a learned Jewish ministry able to interpret Conservative Judaism for American Jews. In addition his dream was to found a great library endowed with the most complete collection of Judaica in the world. In this task he was aided by Alexander

Marx and together they succeeded in establishing the largest Jewish library in existence which had over two hundred and fifty thousand volumes and twenty thousand manuscripts. Almost one-third of the books, but fortunately, none of the irreplaceable manuscripts, were destroyed by a fire in 1966, but it is estimated that within three years the library will once more attain the size and comprehensiveness that Schechter envisioned.

Realizing also the great need in American Jewry for trained teachers, Schechter established in 1909 the Teachers' Institute as part of the Seminary with Mordecai Kaplan as its director. (Kaplan had not yet formulated his concept of Reconstructionism and Judaism as a civilization). The Jewish Theological Seminary of America, under Schechter's stimulating direction, became the center of Conservative Judaism and one of American Jewry's important scholarly institutions.

Schechter brought the Conservative congregations into a union with the United Synagogue of America which was organized in February of 1913. The fear that it would remain weak and small was unfounded. It now includes more than eight hundred and fifty Conservative congregations with a combined membership of almost two million people, the fastest growing Jewish organization in America. The Conservative movement also has its own rabbinical body to promote traditional Judaism, the Rabbinical Assembly, founded in 1901. It now numbers over eight hundred members.

One of the strongest branches of the movement, the National Women's League of the United Synagogue, did not come into being until after Schechter's death, having been founded by his widow, Mathilde Schecter in 1918.

Within past years the Jewish Theological Seminary has expanded to a university of Jewish studies embracing five collegiate departments and two extension departments.

What Schechter had hoped to achieve is now also being carried out not only through almost a thousand schools associated with the Conservative synagogues, but through a system of day schools (appropriately called Solomon Schechter Schools) and the educationally oriented Ramah summer camps conducted by the Seminary in association with the United Synagogue of America to supplement the work of the synagogue schools.

Today the Seminary continues to radiate in many other directions. It sponsors the "Eternal Light" on radio and television, the oldest continuous religious radio program in existence in America; the Jewish Museum in New York, one of the foremost institutions of its kind in the world; and the University of Judaism in Los Angeles, the very existence of which has transformed Jewish life on the West Coast.

Among the Museum's exquisite collections can be found the Torah Ark brought back by Schechter from the Cairo Synagogue in 1896. This Ark dates back to the thirteenth century and is the oldest piece of Jewish ecclesiastical furniture in the world.

Cyrus Adler, the first student to attain a Ph.D. in Semitics in an American university, who became president of the Seminary upon Schechter's death in 1915, carried on the scholarly tradition of his predecessor.

Louis Finkelstein, one of the most original and erudite Jewish scholars of his time, succeeded Adler as president of the Seminary in 1940.

Schechter, Adler, Finkelstein, Mandelbaum and their colleagues became the definitive spokesmen for Conservative Judaism, while their students, the graduates of the Jewish Theological Seminary, became its active ambassadors.

1903 § ALBERT LASKER: He Made Advertising an Art

Albert Lasker, the man who changed the habits of millions of Americans, was the father of modern advertising and of Madison Avenue. For over forty years he owned Lord and Thomas, one of the biggest, most famous, as well as the most prosperous advertising agency in the world.

Some of America's greatest firms were long-time customers: American Tobacco, Frigidaire, Kleenex, Studebaker, RCA, Sunkist, Quaker Oats and Pepsodent.

The revolution in promoting and selling which he started in the early 1900s has swept across and beyond the western world. Lasker himself took out of advertising more money than anyone else before or since—$45,000,000.

Born in Feiburg, Germany on May 1, 1880, Lasker was brought to the United States in infancy. His father, member of the well-known German Jewish family which opposed Bismarck, settled in Galveston, Texas and became the town banker.

When Albert was sixteen years old he was already a veteran newspaper man and had a part-time job as a reporter on the *Galveston News*. He also worked for the *Dallas News* before starting his career in advertising.

A driving energy imbued the clever, cocky Galveston youth, so eager to get out of high school into big city journalism that he never thought of higher education. It marked him throughout the years in Chicago, when he moved up in the advertising house of Lord and Thomas, took it over and enormously expanded its work.

The year 1898, when eighteen year old Lasker got a job with Lord and Thomas, saw the advertising agencies on the brink of a new era. They needed young men of imagination, thrust and creative organizational powers to demonstrate its potentialities. When Lasker showed how to make Wilson ear drums "invisible, comfortable, efficient," Van Camp condensed milk, "you can have a cow right in your own kitchen," and Palmolive soap "keep that schoolgirl complexion" sell in gargantuan quantity, he made himself foremost among these men. In 1903 at the age of twenty-three, he was making $52,000 a year and was well on the way toward taking over the agency.

Lasker did much to persuade businessmen and industrial executives of the wisdom of increasing their appropriations for advertising. He urged his clients in 1912 to appropriate five to ten times as much as before. To back up his promise that he would prove effective he offered to extend a year's credit to advertisers who shared his faith.

He believed in the importance of advertising as a factor in raising American standards of living and preserving American democracy.

"There can be no democratic way of life without freedom of selection and this freedom makes for better goods at better prices," he said.

But strangely, Lasker was seldom if ever the creator of a slogan. When a Lucky Strike cigarette copywriter produced the magical phrase: "So round, so firm, so fully packed," Lasker bestowed a $10,000 bonus on him. Lasker owed much to Claude C. Hopkins who discarded the old repetition-and-reminder principle in advertising in favor of a research-and-reason principle. He had hired Mr. Hopkins in 1908. And Lasker owed nearly as much to John E. Kennedy, a master of persuasion who insisted that every advertisement carry a positive argument.

It was Lasker, however, who, with his gift for amalagamating diverse talents, his copious flow of ideas, his swiftness of action and his boundless enthusiasm that made Lord and Thomas the lighthouse that sent rays far and wide over the new distributive

ALBERT LASKER

industries. Taking the California Fruit Growers Exchange for a client, he conceived of the idea of popularizing orange juice as a drink and made Vitamin C a household word. He helped Hopkins put over puffed wheat—"the grains that are shot from guns" and Goodyear —"the all-weather automobile tires." He formulated the campaigns that made Kleenex a national success, and his labors in behalf of makers of carpet sweepers, safety razors, toothpaste and hosiery mobilized new armies of consumers. Only now and then did he fail, as when he lost a million dollars on a cold cream project.

His feats in breaking down the prejudice against women who smoked in public literally doubled the market for cigarettes. He turned the American housewife from a drudge into a free woman by substituting packaged breakfast foods for hominy grits and by putting most foods successfully into cans. He brought polling and market testing into advertising and the techniques spilled over into the political field. Then Lasker went on to pioneer in radio advertising; to put Amos'n'Andy on the air and help originate the first major soap operas. He ran the first beauty contest for promotional purposes. Along the way Lasker found time for public service and was an influential friend of presidents. He had gotten to know Warren Harding well and worked for his election. He was also a friend of Coolidge and Hoover. He spent two years as chairman of the

United States Shipping Board (1921-1923), ridding the government of a colossal burden of useless tonnage.

As a sportsman he had formulated the plan for supervising baseball in the national interest and induced Judge Kenesaw Mountain Landis to become the first regulator.

Lasker participated in Jewish causes and his two visits to Israel stimulated pride. He was a trustee of the Associated Jewish Charities of Chicago and a member of the executive board of the American Jewish Committee.

At sixty-two, in 1942, Lasker dissolved Lord and Thomas and turned over its accounts to three associates—Messrs. Foote, Cone and Belding. But he did not retire. Instead he and his wife, Mary Lasker, worked concurrently on at least four different causes: the birth control movement, the American Cancer Society, medical research and the Lasker Foundation.

The Lasker Foundation bestows the well-known Albert Lasker Awards. Since 1946, when the first of its citations was made through the American Public Health Association, the Albert Lasker Awards have come to be regarded as one of the highest recognitions given for achievement in medicine. They are given annually in the field of medical research "for a major contribution to the struggle against killing or crippling disease," also for the best medical journalism of the year and the best medical television show. The Albert Lasker Medical Research Award winners each receive $10,000. The Albert Lasker Medical Journalism Award winners each receive $2,500. In addition the winners also are given a gold statuette replica of the Victory of Samothrace. Seventeen Lasker Award recipients have gone on to win the Nobel Prize. The awards are not merely given to provide honors for distinguished work. They are also designated as a means of arousing public and professional interest in new medical endeavors. Lasker knew of the importance of publicity and of the good which such interest would accomplish.

Ironically enough Lasker himself did not live to benefit by the cancer research he himself helped to stimulate. A cancer of the intestine crept upon him unaware at the very moment when needed experiments were uncovering methods of examination that would have spotted the disease a year or two later.

Albert Lasker died on May 30, 1952, leaving half of his estate to the Lasker Foundation. Since her husband's death Mary Lasker has been the driving force behind the Foundation.

In 1960 there appeared John Gunther's brilliant and searching biography, *Taken At the Flood: The Story of Albert D. Lasker.* It is an astute and lively account of the man who transformed advertising into a major industry.

1905 § JACOB SCHIFF: Financier and Philanthropist

Albert Lasker

§152

Jacob Henry Schiff, the most beloved American Jewish philanthropist and internationally respected financier of the 1900's, lived at a time when America was becoming a great industrial power. It was the era of railroads, growing factories and expansion.

Born in 1847 in Frankfurt-am-Main, Germany, he came from an old aristocratic background. The Schiff family tree contained not only successful businessmen and bankers, but distinguished scholars and members of the rabbinate. Jacob Henry studied in the neo-Orthodox school of Samson Raphael Hirsch, who labored to deepen the religiosity of modern Jewry. Schiff never forgot the lessons of his student days nor quite lost the spirit generated in that atmosphere. Nevertheless he chose a business career, and after acquiring the rudiments of banking in Frankfurt he departed at the age of 18 for America.

In New York, Jacob went to work as a bank clerk in a brokerage house; this was the best way of adjusting to a new land and learning its ways. At 20 he formed his own brokerage firm under the name of Budge, Schiff and Company. Six years later he dissolved the partnership and sailed for Europe to console his mother who had become a widow. He offered to remain in Frankfurt, but his mother sensed his deep attachment to America and urged him to return. In 1875 he joined Kuhn, Loeb and Company and began his amazing career as one of the top creative financiers who assisted in the rapid development of industrial America.

The success of Schiff was all the more surprising because he came as an immigrant without money or connections. He was 27 when invited into the firm of Abraham Kuhn and Solomon Loeb, retired merchants from Cincinnati who came to live leisurely in New York and went into commercial banking in 1867 only to escape boredom. They drifted into investments and built up a solid business marketing railroad bonds and government securities. The same year Schiff entered the firm, he married the daughter of the junior partner. By 1885, the thirty-eight year old financier, now head of Kuhn,

Loeb and Company, having replaced his father-in-law Solomon Loeb, upon Loeb's retirement, was deeply involved in transactions of the first magnitude and was a power on Wall Street closely associated with the foremost industrialists, bankers and railroad magnates. His firm loaned hundreds of millions of dollars to business enterprises, foreign governments, trust companies and railroad builders who opened up the empire of the west to settlement. His varied undertakings unrelated in character included Western Union, Armour and Company, American Telephone and Telegraph, Westinghouse Electric and United States Rubber. He floated huge loans for the Pennsylvania Railroad and assisted in realizing the dream of A. J. Cassatt to build the Hudson Tunnel under the Hudson River and the Pennsylvania Station so that trains could penetrate the heart of New York City. His firm was engaged in financial operations that aided such railroads as the Baltimore and Ohio, the Illinois Central, the Chesapeake and Ohio and the Union Pacific Railroad. Through the success of these enterprises his firm became immensely wealthy until it was the second largest private banking firm in the country. In the five years from 1900 to 1905 alone, his firm had sold more than one hundred and seventy five billion dollars worth of securities.

Jacob Schiff

§153

The expert on financial matters, B. C. Forbes, once declared, "Kuhn, Loeb and Company have issued more good investments and fewer bad ones than any other banking concern in America."

The comparatively few errors in the judgement of Jacob Schiff were proof of an amazing grasp of factual data whether practical, economic, industrial, agricultural or international. But he did more than market securities. He investigated thoroughly the prospects, the difficulties, the problems of many corporations and often helped with sound advice and valuable suggestions.

In 1905 during the Russo-Japanese War, his firm loaned huge sums of money to Japan. For floating a bond issue of $200,000,000 for the Japanese government, the most outstanding achievement in international finance since the inception of America, he was awarded the Second Order of the Sacred Treasure, the highest Japanese decoration ever given to an American.

It was as his daughter, Frieda Schiff Warburg, wrote, "not so much my father's interest in Japan, but rather his hatred of Imperial Russia and its anti-Semitic policies, that prompted him to take this great financial risk."

Such an immensely wealthy and successful financier could help Jewish causes on an unprecedented scale if he wished, and he

JACOB SCHIFF

did. During the Russian pogroms of 1903-1905, Schiff helped organize a committee to raise the unprecedented sum of $1,750,000 for relief of the victims of the massacres. The following year he sponsored the American Jewish Committee, the first American Jewish organization concerned with the civic and religious rights of Jews both here and abroad. Schiff was equally interested in the promotion of Jewish learning. A roll call of the Jewish educational activities and institutions that owe their existence or their sound establishment to him would include many of the major undertakings of Jewish scholarship: the Teachers' Institute of the Jewish Theological Seminary and the Hebrew Union College, the Jewish Encyclopedia, the Hebrew Press of the Jewish Publication Society, the Semitic Museum at Harvard, the Jewish Book and Manuscript Collection at the Jewish Theological Seminary, the Library of Congress and the New York Public Library.

In creating these landmarks of Jewish learning, Schiff was guided not only by personal reverence for the traditions and culture of the Jewish people, but by a deep desire to find a means of revitalizing that culture. It was this motivation that prompted him at the very beginning of his career as a patron of Jewish learning to come to the support of agencies dedicated to educating Jewish youth. During its first two decades the New York YMHA found it difficult to gain community support, but when Schiff came to its rescue it soon reached a significant place on the Jewish scene. Schiff was also a factor in the formation of the National Jewish Welfare Board.

Though Schiff was the most remarkable builder of institutions there has ever been among American Jews, he was also interested in general education. When Barnard College was founded, he gave more than $1,000,000 to the new college. At Columbia University, he founded a department in social economics and provided scholarships for students in that field.

Schiff was interested in the cultural and economic development of Palestine and gave $100,000 for the founding of the Haifa Technicum. It is hard to believe that a man who owned so many millions of dollars could have found the time for all the interests which occupied Jacob Schiff. Yet he never forgot the little man. In the Montefiore Hospital in New York, of which he was elected president in 1885, an office he held to his last day, he used to spend many hours conversing with the patients, eating their regular fare with them, not only helping them from the outside, but trying to see the world from the angle of their poverty and misery.

It was the blending of statesmanship and of a stateman's vision with the urgency of his heart that rendered Schiff incomparable among the philanthropists of his period. Although a good deal of his far flung philanthropy was anonymous, none of his gifts went out carelessly. He sat on the boards of many institutions, continually made inquiries about the welfare of those concerned and talked with their workers.

A few weeks before his death, Schiff corresponded on the subject of a loan for Palestine with Sir Herbert Samuel, the High Commissioner. He believed that it was possible to finance a Palestine project then under way and that the country would be rebuilt in accordance with the terms of the Balfour Declaration. His death, unfortunately, put an end to this work.

Jacob Henry Schiff died on September 25, 1920, at the age of seventy-three, if one may be said to die, when so many splendid memorials live on to do him honor.

1906 § OSCAR STRAUS: First Jewish Cabinet Member

American Jews have achieved fame as public servants and gained respect for their ability. They have occupied almost every public office in the land, not always in proportion to their numbers but certainly enough to prove their patriotism and loyalty.

In 1906 President Theodore Roosevelt chose Oscar S. Straus, after whom a memorial was dedicated in Washington, to serve in the newly created Department of Commerce and Labor. For the first time in American history a Jew occupied a cabinet post.

Oscar Straus

§156

Member of the distinguished Straus family who were to own and operate R. H. Macy's department store in New York City, Oscar Straus studied at Columbia College and Law School. At the age of twenty-three he entered private law practice. From that time on his career was rapid and brilliant, in law practice, and business, in schalorship, authorship, and finally in public service.

His devotion to his country led Straus to make a special study of its institutions and the men who laid the foundations of the republic. This resulted in the publication of two notable books. One, *The Origin of the Republican Form of Government*, was the first attempt of its kind to trace with skill and scholarship the rise of American democracy from the Hebrew Commonwealth as expounded in the Bible. The second, entitled *Roger Williams, Pioneer of Religious Liberty in the United States*, earned for him the honorary degree of LHD from Brown University. He later wrote several other books, particularly his autobiography, which he called *Under*

OSCAR S. STRAUS

Four Administrations, referring to the four presidents under whom he held office: Cleveland, McKinley, Roosevelt and Taft.

At the age of thirty-two Straus entered politics as secretary of the committee to re-elect William R. Grace mayor of New York. It was an independent venture that won out against the opposition of an all-powerful Tammany Hall. In 1884, he took part in the presidential campaign that enabled Cleveland to defeat Blaine by the narrow majority. On a business trip to Chicago he happened to meet New York's Senator Gorman, who remarked that the Minister of Turkey was about to resign. Then, to his complete surprise, Gorman stated that he would like to recommend Oscar Straus for the post. Without diplomatic experience and in no position financially for the entertaining that such a position required, he hesitated. But with the warm assurances of support by the entire Straus family he consented.

Three times he was appointed the American representative to Turkey, first by President Cleveland, and subsequently he was reap-pointed to that post by Presidents McKinley and Taft. (Straus was not the first Jew to hold a high diplomatic post, for beginning with the appointment by President Monroe of Mordecai Manuel Noah as consul to Tunis there had been more than twenty Jews in the diplomatic service of the United States.) His success the first time as defender of the Christian missionaries and as intermediary for the Christians and Mohammedans was so marked that he was sent back twice more when danger threatened in the Near East, and he set a precedent that a Jew may prove the most appropriate ambassador to a Mohammedan country.

After his return from his second mission in Turkey, Oscar Straus was appointed one of the four American representatives to the permanent Court of Arbitration at the Hague and was reappointed three times to this position by Presidents Roosevelt and Wilson, holding it for twenty-three years, from 1902 till his death in 1926. He worked with Wilson at Paris in 1918-1919 to make the covenant of the League of Nations part of the Versailles Treaty. It was a deep disappointment to the aging Oscar Straus that the United States did not rise to its historic duty and responsibility in bringing about a permanent peace through the League of Nations. Straus also served as Public Service Commissioner of the State of New York and in this capacity adjusted and arbitrated many labor disputes and either settled or prevented more than a dozen important strikes during the year and a half of his incumbency.

The respect which Straus gained for himself was at the same

time a tribute to the Jewish people, for Straus was known as an active and interested Jew. President Theodore Roosevelt frequently called him to Oyster Bay or to Washington to ask his advice on diplomatic or political questions. In fact, when in December of 1906, President Roosevelt asked him to accept the post of Secretary of Commerce and Labor in his Cabinet, he did so with the words: "There is still a further reason: I want to show Russia and some other countries what we think of Jews in this country."

Oscar
Straus

§158

Straus served in Roosevelt's cabinet, followed him into the Progressive Party, and ran on his ticket for governor of New York State. This intimate friendship lasted until the death of the former president.

As a loyal Jew, Straus was one of the founders and first president of the American Jewish Historical Society. This was not his only Jewish activity. As early as 1874 he had been a leader in the formation of the YMHA in New York. He was a trustee of the Jewish Publication Society of Philadelphia and a member of the executive committee of the American Jewish Committee, a governor of Dropsie College and a director of the Hebrew Orphan Asylum in New York. Above all he was a leader in all activities on behalf of the unfortunate Russian Jews who were the victims of pogroms during the closing years of nineteenth century and the early years of the twentieth.

A liberal Jew, a patriotic American, Oscar Straus was one of the outstanding men of his generation and rendered a lasting service to his country. He died on May 3, 1926 at the age of seventy-five.

1906 § LOUIS MARSHALL: Champion of Civil Rights

In the controversy that surrounds the civil rights movement today, it is easy to lose sight of the fact that the civil rights movement had many great champions in bygone days. Such a champion was the soft spoken and erudite Louis Marshall, a stocky little man with a small round face and Franz Schubert eyeglasses.

Louis Marshall's name is revered both by members of the group to which he proudly belonged, the American Jewish community, and a broad spectrum of non-Jewish Americans who appreciate his broader contributions to human rights generally.

Louis Marshall was born in Syracuse, New York in 1856, the son

LOUIS MARSHALL

of German Jewish immigrants. After graduating from high school he studied law, first in a lawyer's office and afterward at Columbia University and was admitted to the bar as soon as he became of age. He then practiced law for a short time in Syracuse and for the rest of his life in New York City where he won renown as one of the country's foremost constitutional lawyers. Among the cases he argued before the highest Federal and State courts were those concerned with workmen's compensation, segregation of Negroes, alien immigration, and the abolition of private and parochial schools. One of his notable legal triumphs in the United States Supreme Court was a decision which held invalid an Oregon law that denied Catholics the right to send their children to parochial schools. A conservative, Republican, Marshall, nevertheless, was always on the side of minority groups. He wanted freedom for the underprivileged of the earth regardless of race, color or creed.

In 1906, the Kishinev pogrom was raging in Russia and Jews were being persecuted throughout Eastern Europe, Louis Marshall took the lead in creating an organization to help alleviate the sufferings of the victims and to speak for Jews in such crises.

It was felt that an organization of Jews in America capable of coping with emergencies similar to that created by the Russian massacres was essential. Accordingly, following several conferences participated in by such men of distinction as Jacob Schiff, Cyrus Adler, Mayer Sulzberger, and Oscar and Nathan Straus, it was agreed that it was "advisable and feasible to establish a general committee in the United States for the purpose of cooperating with various national Jewish organizations in this country and abroad on questions of national and international moment to the Jewish people."

On November 11, 1906, the first general meeting of a committee of fifty was held (in Jacob Schiff's house) to create such a central communal organization. What emerged from the proceedings was an organization called the American Jewish Committee which from the outset was designed to protect the rights and better the condition of Jews throughout the world.

The Committee was most effective in mobilizing the friendship and support of the American government on behalf of Jews in the United States and Europe. For seventeen crucial years, from 1912 to 1929, the president of the group was Louis Marshall. During his tenure of office as president of the American Jewish Committee, Marshall demonstrated a highly developed talent for shrewd and tactful negotiation. He launched a vigorous assault for Jewish rights wherever he feared they were being threatened. This led him into activities as diverse as defending Leo Frank, courageously confronting the Ku Klux Klan, condemning the establishment of Jewish quotas in colleges, and deploring the release of movies which he felt strengthened the anti-Jewish stereotype. Noteworthy in the latter case were Marshall's actions in seeking to induce Cecil B. De Mille both to soften the overt anti-Jewish stereotyping in a motion picture on the life of Jesus, entitled *King of Kings*, and to prohibit explicitly its distribution in foreign countries where anti-Semitism was already rife, such as Germany, Hungary, Rumania and Poland.

In 1912 after Marshall's eloquent and closely reasoned presentation, the Taft Administration rejected the extension of the 1832 Russo-American Trade Treaty in protest against Russia's refusal to grant entry visas to American Jews carrying American passports. Six years later, he won over the Wilson Administration to the support of Jewish minority rights in Eastern Europe. It was Marshall, too, who persuaded the uninformed industrialist, Henry Ford, to cease publication of the *Dearborn Independent* and to repudiate its notorious articles on "The International Jew" and the insidious *Protocols of Zion*.

After the outbreak of World War I, the American Jewish Committee in cooperation with the Zionist Organization of America sent emergency aid to the Jews in Palestine who had been suddenly cut off from communication with other Jewish communities. In October of 1914, Marshall set up the American Jewish Relief Committee, the largest of the American Jewish relief bodies which was merged with other relief organizations into the Joint Distribution Committee for extending relief to Jewish war sufferers and displaced persons in other countries. By the end of the war it was distributing sixteen million dollars a year, received from various sources.

These were achievments which gave Marshall extraordinary standing and prestige among his fellow Jews. Israel Zangwill once jestingly remarked that American Jewry lived under Mashall Law; someone else called Marshall, Louis XIX.

Louis Marshall

§161

Marshall was interested not only in one party or in another, but in the welfare of all Jews everywhere, and particularly in the advancement of Jewish education. So he was at the same time president of the reform congregation Temple Emanu-El of New York and chairman of the Jewish Theological Seminary of America and of Dropsie College. He held many public offices, being the only man who was a member of three constitutional conventions of the State of New York.

His last great work was the completion of the organization of the Jewish Agency for Palestine in Zurich, Switzerland, in August 1929, just a month before his death. Mr. Marshall, who never joined the Zionist movement, was the leader of the non-Zionists, who arranged this joint organization with Dr. Chaim Weizmann, president of the World Zionist Organization who was to become the first president of the State of Israel. This was a difficult task, for many Zionists objected to taking non-Zionists into the work for Palestine unless they joined the Zionist Organization. But Mr. Marshall prevailed upon his friends, and Dr. Weizmann, and finally the two groups came together and worked out the method by which all Jews the world over might help in the economic and cultural upbuilding of Palestine. Just after this meeting, Mr. Marshall fell ill and died in Zurich at the age of seventy-three.

One of Marshall's interests was in the forests of America. He was a leader in preserving the forests of the Adirondack Mountains in upper New York State. For many years he was chairman of the State Forestry School at Syracuse University. It was under his leadership, as former president Franklin Delano Roosevelt put it, that the school "became recognized as the preeminent institution of its kind in the United States." After his death the new Forestry Building of Syracuse University was named in his honor.

Stephen S.
Wise

§162

A rabbi who for years stood in the foremost ranks of Americans as organizer and fighter for what he believed to be the truth, was Stephen S. Wise. The descendant of a distinguished family of European rabbis, he was born in Budapest, Hungary, on March 17, 1874. When the boy was still an infant, his father came to the United States where he occupied orthodox pulpits in Brooklyn and New York City.

Stephen attended the public schools of New York and Columbia University where he obtained an A.B. degree in 1893 and a Ph.D. degree in 1901. His rabbinical training was secured privately, chiefly under the instruction of his father, Max L. Margolis, Alexander Kohut and other eminent scholars.

As a young man Stephen Wise served as a rabbi in New York City. Then he became rabbi of Temple Beth Israel in Portland, Oregon where he ministered until 1906. From his pulpit he discussed many public issues and told his congregation the truth about the social evils of the city. By the time he had reached his thirties he was already noted for his matchless oratorical power, courage and zest for combat. He was offered the position of rabbi of Temple Emanu-El in New York, one of the most influential congregations in the east. But he felt that he could not accept this tempting post unless he received the congregation's promise that he would be allowed to express his own personal views from the pulpit. This was refused. Through the press of the nation Rabbi Wise denounced the "muzzled pulpit." The startling adjective referred chiefly to the unwillingness of the worshippers to listen to Zionist sermons. His open letter written to the president of the congregation in which he denounced the temple's policy remains a classic plea for freedom of the pulpit.

Rabbi Wise decided that it was time for him to create his own congregation where he would enjoy unlimited freedom to express his own ideas. He thereupon resigned from his post in Portland, returned to New York City and on April 17, 1907, founded the Free Synagogue.

The Free Synagogue was established on the cardinal principle of complete freedom of expression for the rabbi and free unassigned

RABBI STEPHEN S. WISE

pews which opened seats to all worshippers regardless of financial condition. To supplement the aid of the various charitable groups in their care for the stranger, the orphan and the aged, and unite it more closely to Jewish life, Rabbi Wise introduced social service as part of the program of his Free Synagogue. Another one of its successful projects, the adoption of Jewish children, was introduced by the rabbi's artist-wife, Louise Waterman Wise.

Under Rabbi Wise's dynamic leadership the Free Synagogue grew from a congregation of fifty members to four thousand. Sunday services were instituted in Carnegie Hall which frequently was filled with vast congregants eager to hear Wise speak on the burning issues of American and Jewish life.

Considered one of the most eloquent preachers in America, he was in great demand as a lecturer by general as well as Jewish audiences throughout the country. His popular appeal was heightened by involvement in important public controversies—such as his attack on the injustices in the steel industry, labor legislation, municipal reform, the single tax, transit unification, pacifism, the repeal of Prohibition and the League of Nations. He was one of the decisive factors with John Haynes Holmes in driving Mayor Jimmy Walker out of office and into hiding in Europe. Fiorello La Guardia once remarked of Wise that whenever he attacked a politician, steamship business to Europe improved immediately.

Rabbi Wise was at the heart of the Zionist movement and active in its leadership from his participation in the Second Zionist Congress in which he served as secretary. He was a founder of the Zionist Organization of America in 1897, and later in 1917 and 1936-1938 served as its president. He influenced many notable Christians toward sympathetic understanding of Zionism of whom President Woodrow Wilson was the most well known.

Rabbi Wise's attachment to the Jewish masses and his faith in the principles of democracy moved him to assume leadership in the establishment of the American Jewish Congress. At various times he served as president of this organization which was intended to apply the principles of democratic representative institutions to the needs, problems and rights of the Jewish people.

After extensive deliberation, an elective system was evolved and elections held in Jewish communities throughout the country on June 10, 1917. On that day, for the first time in modern Jewish history, 335,000 Jewish men and women went to the polls to choose their representatives to the first American Jewish Congress.

The first session of the American Jewish Congress was finally convened in Philadelphia on December 15-18, 1918. More than four hundred delegates were present. The participants included the most distinguished figures in American Jewish life. The session adopted a program for submission to the Versailles Peace Conference which included the demand for full and equal civil, political, religious, and national rights for all citizens of any territory without distinction as to race or creed, autonomy in the management of their communal institutions by members of the various national and religious bodies, and recognition of the historic claim of the Jewish people to Palestine.

The Congress elected a delegation to represent American Jewry at the Peace Conference which brought some gratifying diplomatic results.

The Congress did not go out of existence after the fulfillment of its mission in Europe. Convinced that it had a mandate from the masses, it set itself up on a permanent basis as the democratic organ of American-Jewish life. Under the leadership of Stephen Wise, who was the organization's president from 1924 with intermissions to 1949, the Congress worked unremittingly to expose and combat anti-Semitism, and in support of Zionism. It endorsed, as well, a wide variety of liberal causes such as public housing, the Fair Employment Practices Commission, the United Nations and UNESCO. Wise organized mass meetings, parades, public boycotts of German-made goods, and large-scale letter-writing campaigns to promote liberal legislation.

Rabbi Wise, who felt that there should be a training school for rabbis and leaders in Jewish education and social service in such a great city as New York, in 1922 founded the Jewish Institute of Religion. He trained its rabbinical students to transcend narrow denominationalism and to accept instead their prophetic responsibilities as social reformers. Today this institution is united with the older Hebrew Union College.

Rabbi Wise lived to see the persecutions of Hitler which doomed six million Jews to death. He gauged the menace of Hitler long befor the world awoke to the danger. "The racial fanatacism of the Hitler Reich is a threat to all races and to all nations," he declared. While Wise's name was still the best known throughout the world and drew the most voluminous correspondence of any Jewish leader, the old man was tired, broken and unable to fight the battles of the world as hopefully as in his youth.

He died at the age of seventy-five on April 19, 1949. His place in history will always be remembered by the causes he fostered and the institutions he built.

An enduring and close friendship grew up between Rabbi Stephen Wise and the Reverend John Haynes Holmes, the great Unitarian minister. They liked one another, disliked the same evils, and became spiritual brothers.

The tandem biography in which their careers and achievements are related is called *Rabbi and Minister*. Written by the Reverend Carl Herman Voss, a Protestant minister, it recaptures the spirit and the excitement which these men produced in millions.

Abraham Michelson

§165

1907 § ALBERT ABRAHAM MICHELSON: First American for a Nobel Prize

Alfred Bernard Nobel, the Swedish engineer, inventor and philanthropist, established five prizes of $42,280 each to be awarded annually on December 10 for the most important discoveries in physics, chemistry, physiology and medicine; also for the best effort to promote peace during the year and for the most distinguished work of literature. While Jews make up less than one per cent of the world's population, they have carried thirteen per cent of all Nobel Prizes. In 1907 Professor Albert Abraham Michelson, professor of physics at the University of Chicago, was the first American and the first American Jew to receive the award. For a number of years the only other American physicists who were Nobel laureates have been associates or students of his.

Abraham Michelson

§166

Born on December 19, 1852, in Streslo, Prussia, Michelson was brought as a child to California by his immigrant parents. When he finished his secondary schooling, the young man journeyed alone from California to Washington, D.C., in order to make a personal plea to President U. S. Grant for an appointment to the United States Naval Academy at Annapolis. Although President Grant had already exhausted his ten appointments-at-large, he was so much impressed with the lad's ability that he made an exception and appointed Michelson.

At the Naval Academy Michelson soon found out that he was not fated to become an admiral. He was outstanding in physics, and upon graduation, was appointed an instructor at the Academy on that subject. There he conducted his epoch-making light measurement experiments. After many years of research, he made one of the greatest scientific discoveries of the age by computing that light travels 186,508 miles per second. This paved the way for the most startling of modern conceptions, Einstein's theory of relativity.

By devising the instrument known as the interferometer, Professor Michelson made it possible for scientists for the first time to measure the diameter of the stars. This marvelous instrument with its exactitude in measuring the tiniest quantities of space and matter could make discoveries of great importance. Our knowledge of radioactivity, vitamins, hormones and their acitivity in the human body, was all made possible by use of this instrument.

The first "Distinguished Professorship" ever granted by the University of Chicago was awarded Michelson in recognition of his remarkable record as original discoverer in the field of physics. In addition to honorary degrees from a large number of universities, membership in scientific societies in this country and abroad, a number of national and international awards, he received every honor that can be given to a scientist, of which the Nobel Prize is the best known.

In 1929 Michelson retired to Pasadena, California, still continuing

ABRAHAM MICHELSON

his work. At his death, two years later, he was mourned as one of the greatest scientists of modern times. Gifted with deep insight and breadth of view, he also had strong artistic leanings. Like Einstein he was an accomplished violinist and his paintings attracted attention.

His major publications include *Light Waves and Their Uses* and *Studies in Optics.* The first represents his Lowell Lectures delivered in 1899; the second consists of a condensed summary of his most important researches.

Up to his time no scientist had ever left his lifework in more complete form. No physicist had ever made more exact measurements, or shown more skill in the design and manipulation of scientific apparatus.

Michelson had not only had an extraordinary long life but a rich life. He had the double satisfaction of seeing his theories embodied throughout physical science and knowing that his startling but balanced philosophy had been accepted throughout the world.

1908 § DR. ABRAHAM FLEXNER: Father of Modern Medical Education

Abraham Flexner

§168

Many a hospital patient owes his very life to Abraham Flexner and his passion for the improvement of medical schools. Dr. Flexner led in revolutionizing the standards of professional training in the medical field; he raised professional standards in all other fields; he quickened the flow of philanthropic gifts to sound educational undertakings and he opened new doors to research and experiment.

It is difficult for us to comprehend the low state of the medical schools in this country when Flexner in 1908 set about the investigation which led to his Bulletin No. 4. There were no admission requirements to speak of, there was no grounding in the basic sciences, no required courses, and teaching was chiefly in the hands of practicing physicians who had a financial interest in maintaining a large number of students but nevertheless regarded their pedagogic responsibilities as distinctly secondary to active practice.

The courage and thoroughness of Dr. Flexner's dissection was equalled by the skill with which he marshalled men and forces to apply a remedy.

Always, he will be remembered as the Father of Modern Medical Education.

Flexner was born in Louisville, Kentucky on November 13, 1866, the son of a German Jewish immigrant who had begun life in America as a peddler. When the boy was nine the family savings were swept away by the Panic of 1873; his father died within the decade; the older boys had to go to work. At fifteen young Abraham began earning his way as assistant in the Louisville library. The Louisville schools, a boys' debating society and the library fed his precocious mind.

His brothers raised enough money to send him to Johns Hopkins University, then in the first flush of its glorious beginnings. There he settled down to the long grind of becoming a teacher. After his preliminary training, in 1886, Abraham found himself teaching in high school. Four years later, in 1890, deciding to put his own ideas into practice, he created almost single-handed one of the most distinguished private schools of the South. Breaking away from established customs, he followed his own methods of no examinations, no records or reports, and no fixed speed of study.

College authorities soon began to notice that Flexner's pupils were reaching their campuses at an earlier age and better prepared. But with success assured, Flexner suddenly gave up the school to continue his own studies at Harvard and in Berlin. In 1908, on his return to America, the Carnegie Foundation asked him to make a survey of American medical schools.

Flexner began ·by reading everything on which he could lay his hands that dealt with the history of medical education in Europe and America. Then began a swift tour of medical schools in the United States and Canada—one hundred and fifty-five in number—every one of which he visited. From this sprang his great opportunity to expose and destroy the scores of fraudulent and incompetent medical schools which annually loosened an army of quacks upon the helpless public.

The publication of his Bulletin No. 4 in 1908 caused wretched medical schools to collapse; in his native Louisville, seven were reduced to one. His subsequent works, *Medical Education in the United States*, published in 1910 and *Medical Education in Europe,* which appeared in 1912, sparked a revolution in the medical world.

Abraham Flexner

§169

ABRAHAM FLEXNER
(Courtesy of the Rockefeller Foundation)

Shortly after the publication of Bulletin No. 4, Flexner became a member of the staff of the Rockefeller-endowed General Education Board and it was through this board that Flexner had his great opportunity to influence the development of medical education in the United States with which his name is irrevocably linked. In answer to his personal appeal, John D. Rockefeller, Sr. gave 45 million dollars to the General Education Board to reorganize medical education. When this board finished its program in 1964, it had given more than 94 million dollars for the improvement of medical education. Many millions more were provided for this same purpose here and abroad by a sister organization—the Rockefeller Foundation. Through the stimulation of matching grants Flexner also induced such great men of wealth as Andrew Carnegie, Julius Rosenwald, George Eastman, J. P. Morgan, Albert Lasker and others to give more than half a billion dollars to medical schools both in America and Europe.

During these years as a trustee and officer of the General Education Board, Flexner's lively interests extended in many directions and in 1915 he framed a plan for a model grade school which was subsequently established as the famous Lincoln Experimental School of Teachers' College, Columbia University.

Dr. Flexner's next great achievement was the founding of the Institute for Advanced Study at Princeton. After delivering a series of lectures at All Souls College, Oxford, in 1928, he observed that the fellows, a select group of men exempt from teaching duties, made the most of an atmosphere singularly favorable to advancing the frontiers of knowledge. He was familiar with the great achievements of the several Kaiser Wilhelm Institutes and of the original Collège de France in Paris. Why could not America have a nurturing home for advanced research which embodied the spirit of these two seats of learning and of all Souls? With this vision he persuaded Louis Bamberger, the celebrated department store owner, and his sister Mrs. Felix Fuld, to give eight million dollars for the establishment of the Institute for Advanced Study at Princeton University.

The Institute opened its doors in 1933 under Flexner's direction. He brought to it many of the most brilliant minds in the world. Above all, by tactful persuasion he enlisted Albert Einstein to come to the United States. Flexner remained its director for nine years, until he retired so that he could be free to travel and lecture.

Flexner's autobiography, *I Remember*, a wise, humane, and adventurous story of a beloved leader in the "aristocracy of excellence," appeared in 1940. Almost twenty years later, in a revision, he was able to rearrange some of its parts and bring the story down through his later activities as head of the Institute to his final placid years in New York and Washington, rich in meditation and friendships.

Dr. Flexner was among those who helped the founders plan the medical school of the Hebrew University in Palestine.

On September 21, 1959, Dr. Flexner—then nearing ninety-three—died in his home. The news of his death saddened the country, for it had been recalled the causes he had led and the adventures in which he shared.

Two other brothers were also famous, Bernard as a lawyer and Jewish leader, and Simon as a bacteriologist and pathologist. Dr. Simon Flexner served as the first director of the Rockefeller Institute for Medical Research. This organization has since been reorganized as the Rockefeller University. Under his leadership it was to develop into the outstanding medical research institution in the country.

1908 § ABRAHAM ARDEN BRILL: First Psychoanalyst in America

Few people today entirely escape the consequences of the conflicts and frustrations of modern life. Anxiety, emotional tension and fear have become symptoms characteristic of our time.

Many hold that psychoanalysis is an introduction to a more satisfying life for it is the master key to the understanding both of one's self and human nature.

Dr. Abraham Arden Brill was the "father of American psychoanalysis." It was due to his efforts that psychoanalysis became an accepted treatment for mental and nervous diseases in this country. In the more than forty years of his practice, he once estimated that he had personally taken case histories of more than 50,000 men and women. Drawing upon his vast experience, he set forth not only the tenets and theories of psychoanalysis, but also illustrated the practical application of that knowledge in hundreds of specific cases. His examples were always alive and brilliantly interlaced with a critical digest of a heterogeneous storehouse of knowledge. His case histories read like interesting romances and he gave to authors many a "plot" which came to his attention from patients. His book *Basic Principles of Psychoanalysis* is one of the most readable as well as the most authoritative works in the field.

Abraham Arden Brill was born in Kanczuga, a small town in Austria on October 12, 1874. His father was a tradesman and when the child was six, the Brills moved to New York. As a schoolboy he consistently led his class without difficulty and was considered a model pupil in every way. When he entered New York University, he was still undecided about his future career, although he had thoughts about becoming a medical student. While still an undergraduate he was a demonstrator in physiology. This was in 1894, when Brill was twenty.

As a medical student at the College of Physicians and Surgeons of Columbia University, Brill studied psychiatry and clinical neurology. Having qualified for his M.D. degree in 1903, young Doctor Brill decided to go into the field of psychiatry. He began to work at the Central Islip State Hospital in Long Island, studying certain brain and nervous diseases. In 1906, he was appointed Lecturer in Psychiatry at Columbia University.

Perhaps this appointment made him feel that he needed more training in psychiatry—perhaps not. At any rate, right after he was appointed, he took off for Vienna in the fall of 1907 to work under Sigmund Freud who was exciting the medical world by his use of psychotherapy at his neurological clinic. Freud tried both to cure patients of certain diseases and to find out if these diseases were caused by psychological rather than organic illness. He also discovered that in hysterical people he could induce symptoms—such as temporary paralysis—by merely suggesting these symptoms while the person was hypnotized.

Brill accepted Freud because he found his theories applicable in his clinical material and because it shed light on hitherto obscure problems.

He attended Freud's clinics until the spring of 1908. Then he went back to New York to take up his work at Columbia. His use of psychotherapy on patients and his theories about it caused an uproar. No matter how carefully he examined and revised Freud's findings he followed him for the rest of his life. He explained and expanded Freud's theories of the unconscious mind and his method of bringing "repressed" thoughts to the conscious mind. This method as formulated by Freud was called "free association," which means saying the first thing that comes to your mind when a word is suggested to you. He tried this new and hazardous approach and discovered that by inducing the patient to recall his past through "free associations" he could revive the patient's hidden memories and thus cure him.

Brill conducted further important original studies relating to mental and nervous diseases, applying Freud's theories. He added modifications and refinements to Freud's own revisions.

Brill focused attention on the system with his thousand page compilation of *The Basic Writings of Sigmund Freud.* It consisted of *The Psychopathology of Everyday Life, The Interpretation of Dreams, Selected Papers on Hysteria, Wit and Its Relation to the Unconscious, Totem and Taboo* and *The History of the Psychoanalytic Movement.*

In an introduction to Brill's translation of his work, Freud wrote: "If psychoanalysis now plays a role in American intellectual life, or if it does so in the future, a large part of this result will have to be attributed to this and other activities of Brill's."

Brill also translated Carl Jung's book *Psychology of Dementia Praecox* and most of the works of the other early exponents of psychotherapy.

Psychoanalysis is now accepted in one form or another by most psychiatrists throughout the world as an indispensable tool in the treatment of mental and nervous disorders.

For forty years in which Brill was actively functioning as an expositor of psychoanalysis, he profoundly influenced the medical profession. As the first American psychoanalyst, he was the teacher of two generations of psychiatrists and psychoanalysts.

Of interest is Brill's statement on the humor of Abraham Lincoln in which he asserted that the great emancipator was one of the greatest wits of this country and that he used his wit as a safety valve for his pent-up emotional tensions.

In 1911 Brill founded the New York Psychoanalytic Society, the first meeting of which was held in his home. A few months later, he organized the American Psychoanalytic Association. It now has branches in most states.

After a lifetime of controversy, as with Freud, honors began to pour in on him in his later years. His work was dissected, disputed and finally acknowledged.

To accumulated and often confusing experience he added a bitter but liberating wisdom. But his real significance is that in a time when man's whole interest was directed toward an increased mastery of external work, he tried to bring an understanding of man's relationship to man.

He died in New York on March 2, 1948.

"Brill" is now a word in the medical dictionary.

Abraham
Arden
Brill

§173

*Victor D.
Brenner*

§174

The first coin bearing the facsimile of the head of a president of the United States, the Lincoln penny, issued by the Treasury Department on August 2, 1909, was designed by a Jewish artist, Victor David Brenner, whose initials, VDB appeared on the first 28,000,000 of these coins. This was the first portrait coin ever used in American currency.

Brenner, born in Lithuania in 1871, came to the United States in 1890. As a boy he obtained employment as a die cutter and engraver of badges in an Essex Street shop in the Lower East Side of New York City. At night he attended art classes at Cooper Union and later at the National Academy of Design and Art. In 1893 he set himself up as a die cutter and engraver for jewelers and silversmiths, prospered, and sent for his family.

One day while Professor Ettinger, a well-known coin collector of the City College of New York, was browsing around the East Side, he entered Brenner's shop and was attracted by a head of Beethoven which Brenner had done for a musical society. His interest in the young immigrant resulted in an introduction to the Numismatic Society through which Brenner won the commission to design a medal which brought him into prominence. He was enabled to study in Paris under Louis Oscar Rotz, ranking medalist of Europe, and Alexandre Charpentier, member of the Rodin group. Under these new influences Brenner's work developed in scope. He won a bronze medal at a Paris exhibition and several other awards in American cities.

After extensive travel through Europe, Brenner came home to throw himself at once into the battle being waged by the Numismatic Society for better American coins. The movement met with hearty approval from President Theodore Roosevelt whose head was being modeled by Brenner for the obverse side of the Panama Medal awarded to every workman who put in two years of labor on the canal. During one of the sitting sessions, Brenner showed Roosevelt a design of a Lincoln plaque which so impressed the President that he urged the Treasury Department to adopt it as a first step in reforming the United States coinage. But to Brenner this was more than a

JULIUS ROSENWALD

chance commission. He expressed the desire that the design be used on a one cent piece, in order that it have the widest circulation possible and thus familiarize even the most humble with President Lincoln's face.

In 1910 Brenner wrote *The Art of the Medal*, a leading book in the field. He achieved further prominence with his bust of Charles Eliot Norton, which is in the Fogg Museum at Harvard. His famous bas-relief of Washington may be seen today in the Federal Building in Pittsburgh and his bas-relief of Lincoln in the Washington Irving High School in New York City.

1910 § JULIUS ROSENWALD: Practical Humanitarian

Jews have never felt that their charitable duties were discharged by providing for the needs of fellow Jews. The Talmud goes beyond the Bible in its insistence on generosity. They have borne their full share of the philanthropic burden of the general community.* It is to be

---

* American Jewry has provided with care and intelligence for its sick, home-less, orphaned and aged. Many of the techniques employed and the organiza-tions they have developed in the United States have been exemplary and have served as a spur to the workers in the general field of philanthropy. Jewish organizations have pioneered in introducing the transportation rules for tran-

expected that a wealthy Jew will share his affluence with his less fortunate brethren. And yet, the benefactions of Julius Rosenwald hold a unique place in Jewish philanthropy. For Rosenwald raised the standards of giving to charitable purposes in his own community and the country to unprecedented levels by matching his own contributions with those of others, thus stimulating them to give more and more. He was especially interested in the welfare of the colored people. By his munificent contributions to their educational institutions he helped to create facilities for leader training which they otherwise would not have had, and called attention to the discrimination practiced against the colored people in educational institutions.

Julius Rosenwald

§176

Rosenwald made another outstanding contribution through his espousal of a type of liquidating foundation. His idea, in brief, was that each generation should meet its own needs and that foundations should be set up to last only twenty-five or thirty years and should spend their capital as well as their income. He set up the Julius Rosenwald Fund to finance his charities on that basis. There is still considerable controversy about the social soundness of his idea. But it made people think about foundations, their programs and their influence, as few ideas about foundations have.

Julius Rosenwald was born in Springfield, Illinois on August 12, 1862, in a street where Abraham Lincoln once made his home. His father, a German Jewish immigrant, was a storekeeper, and while the millionaire business leader could say in later years he had never known poverty, his family's means were limited.

Young Rosenwald attended the high schools of Springfield for two years until he was sixteen. Then in 1879 he went to New York City to serve an apprenticeship in the clothing business with his uncles, the Hammersloughs who were leading clothing merchants. With the aid of his father's capital and his uncles' experience, he opened a small retail shop of his own in 1884 when he was twenty-three. The shop had indifferent success. But a year later, in 1885, the realization that the midwestern sections of the country needed more men's light-

---

sients; the subsistence homestead; cooperative credit among farmers; labor information bureaus for immigrants; the elevation of relief standards and the unionization of social workers. Perhaps the most important area of contribution in the social services field which Jews have been able to make was of central fund raising and distribution. As such the association of Jewish Welfare Federations and Welfare Funds has developed as a uniquely American Jewish voluntary organization. The first Federation founded in Boston in 1895 was emulated by other Jewish communities and was followed twenty years later by the first community chest for the total community.

weight garments than the East could supply, sent Rosenwald to Chicago where the clothing factory of Rosenwald and Weil was established.

In 1893 Richard Warren Sears and Alvah Curtis Roebuck founded the watch firm of Sears, Roebuck and Company in Minneapolis, doing business through the mails. Others items were gradually added to the stock. In the following year the firm moved to Chicago. An order for 10,000 suits which Mr. Sears wanted to place with Rosenwald and Weil led to a meeting with Rosenwald. The result was that Rosenwald obtained a chance to buy into a partnership with Sears, Roebuck and Company with another man, each putting in an investment of $35,700. The additional captial financed an expansion of business and in 1896 Rosenwald transferred his entire activities to the firm. In 1897 he became vice-president of Sears, Roebuck and Company which grew to be the world's largest mail-order house and chain of retail stores. In 1910 he succeeded Sears as president, a position he held until 1925, when he became chairman of the board.

Because of the volume of its trade, Sears, Roebuck was able to buy goods cheaper and to sell them cheaper than its country competitors. It was able to set up its own factories for the manufacture of some of the goods it sold and to take a financial interest in other factories by means of its surplus profits. It set up the first testing laboratory for merchandise in this country. It lengthened its mailing lists so that some fifty million copies of the Sears, Roebuck catalogues came to be distributed annually. Hardly an item for personal or general use was omitted.

Convinced that they would get their money's worth the farmers of the country and their wives began to go through the company's huge catalogues as their city cousins would go through a department store. There is no doubt that the mail-order business became a powerful factor in raising the standards of living in rural communities.

Due largely to a policy which Mr. Rosenwald originated, the "money-back if not satisfied" guarantee and truth in advertising, he developed the company to its present enormous size (sales jumped from $11,000,000 a year in 1900 to more than $50,000,000 in 1906 and crossed the $100,000,000 mark in 1914. By 1927 it became $270,000,000 and has steadily grown to its present annual turnover of over $6,000,000,000.

Rosenwald's own fortune grew by leaps and bounds until in the peak of 1929 it was estimated at between $200,000,000 and $300,000,-000.

He did not believe that every American boy could not attain what he had and seldom lost an opportunity to stress the part that luck played in his career.

He made the following statement to a newspaper reporter in New Orleans and the words went around the country: "I believe that success is ninety-five per cent luck and five per cent ability."

Having made a great fortune, Rosenwald made strenuous efforts to distribute his money wisely to innumerable causes, movements and organizations which he considered worthy of support. He set up a staff of experts to advise him on his benefactions, to make sure they would do the most good.

Julius Rosenwald

§178

He gave to hospitals, schools and libraries. He helped to build the University of Chicago into a great institution and financed the Museum of Science and Industry. But help to the Negro became his most outstanding life work.

How he became interested in the Negro was indicated in an address made in 1911: "Whether it is because I belong to a people who have known centuries of persecution," he said, "or whether it is because naturally I am inclined to sympathy with the oppressed, I have always felt keenly for the colored race."

His first notable offer was made in 1910 when he promised to give $25,000 toward the construction of a YMCA building for colored people in any community where $75,000 was raised by the white and colored population. By 1926 twenty-five cities had taken advantage of his offer, and three additional YWCA buildings for colored women had been built in New York City as a result of his subventions. He also gave funds for the construction of fifty other small buildings for the recreational use of the Negro in the South. With the help and approval of Booker T. Washington, the eminent Negro leader and educator, he worked out a plan for building rural schools. He offered to give substantially for the construction of schools for Negro children in any community that would raise a certain amount by its own efforts and guarantee to keep up the building. Under this plan there grew up over five thousand Rosenwald schools in fifteen southern states. In addition to the regular elementary school subjects the Negro children were also taught a trade.

In 1917 he established the Julius Rosenwald Fund, which was to supervise most of his contributions to Negro welfare. It was created as a liquidation fund to be terminated within twenty-five years after his death. At the time of its reorganization in 1929 the capital fund totalled about $30,000,000. Apart from the educational and welfare work undertaken by the Rosenwald Fund, Rosenwald set aside $2,-

700,000 for use in the building of model housing for the colored people of Chicago.

For this and other work to better the condition of the Negro, Rosenwald received the Gold Medal of the William E. Harmon Foundation for Distinguished Achievements in Race Relations in 1927.

Rosenwald took an active part in Jewish life, being an officer of Sinai Temple of Chicago, and the honorary president of the Jewish Charities of Chicago.

Rosenwald contributed to many Jewish causes. He gave half a million dollars for the Hebrew Union College Endowment Fund.

His wealth was expended not only here but in distant countries. Decorations, honors and tributes of all kinds came to him from virtually every corner of the earth.

After a brief illness Rosenwald died in his sleep on January 6, 1932 at the age of sixty-nine.

The immediate members of his family were present at his bedside. Relatives in Germany, Negroes in the southern states and Americans throughout the country listened in sorrow to the radio announcement that one of the world's greatest humanitarians was dead.

A resolution unanimously adopted by the Board of Directors of the Chicago Public Library epitomizes Rosenwald's contribution to human welfare:

"A humanitarian with world-wide sympathies, Julius Rosenwald not only merited and received the grateful recognition of his own generation but made his name endure forever as the symbol of the wise and generous benefactor in the promotion of the many causes in which he sought and found the fulfillment of his ideals."

1911 § IRVING BERLIN: In Tune With America

Irving Berlin rose from the sidewalks of New York and object poverty to become the world's most famous writer of popular songs. For better than five decades, he has been turning out song hits with metronomelike regularity, furnishing happy lovers with lilting praise of Cupid, sad lovers with melodic regrets, sentimental folk with tuneful nostalgia, patriots with pulse-stirring psalmody, and all kinds of people with lighthearted strains for light-footed dancing.

Strangely enough Berlin can scarcely be called a composer. He never acquired dexterity at the piano and even today finds it difficult to give fluent pianistic expression to the melodious creations of his mind. He plays in only one key—F sharp. He has never had any musical education. As a matter of fact his entire education consisted of two years of schooling as a child. Yet his simple music and lyrics have supplied the people of two generations and three continents with endless pleasure.

Irving Berlin

§180

As of 1966, Berlin, a thin, little man, with a dark leathery face, seventy-eight years old, had written over 900 songs, among them some of the most outstanding successes in the history of Tin Pan Alley.

Back in 1911, came the song, words and music both by Berlin, which swept the world—a syncopated creation that set a new style in song and took rank with the greatest native American works— "Alexander's Ragtime Band." By 1915 it has sold over 2,000,000 copies and it is still selling. It had a strong influence on contemporary composers. Jazz concertos and jazz symphonic works were unknown before its appearance, but when serious musicians were caught up in the sweep of its irresistible melody, they began to sense a new idiom in American music.

And the sales of this song were multiplying when he repeated with three more the same year. Four such hits in one year from the same songwriter who wrote both the words and music startled the music publishing world.

Up to 1914, Berlin had written songs for various shows, but that year, Broadway heard the first all-Berlin score in "Watch Your Step."

In 1918, Berlin a sergeant of infantry at Camp Upton, Long Island, wrote, produced and appeared in the all-soldier show "Yip, Yip, Yaphank." One of the unforgettable songs to come out of the show was "Oh, How I Hate To Get Up In The Morning," a comic lament which has been echoed by soldiers and civilians ever since.

It was in the twenties that Berlin wrote some of his most memorable ballads, such as "Always," "Remember," "A Pretty Girl Is Like A Melody," and "Blue Skies."

In the thirties he did "Easter Parade," "Cheek To Cheek," "Say It Isn't So" and "How Deep Is The Ocean," standard numbers on every hit parade.

In 1935 Berlin was called to Hollywood by R.K.O. Pictures. The first of the moving pictures hallmarked with the Berlin name was "Top Hat," a starring vehicle for Fred Astaire and Ginger Rogers.

In the forties he did such numbers as "I Left My Heart At The

IRVING BERLIN

Stage Door Canteen," and "Doin' What Comes Natur'lly," tunes on almost everyone's lips. And he wrote "White Christmas," one of the biggest hits of all time. More than 8,000,000 recordings of it and some 7,000,000 copies of its sheet music have been sold.

His score for *Annie Get Your Gun* written in 1946, included such gems as "They Say It's Wonderful," and "There's No Business Like Show Business,"

This show was followed on Broadway by *Miss Liberty* in 1949, *Call Me Madam* in 1951 and *Mr. President* in 1962.

In 1966 the prolific and popular song writer added two new songs to *Annie Get Your Gun* which starred Ethel Merman as it was being readied for its New York revival at Lincoln Center.

That same year, at the age of seventy-eight when most men entertain thoughts related to the tranquility of retirement, Mr. Berlin's productivity had shown no signs of abating. Mr. Berlin planned to "be as active as my health will allow me to be." And he added, "My health is pretty good."

He was born Israel Baline in Temun, a Russian village near the Siberian border on May 11, 1888. His father Moses Baline, was a rabbi and cantor who sang in a synagogue during the High Holidays. During the rest of the year he taught Irving and the other boys of the neighborhood the hymns of his faith. In 1892, after a pogrom in Temun, Mr. Baline brought his wife and four of their children to this country. A married daughter and an older son remained behind.

The family settled on the Lower East Side of Manhattan—first on Cherry Street and then on Monroe Street. His father died when he was eight. Irving sang on stret corners for pennies. At fourteen he ran away from home—four blocks west to the Bowery, where he worked as assistant to an itinerant singer and occasionally sang himself.

Irving Berlin

Izzy Baline became Irving Berlin, a singing waiter at the Pelham Cafe at 12 Pell Street, in New York's Chinatown. M. Nicholson was pianist at the Pelham Cafe. The singing waiter and the pianist were inspired to original composition one day when a similar team in a nearby cafe created a successful song, "My Marinucci Taka Da Steamboat," an Italian dialect comic recital. Berlin wrote the words, Nicholson the music of "Marie From Sunny Italy," a song that appeared in 1907. It was Berlin's first published number and his total royalties reached thirty-seven cents. Undismayed Berlin continued writing lyrics for songs.

§182

He had great difficulty in getting this number published. "Too long," some publishers said of it. "Unsingable," others declared.

However, he finally got George M. Cohan to introduce it at the "Friars' Frolic" of 1911 and immediately it—and Berlin—were "made."

By 1912 he was a celebrity both as a "composer" and as a vaude-villian.

Berlin's forte was the invention of melodies of simple charm and the fabrication of lyrics of equal simplicity which combine to voice expressions in songs of universal appeal.

Soon he was being asked to write scores for Broadway shows and he did such hits as "Watch Your Step" in 1914 and "Century Girl" in 1916. Out of these productions came songs all still popular today.

Since then he has turned out one hit after another, including several *Ziegfeld Follies, Music Box Reviews, As Thousands Cheer,* and *Louisiana Purchase,* in addition to a long list of musical films.

Mr. Berlin has probably made more money for his work than any other writer of music. His twelve-and-a-half per cent gross of the movie *Blue Skies* totaled $1,250,000 while his score for *Easter Parade* brought him $600,000. On one record alone he was paid $63,000 for just a three months sales period. In 1919 he formed his own music publishing company so that, in the case of *Annie Get Your Gun,* he not only received $2,500 a week in composer's royalties for a year or more, but he also made close to half a million dollars as the publisher of its score.

Generous with his money, Berlin turned over the royalties from his ever-popular "God Bless America" to the Girl Scouts and Boy Scouts of America, netting them more than $309,044 to date. His "I Threw A Kiss In The Ocean" made over $20,000 for Navy Relief. During World War II, he volunteered his services to write, stage and act in a new soldier show, *This Is The Army*. It earned $9,761,000 which was turned over to Army Emergency Relief.

Of his work, the *Saturday Review* has said as much in truth as in jest, "By providing lovers with theme songs for the past fifty years, he has increased the population of the world by millions. He has been masseur to lonely hearts, has staved off many varicose veins by inciting to dance, and the Lord knows what other miracles his monosyllabic poetry, set to horizontal music, has performed."

1913　§　SAMUEL GOLDWYN: Motion Picture Magnate

Ever since 1894, when the Holland brothers opened up the first penny arcade and peep show on Herald Square, the citizens of New York could not stay away from the nickelodeons. The pictures they saw were only a few minutes long—"Bronco Billy" chasing a train and falling on his face, children throwing pillows, or a couple of drunks running away from each other.

In 1896, a fourteen year old boy who was born in poverty in Warsaw, Poland, came to the United States. Little did Samuel Goldfish, as he was then called, realize that he was destined to become one of the foremost motion-picture producers. During his early years in New York, he became a glove salesman. So capable did he prove to be that in his early twenties he became chief sales executive for the glove company at the then fabulous salary of $15,000 a year.

Drawn into the moviemania of the time, he frequented the nickelodeons. Sam was completely enthralled. He would come home and pester his brother-in-law, Jesse Lasky to go into the motion picture business with him. He had an idea that full-length stories and plays could be made into motion pictures.

In those early pioneering days, all motion pictures were made in the East, mostly indoors. Samuel Goldfish, full of enthusiastic plans for picture-making, wanted to find a more suitable place with good climate for the making of outdoor movies the year round. He went

SAMUEL GOLDWYN

West and found such a place. It turned out to be Hollywood, now the foremost world-center for movie making.

By 1913, he had left his successful business career to help produce the first feature-length moving picture made in Hollywood, an epic of American Indians and London high society called *The Squaw Man*. The picture was produced in a rented stable near the present intersection of Sunset Boulevard and Vine Street. At night coyotes came down from the hills to prowl around the building. Cecile B. De Mille, the director, shot a couple of them and nailed their skins to the wall.

De Mille was one of Goldfish's partners in this pioneer enterprise. So was Lasky, who started as a cornet player and became one of the best-known vaudeville and cabaret impressarios in America. Arthur S. Friend, a theatrical lawyer, was the fourth member of the group. Each invested $5,000 in an organization known as the Jesse Lasky Feature Play Company. Another $5,000 in stock was set aside for general sale, while $5,000 more went to Dustin Farnum as salary for playing the lead in *The Squaw Man*. At the last moment, Farnum backed out and demanded his $5,000 in cash. He got his money, but three years later the stock he refused was worth more than a million dollars.

De Mille and Lasky kept their stock and eventually became multimillionaires. For many years they were prominent producers and leading figures in the Hollywood motion-picture industry.

In 1916, the producer joined with Edgar and Arch Selwyn and the new organization was called the Goldwyn Pictures Corporation, a name derived from the first syllable of Goldfish and the last syllable of Selwyn. The more Goldfish saw and heard the name Goldwyn, the more he liked it and he annexed it for his personal use.

Goldwyn became the most legendary and the most fantastically successful independent motion picture producer in history. For over fifty-five years, he made the finest pictures in the world, and he produced many screen classics such as: *Street Scene, Arrowsmith, Dead End, Wuthering Heights, Dodsworth, The Dark Angel, The Little Foxes, Stella Dallas*, and *The Best Years of Our Lives*. The latter, produced in 1946, was acclaimed one of the best pictures of all time and received an unprecedented total of nine academy awards.

No one spent as much to get the best actors, writers and directors as Goldwyn. He was the first to pay as much as one million dollars for the rights to film a story. Although he introduced to the world many of the most famous screen stars in motion picture history, he has remained the only producer whose name on a theater marquee means as much as the stars.

On August 27, 1967, Samuel Goldwyn celebrated his eighty-fifth birthday. While others of early motion picture fame have been retired on their earnings and prestige, Samuel Goldwyn continued to turn out the best pictures he knows how to make and each year the industry looks to him to set the pace.

1914 § PAUL M. WARBURG: A Creator of the Federal Reserve

Paul M. Warburg stemmed from an aristocratic family of rabbis and businessmen who for three hundred years had engaged in commerce and banking in Europe in addition to following numerous other pursuits. The family bank of M. M. Warburg and Company in Hamburg was an ancient enterprise founded in 1798, which lasted well into the Hitler era, when it was forcibly confiscated by non-Jews in 1938.

Following the Jewish tradition of acquiring learning Paul graduated at eighteen from the Real-Gymnasium, which is equal to two years of an American college. The young student would have preferred continuing his studies at the University, but the Warburgs had a career at the family bank awaiting their son. German thoroughness prescribed a period of apprenticeship. To become a qualified financier one had to know the intricacies of merchandising, shipping and exporting. Paul received a thorough drilling in menial tasks on the busy polyglot docks of Hamburg while working for an export firm.

He spent two years in England and for several months rounded out his experience in a London broker's office learning about the losses and profits of stock speculation. In France he widened his knowledge of solid banking. After further experience in the banking business in the ancestral bank in Hamburg, he went off on a world tour. In New York he met a daughter of Solomon Loeb of Kuhn, Loeb and Company, and married her two years later. A trained banker, cosmopolitan in viewpoint, and thoroughly drilled in domestic and international financial operations, Paul M. Warburg was admitted into the Hamburg firm founded by his great-grandfather in the eighteenth century.

Paul M. Warburg

§186

At home and completely integrated into the life, cultural interests and commerce of Hamburg, Paul Warburg became a member of the local legislative body and served on the arbitration court for settling mercantile disputes. Rapidly emerging as a recognized power in the financial district, he had no thought of leaving his birthplace despite some underground rumblings of anti-Semitism. But his wife's parents suffered from ill health and desired to have their daughter near them. Strongly urged by his in-laws and offered a flattering partnership in Kuhn, Loeb and Company, Paul Warburg finally yielded to their pleading and settled in New York in 1902.

Warburg's colleagues could observe at first hand the wide knowledge and sound judgement they read in his articles on the need for reform in American currency and banking. Something was obviously wrong with a system that permitted the rise of call money to over 20 per cent on Wall Street when the banks in California might be bursting at the same time with an oversupply of ready cash. Banks throughout the land held promissory notes frozen in their vaults, yet sound paper might be rediscounted at some national institution and liquid funds could circulate in trade channels to the advantage of business all over the country. About 20,000 state and national banks were operating independently without overall direction or supervision. To Warburg a portent of disaster lurked in such a situation.

As an expert in finance, Warburg came to the conclusion that a central organization should credit the banking system of the nation, regulate currency and credits and restrain speculation. In Germany, the Reichsbank had such powers. He had witnessed the successful operation of the Bank of England in the world's financial center.

The Banque de France exercised similar functions. Then why should the United States not have a similar institution?

In 1911 Warburg began working with Senator Nelson W. Aldrich of Rhode Island on a complete reorganization of American banking system.

On December 23, 1913 the Glass-Owen Federal Reserve Board Act went into effect. It was not the complete realization of Warburg's plan, yet his ideas are in substance reflected in its preamble: "To provide for the establishment of Federal Reserve Banks, to furnish an elastic currency, to afford means of rediscounting commercial paper, to establish a more effective supervision of banking in the Uinted States and for other purposes."

Paul M. Warburg

§187

The Act represented a careful compromise in that the 12 Reserve Banks became centralized each in its own district, yet the system remained decentralized as to the country at large. Each branch became the bank that served the nation or state banks of its district in the same manner as the individual institutions served their depositors.

The entire system was governed by the Federal Reserve Board consisting of eight members of whom two were government officials.

PAUL M. WARBURG

Recognition of the service rendered in drafting the act impelled Woodrow Wilson to name Paul M. Warburg a member of the first Federal Reserve Board.

Warburg's service on the Board for four years coincided with the momentuous period of World War I. Economists wondered how victory could have been achieved without the Federal Reserve System.

Warburg's labors were again appreciated when the Board elected him vice chairman for the last two years. President Wilson was ready to appoint him for another term, but the war stirred up intense bitterness against German Americans, to whom Theodore Roosevelt applied the epithet "hyphenated Americans." Warburg, feeling that his reappointment would excite xenophobic criticism embarrassing to the president, declined nomination.

On resuming private life Paul Warburg rejoined Kuhn, Loeb and Company, founded the International Acceptance Bank and continued his civic and cultural interests. In his spare time he wrote a monumental history of the Federal Reserve System and a number of sad introspective poems.

Actively in touch with industrial conditions as Chairman of the Economic Commission of the American Bankers Association, he was virtually the only financial authority to warn the public of the impending danger of overspeculation in Wall Street that could bring about a general depression involving the entire country. Early in 1929 he foresaw the crash of the stock market that followed barely seven months later. Tribute to his understanding of the basic economic factors responsible for the "ultimate collapse" was paid him by the *New Republic* in its issue of January 21, 1931.

By 1932 the 64 year old Paul M. Warburg was dead. Formerly universities had conferred honorary degrees upon him and now the most eminent uttered their eulogies. But unexpected praise came from the *Nation,* a publication without affection for wealth or privilege, in its obituary: "No one in a similar influential position excelled Mr. Warburg in his feeling of responsibility to the public," it declared.

David B.
Steinman

§189

On September 6, 1952, a special postage stamp was issued by the United States Post Office to mark the one hundredth anniversary of the founding of the American Society for Civil Engineers.

The design of the stamp portrays the advancement made in one phase of civil engineering—bridge building—during the past century. In the lower left hand corner of the stamp is a replica of a typical covered wooden bridge of the 1852 period. Dominating the right and central portion of the stamp is a reproduction of the George Washington Bridge with the New York City skyline in the background. Directly above the drawing of this bridge appear the hands of David Bernard Steinman. It is a fitting tribute to one of the world's leading authorities on bridge construction who designed and built bridges for nearly half a century.

All in all David Steinman built more than 400 bridges on five continents. His bridges, rising triumphant over obstacles and difficulties, have won the highest awards for excellence. They are artistic as well as engineering masterpieces. Their piercing granite towers, the graceful arcs of their main cables, the gossamer network of their lighter cables and the arched lines of their roadways combine to produce matchless compositions expressing harmonious beauty in steel. They are things of enduring beauty.

Born in the shadow of the Brooklyn Bridge on the Lower East Side on June 11, 1886, David Steinman was one of the seven children of Eva and Louis Kelvin Steinman, a factory worker. At thirteen he entered New York's City College and in the same year won a special pass allowing him to climb the steelwork and observe the engineering wonders of the nearby Brooklyn Bridge spanning the East River. Young David loved to walk over its span and to explore its marvels. He was awed by its vastness, by the majesty of its towers, by the power of its cables and he was fascinated by all the details of its construction. When he would return from these pilgrimages, he would recount to his friends and elders the wonders he had seen. To him it was truly a "miracle bridge" and he wondered how so marvelous a work could have been created. He was fired with the ambition to become a builder of suspension bridges himself. This far-

DAVID B. STEINMAN

flung ambition seemed beyond the boy's reach, but the spirit of the bridges and later the story of its builders entered the boy's heart and mind and his dream came true.

At City College Steinman was an extraordinary student. He graduated with the highest honors and three scholarships which enabled him to continue his studies at Columbia University where he obtained a degree in civil engineering as well as a Ph.D. While pursuing his studies there, he taught civil and mechanical engineering at City College in the evening. Later, he was to teach at several other universities and engineering schools.

His Ph.D. thesis on "The Design of the Henry Hudson Memorial Bridge as a Steel Arch," written in 1909, became a standard textbook and sold many editions. A quarter of a century later, Steinman, with a few modifications, actually built this bridge, the longest hingeless arch bridge in the world, and one of the most beautiful. (This structure, spanning the Harlem River, and often referred to as "The Scenic Gateway to Manhattan," doubles the traffic capacity.)

At the age of twenty-three Steinman joined the faculty of the University of Idaho as the youngest professor of civil engineering in the country.

In 1914, a few years later, he launched his career in the individual construction and design of bridges. He helped build the Hell Gate arch bridge over New York's East River which was considered an engineering feat of unusual proportions for its time. He designed the Sciotoville Bridge over the Ohio River, establishing a new record for length. He constructed the magnificent $100,000,000 five-mile Mackinac Straits Bridge, connecting the northern and southern parts of Michigan.

In the plans for the bridges he built, he incorporated revolutionary ideas offering greater rigidity while reducing the amount of steel normally used. His fame grew, and Steinman found himself being called upon by every country in the world.

He took part in the design and construction of the Florianopolis Bridge in Brazil, the largest bridge of its kind in South America. In California he built the Carquinez Straits Bridge, the longest cantilever bridge in the United States, the first constructed especially to withstand earthquakes. In Rhode Island he built the longest bridge in New England, the Mount Hope Bridge between Providence and Newport, "to take the island out of Rhode Island." For this he received the award from the American Institute of Steel Construction for the most beautiful long-span structure of the year. Other such award-winning works of his are the St. John's Bridge in Portland, Oregon; the Waldo-Hancock Bridge in Bucksport, Maine, the most beautiful American bridge ever built for less than one million dollars; and the Charter Oaks Bridge over the Connecticut River in Hartford which represented an advance in the science and art of bridge design. Then there was the Thousand Islands Bridge over the St. Lawrence, which links the United States and Canada, the first modern suspension bridge to be built with scientific features to provide stability against aerodynamic forces.

Steinman constructed beautiful suspension bridges in England, Italy, Holland, Spain, Denmark, Germany, Australia, Bolivia, Siam, and in many, many more countries all over the world.

In his native city of New York, he helped design the famous Triborough Bridge which connects the three boroughs—Manhattan, the Bronx and Brooklyn. He was consultant on the construction of the George Washington Bridge spanning the Hudson River between New York and New Jersey.

In 1948, at the peak of his fame, he was asked to modernize the Brooklyn Bridge. It was the constant sight of this bridge that made him first think of building bridges when he lived nearby as a boy.

Steinman was the author of 750 publications, including fifteen textbooks, some of which are standard textbooks for engineers today, books about bridges for juveniles and many volumes of poetry, frequently on the subject of bridges. Some of his most popular works are: *Suspension Bridges: Their Design, Construction and Erection* (1923); *A Generalized Theory for Suspension Bridges* (1934) and *Bridges and Their Builders* (1941). He was an associate editor of the *Engineers Handbook Library* which first appeared in 1921 and went through many subsequent editions.

David Steinman was the recipient of many honors, prizes, medals and awards (eight in all for the most beautifully constructed bridges in America). He held eighteen honorary degrees and was decorated with the French Legion of Honor. He was the founder of the National Society of Professional Engineers, and held membership in many other scientific organizations.

Steinman died at the age of seventy-four on August 21, 1960. His bridges remain among the finest monuments of their age. The success which crowned his achievements conveys some measure of the tremendous reservoir of ability released when our Jewish citizens found here the opportunities that the Old World denied to most of their parents.

1915 § MOSES ALEXANDER: The Governor from Idaho

Many American Jews have taken part in municipal, state, and national affairs. Some have risen to high public office. Four western states, which have very few Jews, have elected Jews as governors in recent years.

The first Jew to hold this position was Moses Alexander, who was governor of Idaho for two terms, from 1915 to 1919.

Alexander's family emigrated to the United States from Bavaria in 1868 and settled in Chillicothe, Missouri. Here young Alexander attended school and obtained his first position as a clerk in a clothing store. A few years later he owned the store. He became interested in local politics, and in 1886 served on the city council of Chillicothe. In recognition of his record, he was elected mayor, and then saved the town from bankruptcy.

In 1891, because of ill health, Alexander was forced to leave Missouri and went to Boise, Idaho. He opened a clothing store which soon developed into a thriving chain-store business with branches in Lewiston and Pocatello.

No other Jew in Idaho achieved anything like his reputation. When a Reform Party invited him to be its mayoralty candidate, he accepted, and was elected in 1897. Alexander declined to succeed himself, but his reelection in 1901 on a coalition ticket made him a leader of the Democratic party. Defeated in his first try for governor in 1908, he ran again in 1914 in a campaign that made political history.

When he took office in Idaho's twenty-fourth year of statehood, he had to contend with a hostile legislature. Nevertheless, he gave the state a business-like administration that won him many friends, and as one writer put it, "more enemies than any man has a right to expect." At the end of his first legislative session, he was faced with a huge stack of bills. When asked what he was going to do with them, Alexander riffled through the pile and replied, "I think I'll sign the thin ones and veto the thick ones."

Moses Alexander

§193

He was reelected in 1917, this time with a Democratic legislature, and pushed through legislation that gave the state its first workmen's compensation law, paved the way for a state highway system, created much-needed irrigation, reclamation, and waterway projects, and established prohibition. He retired from public life at the end of his second term, in 1919, but was prevailed upon to run again in 1922, only to be defeated.

The year Alexander became governor, another Jew, Charles Himrod, was mayor of Boise, and two others, Max Mayfield and Leo Greenbaum, were Boise councilmen. Shortly afterward, Simon Bamberger, a Jewish merchant of Salt Lake City, was elected governor of Utah. He was the first Democrat and non-Mormon to become governor of that state. The only existing railroad named for a person, the Bamberger Line of Utah, was founded by him.

When President Franklin D. Roosevelt took office in 1933, there were four Jewish governors in the United States. They were Herbert Lehman of New York, Henry Horner of Illinois, Julius Meyer of Oregon, and Arthur Seligman of New Mexico.

Today the governor of the Virgin Islands is Ralph Paiewonsky. Governor Paiewonsky is presently the only American Jew occupying a governor's seat.

Louis D.
Brandeis

§194

Both in private practice and on the bench, American Jews have risen to high eminence in the profession of law.

It was on January 28, 1916 that President Woodrow Wilson made the precedent-breaking appointment that saw the first Jew in history named as a member of the United States Supreme Court. The choice could have fallen on no better man than Louis Dembitz Brandeis, already described as "friend of justice, and friend of man." For Brandeis, prior to his nomination, inveighed forcefully against the establishment of his day, for its callousness, its exploitive practices, its mad scramble for power and profit. He was a militant crusader for social justice whoever his opponent might be.

Brandeis was born in Louisville, Kentucky, in 1856, to a young immigrant couple who had rebelled against their native Austria's lack of equal opportunity and left their fatherland to find freedom in America. His uncle, after whom he was named, was a member of the national convention that nominated Lincoln for president, and was well-known as a scholar and writer on Jewish topics.

As a young man Brandeis studied law at Harvard University. Upon graduation he formed a partnership with Samuel Warren and set up the first really modern law office that Boston had ever had. Within a short period of eight years he became the leading barrister of that city. By representing liberal causes before the courts and "little men" against great corporations, he became known as the "People's Lawyer." He worked out such splendid projects as the Massachusetts system of savings bank insurance and pensions for wage earners. In 1910 he was asked to act as arbitrator in the New York garment workers' strike, the largest New York had ever seen. In this capacity he originated constitutionalism in disputes between employer and employee. Here for the first time Mr. Brandeis became interested in Jewish problems and was led to an intense study of Zionism. The idealist in him warmed to the thought of making Palestine once again the homeland of the Jewish people, and he became a leader in the fight to reawaken the Jewish spirit and safeguard Jewish rights. In his uniquely terse and powerful style he set down a credo that has become classic: "Loyalty to America demands that every Jew should be a Zionist." When President Wilson appointed Mr. Brandeis to the Supreme Court, he was president of the Zionist Organization.

Although the President at first was assailed for naming Brandeis to the highest court in the land, after a few years Brandeis was hailed as one of America's greatest jurists and among the greatest lovers of justice the world has ever known. After a great career in both Jewish and American life, he died in 1941, at the age of eighty-five.

Louis D. Brandeis

Justice Brandeis served on the Court for twenty-three years. Although in many of the more than six hundred decisions he rendered during this time he was in the minority, prior to his retirement, he saw his beliefs and prophecies welded into the framework of the law.

§195

Oliver Wendell Holmes was 75 years old when Brandeis joined him on the Court. Almost at once the famous phrase, "Holmes and Brandeis dissenting," began to make legal history. To the vast annoyance of the majority members of the Court, the opinions written by the two dissenters were more influential than the actual decisions of the Court itself. In case after case, one session's defeat became next session's law. Chief Justice William Howard Taft fumed: "I think the two gang up together out of sheer deviltry!" Actually, however, the two "dissenters" voted with the majority of the Court far more often than they voted against it.

LOUIS D. BRANDEIS

Holmes and Brandeis were old friends who enjoyed one another's company, but in court matters they arrived at their conclusions by very different routes. Holmes frankly regarded Brandeis's lengthy, fact-stuffed opinions as a great bore. One day when Brandeis sent over an opinion which was even more ponderous than usual, Holmes regarded it gloomily, then scribbled a response in the margin. "This morning I took a walk along the canal. I saw a robin. Spring is here at last. By the way, I concur."

Franklin Roosevelt admired Brandeis and considered him both friend and political ally. But when Brandeis voted to send most of the President's early New Deal legislation to the wastebasket, F. D. R. felt betrayed. He included Brandeis in his bitter denunciation of "nine old men." Brandeis was pained. He explained his stand: "You can't solve the problems of today by creating tyranny for tomorrow."

During his final years on the bench, Brandeis seemed to grow more and more conservative. When he defended the right of a worker to refuse to join a union, the union leaders were bitterly angry. "I have defended the working people, when they need it, against tyranny of industry," Brandeis said cooly. "I do not now propose to see anyone subjected to a tyranny of labor." He still objected to bigness in any form—unions, banks, industry or government. "Equal bargaining power for all," he argued. Many said Brandeis had changed, but it was the world that had changed—and he had helped to alter it.

In Israel, a colony was established which bears the name of Kfar Brandeis after the late justice whom the Jews of America were delighted to honor. In Waltham, Massachusetts, in 1948, another tribute was paid to his memory by naming a university after him.

Today, Brandeis University, the first Jewish sponsored institution of higher learning in this country, which welcomes students of all races and religions, takes its place as a pre-eminent member of the American family of universities.

1916 § SAMUEL A. LEVINE: He Was the First to Diagnose Coronary Thrombosis

American Jews have made notable contributions to medicine in many of its branches. Several have won Nobel Prizes and large numbers are engaged in medical research and as laboratory technicians.

The recognition, diagnosis and treatment of coronary thrombosis and many other forms of heart disease was one of the big question marks of medical science until Dr. Samuel Albert Levine turned his mind to answering it. Before his time a "coronary" was not recognized as such until the patient died and an autopsy was performed; if he lived, it was assumed he had not had a coronary attack for it was thought incompatible with survival.

Today because of Dr. Levine's work, a great deal is known about cardiovascular disease.

Tens of thousands of people who suffered serious heart attacks have been properly diagnosed and are alive today because of his work.

Samuel A. Levine

§197

Dr. Levine's big findings in cardiology started in 1916. It resulted in his publication in January, of that year of the first monograph on clinical coronary thrombosis to appear in medical literature. The only one who had previously described the condition was Dr. James B. Herrick of Chicago, and his work was known to but few physicians.

In his early work Dr. Levine established that coronary thrombosis was a complete entity that could be recognized clinically. He described many of the detailed clinical and electrocardiographic features of the disease which permits its early recognition. He described its complications. He also showed that loud systolic murmurs are always associated with some form of cardiovascular disease.

After that Dr. Levine made equally great advances, diagnosing and devising the treatment of one form of heart disease after another.

In more recent years he showed that chair rest, instead of bed rest, aids the recovery of patients suffering from coronary thrombosis—a departure from the long accepted practice of keeping coronary patients in bed for many weeks—and that chair rest is preferable to bed rest in the treatment of many other types of heart disease. His studies in digitalis therapy and his recognition of hyperthyroidism which masks itself as heart disease are also milestones in the care of the cardiac.

Dr. Levine wrote what are considered the outstanding texts on heart disorders. His book *Coronary Thrombosis*, which first appeared in 1929, still remains a classic. His volume *Clinical Heart Disease*, originally published in 1936, became a standard work in the field and is now in its fifth edition. Dr. Levine also authored more than one hundred and eighty articles on various phases of heart disease—many of them "firsts" in content that are widely quoted in international medical literature.

One of the country's foremost exponents of "simplification of med-

DR. SAMUEL A. LEVINE

ical diagnosis," Dr. Levine stressed the diagnostic value of clinical bedside methods, especially auscultation (the detection and study of sounds arising from various organs, chiefly the heart and lungs). He always insisted upon the importance of the use of the stethoscope and bedside examinations, noting that a cardiogram should be used to supplement trained ears.

He stimulated considerable discussion among doctors by propounding the theory that heart disease was far less frequent in China because of the diet or philosophical view of life. His general medical curiosity led him to the initial discovery that sufferers of pernicious anemia never have acid in their stomachs, a finding which aided greatly in the diagnosis of this disease.

Born on January 1, 1891 in Lomza, Poland, Dr. Levine rose to prominence in the field of medicine from humble beginnings. His parents immigrated to the United States and settled in Boston when he was three. A child prodigy Dr. Levine reached the sixth grade in school at the age of eight. He sold newspapers in the streets of downtown Boston as a member of the Newsboys Union in his school days and prior to his graduation from high school.

He became the recipient of a Harvard College scholarship set up by the Newsboys Union. At Harvard he set his mind on a medical career after graduating from college in 1911. He attended the Harvard Medical School obtaining his medical degree in 1914 at the age of twenty-three. He was the first medical student to work at the then newly opened Peter Bent Brigham Hospital in Boston as a volunteer worker in the Out Patient Department. Following his graduation he became a member of the early medical staff of the hospital embarking on his long association with that institution as physician and consultant in cardiology which was to continue for the next fifty years. He also did additional graduate work at Harvard, and in 1930 was taken on its faculty as assistant professor of medicine. He was named clinical professor of medicine at Harvard, a post he occupied from 1948 until 1958, when he became professor emeritus.

Dr. Levine conducted a summer postgraduate course in cardiology for thirty-six years, from 1921 to 1956, the longest in the history of the Harvard Medical School, which was attended by physicians from all over the world. In 1954 the Samuel A. Levine Professorship in Medicine was established with a grant of $450,000 at the Harvard Medical School by a grateful patient and personal friend, the New York investment banker Charles E. Merrill, an honor which carried with it at that time the largest endowment for any single chair in the history of that institution.

In 1956 the Samuel A. Levine Cardiac Center was opened at the Peter Bent Brigham Hospital. The Center is an intensive care unit for patients who have suffered acute coronary occlusions. Using sophisticated electronic instrumentation, a team of specially trained nurses and physicians continuously monitor vital body functions during the few critical days following a coronary attack.

When asked what seemed to him most significant in his long and distinguished career, Dr. Levine replied: "My work as a teacher. I love to teach. If I know anything, I want everyone to know it."

Many organizations and universities honored him. He received the Gold Heart Award of the American Heart Association and an honorary Doctor of Humane Letters degree from Yeshiva University in 1959. He was awarded the American-Israel Freedom Award in 1960.

Dr. Levine died on March 31, 1966 at the age of seventy-five. His special gifts to relieve others of suffering and to prolong their lives will reach deeply into the future and into many lives.

1919 § DAVID SARNOFF: Communications Pioneer

David Sarnoff, chairman of the board of directors of the Radio Corporation of America, is recognized throughout the world as a pioneer in the development of radio, television, and electronics.

He is chairman of a corporation whose gross annual sales volume is more than two and a half billion dollars. Its thirty-four manufacturing plants in the United States and twenty plants in nine foreign countries turn out products ranging from tiny ferrite cores for computers to huge radars used in tracking missiles and satellites. It employs more than 120,000 people.

In addition to its manufacturing interests, RCA is engaged in broadcasting through its subsidiary, the National Broadcasting Company; in servicing electronic equipment through the RCA Service Company; in international communications through RCA Communications, Inc.; in publishing through Random House, Inc.; and in education through RCA Institutes. Its David Sarnoff Research Center at Princeton, New Jersey, is one of the world's foremost radio, television and electronics laboratories.

The RCA Astro-Electronics Division, also in Princeton, develops and builds major units for space systems as well as entire satellites. Its achievements include the famous TIROS weather observation series, the Relay communications satellites and the television systems that provided the first close-up views of the moon aboard the Ranger 7, 8 and 9 spacecraft.

General Sarnoff was elected president of RCA in 1930, at the age of thirty-nine. In 1947, he was elected chairman of the board and chief executive officer. In 1966, he relinquished the post of chief executive officer, while continuing to serve actively as chairman of the board.

There is no better example of the American way to success than the story of David Sarnoff. Born on February 27, 1891, in the small village of Uzlian, near the city of Minsk, Russia, he was brought to this country at the age of nine. Soon afterward, with the death of his father, a poverty-stricken house painter, he became the main support of the family in New York's Lower East Side.

He sold newspapers, worked as a delivery boy, and at the age of fifteen was hired by the Commercial Cable Company as messenger. He saved enough money to purchase a telegraph instrument, and soon learned the Morse code.

Fascinated by reports of the new means of communications known as "wireless," Sarnoff was quick to follow the suggestion of a telegraph operator who pointed out that there might be a new field of opportunity with the Marconi Wireless Telegraph Company of America. Sarnoff went to the Marconi office at 27 William Street in New York City and applied for a job as operator. There was no wireless operator's job open, but there was need of an office boy.

DAVID SARNOFF

Sarnoff saw an opportunity to "get his foot in the door," and took the job at $5.50 a week. That was on September 30, 1906.

At seventeen, Sarnoff seized at a chance to become an operator at a lonely wireless station maintained by the Marconi Company at Siasconset, on Nantucket Island, Massachusetts. The station's excellent technical library was an added attraction to the $60-a-month pay. Then, too, at that station he had an opportunity to communicate with some of the operators on the transatlantic liners.

Before long he went to sea on the S. S. *Beothic* as the ship's first wireless operator, for a seal-hunting expedition to the Arctic ice fields. One day, he picked up a message about a sailor on a ship a hundred miles away who had suffered internal injuries. Sarnoff immediately notified the ship's doctor who prescribed the treatment via wireless and the man recovered. The Marine Medico Service is generally regarded as a direct outgrowth of his pioneering.

Eagerness for more study led him to request a transfer to the Marconi Station at Sea Gate, New York, not far from Pratt Institute in Brooklyn, where he enrolled for a special evening course in electrical engineering.

While attending Pratt, Sarnoff became wireless operator at the Marconi station atop Wanamaker's Store in New York. It was in this position that both Sarnoff and wireless were brought to the attention of the nation and the world. On the night of April 14, 1912, Sarnoff was on duty when the S. S. *Titanic*, en route to New York on her maiden voyage, struck an iceberg and sank with a loss of 1,517 lives.

Sarnoff picked up the message reporting the *Titanic's* distress signal and sinking. He promptly made the news available to an anxious world. From the rescue ship *Carpathia*, Sarnoff received the list of survivors and other news related to the disaster. He stayed on duty continuously for seventy-two hours, during which time President William Howard Taft ordered every other wireless station along the East Coast silenced in order to prevent interference.

With the loss of the *Titanic,* Congress quickly passed a Radio Act that made it mandatory for ships carrying more than 50 persons to install radio and to maintain a constant watch at sea. The Marconi Company maintained a training school for radio operators at which Sarnoff became an instructor, in addition to his rapidly expanding responsibilities with the company.

It was Sarnoff who first saw the full posssibilities of wireless for household use. A memo he drafted at the Marconi Company in 1915 proposing the development and promotion of the "radio music box" . . . "to bring music into the home by wireless" led to the first mass production and sale of household radios.

In 1919, the Marconi Company was absorbed by the newly formed Radio Corporation of America and Sarnoff was appointed Commercial Manager of the new company.

It was Sarnoff who paved the way for the establishment of national radio and television networks. He started the first radio network, the National Broadcasting Company, in 1926 with only twenty-four affiliated stations, but under his guidance it has grown to include over two hundred stations.

Through Sarnoff's faith, foresight and leadership, television developed into the greatest system of mass communications the world has ever known. Television became a major industry and a new art and service of widespread proportions.

Under his direction, the Radio Corporation of America spent more than fifty million dollars on research in the development of black-and-white television before there was any financial return on the investment. The expense proved fully justified when RCA's research engineers pioneered in the development of the iconoscope and the image orthicon, the electric eye of the television camera, and the kinescope—the picture receiving tube.

The first postwar television receiver was introduced by RCA in September of 1946. By late 1958, there were one hundred and eighty television stations in the United States and RCA had produced its ten millionth television receiver.

RCA also pioneered in the development of compatible, all-electronic color TV and by the end of 1960 had spent more than one hundred and thirty million dollars in developing and promoting color TV and providing facilities and color programming.

During World War II, Sarnoff achieved wide recognition for his efforts in military communications and was assigned as Special Consultant on Communications to General of the Army Dwight D. Eisenhower at SHAEF Headquarters in Europe. On December 6, 1944, he was elevated to the rank of Brigadier General.

As a radio and television pioneer, David Sarnoff is a man with many "firsts" to his credit. Because of his efforts, the first national political convention was broadcast and televised, as was the first college football game, the first major league baseball game, and the first prize fight. He introduced radio's first classical music appreciation hour and arranged for the first broadcast of an opera from the Metropolitan Opera House. Also, he laid the groundwork for today's extensive radio and television news coverage.

General Sarnoff has received many honorary doctoral degrees, military honors, and awards from scientific, industrial, civic, and cultural organizations, both at home and abroad.

The Television Broadcasters Association, in recognition of his work in introducing and developing television in the United States, conferred on General Sarnoff the title of "The Father of American Television" in 1944.

In 1951, on the occasion of his forty-fifth anniversary in radio, the RCA Laboratories in Princeton, N. J., was named the "David Sarnoff Research Center." A bronze plaque was unveiled which included the following inscription: "David Sarnoff's work, leadership and genius comprise radio's pre-eminent record of the past, television's brilliant performance of the present, and a rich legacy in communications for the future."

On September 30, 1966, when he was 75, more than 1,500 industry leaders and outstanding Americans in all walks of life gathered to honor Sarnoff's sixtieth anniversary in communications and electronics. Sponsoring the "Salute to David Sarnoff" were three national organizations representing the electronics industry, electronics research, engineering, and broadcasting. It was the first time that these organizations had united in such a tribute.

The extraordinary story of General David Sarnoff, the immigrant boy who became an industrial giant, is one of the most spectacular in our annals. As head of RCA and pioneer in communications and electronics, he has probably affected our daily lives more than anyone since Edison.

Edna
Ferber

§204

Jews have made many and varied contributions to American litera-ture. Their numbers include many novelists, critics, poets, play-wrights and journalists. Some of the better known contemporaries are Herman Wouk, Elie Wiesel, Walter Lippmann, Robert Nathan, Fannie Hurst, Lillian Hellman, Louis Untermeyer and the late Ludwig Lewisohn. Of this group, Edna Ferber, whose name betokens story-telling magic, gained a place among the most popular women writers of this country.

Edna Ferber was born on August 15, 1887, in Kalamazoo, Michigan. When Edna was a little girl, her father, a Hungarian Jew, gave up the struggle of operating a store in Kalamazoo and for a year lived in Chicago before trying again in Ottumwa, Iowa. It was in Iowa and Wisconsin that Edna Ferber spent her girlhood where she was to learn to know and love the Middle West and the hardy Americans about whom she was later to write in her novels. While still in her teens, her father went blind. To help the family finances young Edna accepted a position as a local reporter on the town paper for three dollars a week.

Before long a new city editor discharged her and she went on to Milwaukee where she obtained a somewhat better position on the *Journal*. When her father died four years later the mother and two daughters moved on to Chicago where she became associated there with the *Tribune*. She fascinated her readers with a condensed, almost conversational, idiom. In her free time she tried her hand at creative writing. She completed a novel, which she called *Dawn O'Hara*, but did not like it and put it aside. *Dawn O'Hara* told of life as she saw it while a newspaper reporter in Milwaukee describ-ing among other things the boarding house where she had stopped. Her mother rescued the manuscript from the wastepaper basket and sent it to a publisher. Recognized as a gigantic masterpiece, it was published in 1911 and sold over 10,000 copies. A great career had been launched.

From that time on, many other short stories, plays and novels followed, for Miss Ferber has been an industrious as well as care-ful writer.

Her short stories appeared in leading magazines and were later gathered into four volumes, the best liked, perhaps, being *Buttered Side Down* which told about a delightful and witty travelling woman "salesman" of petticoats named Emma McChesney. A play entitled *Our Mrs. McChesney*, of which Miss Ferber and Victor Hobart were the playwrights, in which Ethel Barrymore appeared as the star in the role of Emma McChesney, had a long run on Broadway.

In 1915 Miss Ferber turned again to the writing of a novel. In *Fanny Herself*, the author described her own school days in the little town of Appleton, Wisconsin. The old rabbi was drawn from life; the hard-working, self-sacrificing Jewish mother was the novelist's own mother. This proved a very different story from the many tales of Ghetto life which had appeared up till this time; readers were at once interested in this account of a few Jewish families living in a small town.

The Girls, her next novel, gives a most interesting picture of life in Chicago, extending from Civil War days to the First World War. In 1925 Miss Ferber received the Pulitzer Prize, awarded for the leading novel of the year, *So Big*. It was the story of a boy whose mother spent her life working for him in a truck farm outside Chicago. It served as the basis of two motion pictures, one silent and one "talkie" and has been published on every continent, in every language and in every country of the civilized world. Among her

EDNA FERBER

other novels are such well-known best sellers as: *Show Boat, Cimarron, American Beauty, Saratoga Trunk, Giant* and *A Kind of Magic.*

In 1939 Edna Ferber's autobiography, *A Peculiar Treasure* (whose title was taken from *Exodus* 19: 5-6), appeared. It is a story not only of her American Jewish family and its place in the land of the free, but also a powerful indictment of the anti-Semitism which had almost destroyed Europe and threatened an unwary America. In spite of the fact that this book was published over a quarter of a century ago, it is still timely, alive and engrossing. In 1960, a new edition was brought out in testimony to its interest and appeal to this generation's readers.

As a playwright in collaboration with George S. Kaufman, she won over Broadway with such outstanding hits as *Dinner At Eight, The Royal Family, Stage Door, The Land is Bright* and again *Show Boat*, which proved to be one of the greatest stage and film stories ever seen or heard.

Edna Ferber received many honors as one of America's leading literary figures, among them membership in the National Institute of Arts and Letters and an honorary degree from Columbia University. Her stories are of North American background, trenchant, highly readable and basically critical of their subject matter. Her plots turn on the development of the characters as they meet the vicissitudes of life; and both characters and vicissitudes are so natural that they suggest sketches from life rather than works of fiction. Without preaching she drives home moral lessons and champions the cause of those who have had less than a fair share of life—the uncomplaining supporters of selfish wives and sisters, the women who are compelled to become breadwinners, the homely girl, the humble immigrant, the old father who is no longer able to work and who must live with his relatives. She felt, however, that many readers missed the special message her novels and short stories contain. They are such easy reading that one scarcely expects the undercurrent of seriousness. As William Allen White has said: "The historian will find no better picture of America in the first three decades of this century than Edna Ferber has drawn."

An unabashed, lifetime love affair with all—or most—of America, Edna Ferber's prime importance lies in her exploration of the American literary frontier. She discovered and charted an entirely new domain. What she accomplished is not only expressed in the broadly democratic character of her books—books which palpitate with vigor, customs, fears, dreams and hopes of these States—but is reflected in the native works of others following her.

She died on April 16, 1968, widely acclaimed and mourned as one of the best-read novelists in the nation.

1925 § GEORGE GERSHWIN: He Changed the Pattern of Popular Music

American Jews have shown unusual aptitude for the theater and music. One of the first to be drawn into the new stream of popular music was a Jewish boy by the name of George Gershwin. Gershwin was to prove himself one of the most brilliantly creative geniuses America has yet produced. Before his tragically premature death at the age of thirty-eight, George Gershwin had not only changed the pattern of popular music in this country but had quickened the pulse of music throughout the western world. Gershwin was born in Brooklyn, New York on September 26, 1898, the second son of Morris and Rose Bruskin Gershwin.

It was by pure accident that Gershwin, who stemmed from a family lacking in musical talent, became a song mill, who carefully converted his own vitality and love of life into a series of carefully written scores, all jazz, the only music he ever wanted to write.

With the purchase of a piano bought more for decoration than with the thought of having it played, he mastered all the knowledge his twenty-five cents a lesson teacher could impart. Before long he began writing his own musical compositions and left school to devote himself entirely to a musical career. At fifteen he became a "professional" employed by a music publishing firm at fifteen dollars a week. He accompanied the "song pluggers" in Tin Pan Alley, the Broadway section of New York, where popular songs are born. He toured vaudeville houses to report on acts and tried to write popular tunes. When he was eighteen he succeeded in getting a song published. At twenty-one he composed the entire score for a musical comedy *La La Lucille.* In the same year, 1919, he wrote a song called "Swanee" and became rich and famous overnight when the singer Al Jolson rocked the country with it.

Gershwin always insisted that "jazz is American folk music," and was to prove to the world that popular songs could be planned as carefully as more formal compositions and could be as musically artistic.

Following the success of his first Broadway musical productions, *La La Lucille* in 1919 and *The George White Scandals* in 1920, he was asked by Paul Whiteman, leader of the country's finest dance

GEORGE GERSHWIN

orchestra, to write a composition with a piano part to be played by him, accompanied by the Whiteman band. Thus came to be written *Rhapsody in Blue,* the emotional melody with the variety of moods which was forever to dispel prejudice against the use of jazz in symphonic music. Everyone talked about it. It became an American trademark; nothing ever composed in the United States was so universally performed.

In 1925 Gershwin continued to make musical history when he was commissioned by Walter Damrosch, conductor of the New York Symphony Orchestra, to write a concerto in which the piano played the solo part accompanied by the orchestra. This major composition, the first piano concerto created in jazz—Gershwin's so-called *Concerto in F*—was orchestrated by Gershwin himself and presented for the first time in Carnegie Hall on December 3, 1925, with the composer playing the piano part. For thirty minutes Gershwin poured forth music full of enchanting tone subtleties with a sincerity which moved the audience to tears and cheers.

By the time Gershwin was thirty, he had become internationally famous and a nation hummed and whistled his immortal songs such as: "I Got Rhythm," "Somebody Loves Me," "Maybe," "Liza," and "Our Love is Here to Stay." All of these numbers bristled with his brother Ira's gleefully ironic lyrics. Before his early death in 1937, he had composed the music for *An American in Paris, Porgy and Bess* and *Of Thee I Sing,* the first musical comedy to be published in book form and to receive the Pulitzer Prize for the best play of the year.

The appearance of *Of Thee I Sing*, the great Gershwin show in 1931, signalized the tone of the thirties. A marvelous story, serious and funny in a way no show had ever been before; glorious songs, perfectly integrated into the scheme; a highly American subject; natural American speech; sharp and brilliant lyrics; an all over unity of style embodying wide variety, it marked a point of culmination in the history of American musical comedy.

In 1940, a few years after Gershwin's death, the great English conductor, Albert Coates, listed the fifty best musical works of the generation. Only one American composition was included and but one American composer—George Gershwin and his *Concerto in F*.

Gershwin's memory is still verdant and his music continues to enjoy enormous popularity not only in his native land but also in countries of several continents. An American production of *Porgy and Bess*, officially blessed by the State Department, opened early in 1952 in Vienna and was received ecstatically. It then moved on to Berlin, where it was the highlight of the September Festival of Arts put on by the Western powers. In 1956 it pierced the Iron Curtain and was presented for the first time in Russia.

On July 12, 1953, the first jazz concert ever held in Florence, Italy, took place in the city's five hundred year old Pitti Palace. The main item on the program was Gershwin's *An American in Paris*, played by the Florentine Municipal Orchestra.

Three decades after his death, Gershwin's music is performed more often and is more widely acclaimed than ever.

Record companies ransacked his old scores for forgotten numbers and songs that had not been heard in forty years not only were rediscovered but, with a new generation, attained a new popularity. It was now conceded that, besides creating a vivid musical vocabulary, Gershwin had performed a valuable and unprecedented function. He had broken down the barrier between popular and classical music. He had the tone and the tempo of his age; he had given music a new racy speech and, for the first time in history, an American accent.

Other great American Jewish composers who caught the voice of American and enshrined it immortally in their songs are: Sigmund Romberg, Richard Rodgers, Aaron Copland, Ernest Bloch, Marc Blitzstein, and Leonard Bernstein.

*Al
Jolson*

§210

Alike on the stage, screen, and radio, American Jewish artists are known and loved as entertainers. One of the most enduring contributions in the field of entertainment was made by a Jewish performer by the name of Al Jolson.

Al Jolson, who was born Asa Yoelson, in 1886, in Russia, was brought to this country at the age of seven. As a youngster struck with the lure of the stage lights, he traveled with vaudeville and minstrel shows, sang in cafes and saloons, and followed circuses. He made his first stage appearance in 1899 at the Herald Square Theater in New York, as one of the mob in Israel Zangwill's production, *Children of the Ghetto*. After a long period in vaudeville, he achieved major stardom in the *Winter Garden Shows*.

At about this time the Warner Brothers, a family of Jewish immigrants who had established themselves as producers and distributors of motion pictures of the early nickelodeon type, were the first to sense the possibilities of the use of sound as applied to motion pictures. After witnessing the demonstration of a new device, they acquired the vitaphone and produced the first full-length sound picture, the historic *Jazz Singer*. It was based on Jolson's struggle for a career, dramatizing the plight of the singer torn between his own desire to be in show business and his father's plans to perpetuate a long line of cantors. Jolson, in the starring role, caused a revolt in the motion picture industry. Before the showing of this picture "talkies" were only an experiment. After its release they were put on a sound basis. Bringing to the industry the talents so essential for theatrical undertakings, Jolson also starred in *The Singing Fool* and *Mammy*, the next two "talkies."

In 1932 after several other stage successes, Jolson began his radio career as star of the first program in which running monologue was interspersed with song.

With *The Jolson Story* in 1947 and *Jolson Sings Again* in 1949, two great Hollywood successes produced by Sidney Skolsky. Jolson skyrocketed to even greater heights.

AL JOLSON

When Jolson sang, something happened to audiences. He had a spirit, a quality, that brought him close to every person who saw and heard him. Audiences felt what he felt. When he was sentimental, audiences wept—and frequently Jolson cried himself. When he shot onto a stage bursting with vitality and happiness, audiences grew suddenly happier. It was that quality that made him probably one of the most popular and most successful entertainers in American history.

Jolson died on October 23, 1950, in San Francisco. He had just returned from Korea, where he had given performances for soldiers. Twenty thousand persons jammed Hollywood Boulevard for his funeral. President Harry S. Truman sent a message that began:

"We have lost our Al"

Jolson wrote a will in which he left nine tenths of a $4,000,000 estate to charity, the money to be divided among Jewish, Catholic and Protestant causes.

To perpetuate Jolson's memory the movie industry has established the Al Jolson Award which is given annually to the showman who has contributed most during the current year toward the entertainment of servicemen.

In 1952 the first Al Jolson Award, a gold medal, went to Bob Hope, America's beloved movie, radio and television star.

A thousand legends sprang up about Al Jolson. Always, behind them was the sure magic of his art. But his own life had been his greatest performance.

Bernard Revel

1928 § BERNARD REVEL: Yeshiva University is His Monument

§212

From the beginning higher education in America was based on the theological school. To it were added liberal arts courses in sciences and graduate schools in many fields of learning leading to the great universities. The record of Yeshiva College, the first college of liberal arts and sciences under Jewish auspices in the entire history of the Diaspora, is in this tradition.

In 1897 a group of Jewish immigrants founded a small Yeshiva in New York's teeming Lower East Side for the study of the Torah and Talmudic literature. They named it the Rabbi Isaac Elchanan Theological Seminary in order to perpetuate fitly in America the memory of the celebrated Rabbi of Kovno, Lithuania, Rabbi Isaac Elchanan Spektor, who had passed away shortly before the founding of the Seminary.

The Rabbi Isaac Elchanan Theological Seminary was the first Yeshiva in the traditional sense to be established on the North American continent. While use of the designation Yeshiva in America dates back to 1728, when the Sephardic Congregation Shearith Israel opened its school under the name Yeshibat Minhat Areb, that school as well as the second known Yeshiva to be established here, the Machzike Jeshibath Eitz Chaim, founded in 1886, were elementary schools for children, which provided instruction in the general or secular studies along with the Jewish studies.

Early in 1915, the Boards of Directors of Rabbi Isaac Elchanan Theological Seminary and the Yeshiva Eitz Chaim decided upon a merger. Dr. Bernard Revel, the first American Orthodox rabbi to become a doctor of philosophy, was called in to preside over the merged institutions. Dr. Revel, a young and prosperous man, embodied in his own person the synthesis of Jewish learning and general culture, which the institutions were designated to inculcate. Foreseeing the increasingly important role America was to play in the activities of world Jewry he was determined to prove that it

DR. BERNARD REVEL

was possible to practice Orthodox Judaism in the midst of western civilization. All Jewish life could be based on the Torah as the hub from which all knowledge would radiate, with scientific knowledge as one of the spokes. Furthermore a dynamic and creative Torah life, clothed in the habiliments of science and humanistic learning, could prevent the slow demoralization of the Orthodox Jewish community by a mechanistic scientific environment. He sought to make Orthodox Judaism a living vibrant faith in a new world where competing philosophies were deflecting faith from the ancient heritage of Judaism.

The Jewish learning of the new president was indeed remarkable. The illustrious spiritual leader of Kovno's Jewish community, Rabbi Isaac Elchanan Spektor, predicted a brilliant future for Dov Revel after he examined the youngster in Talmud. Dov was the son of Rabbi Spector's colleague, Nachum Shraga Revel, the Rabbi of Pren. Born on September 17, 1885, Dov was pronounced the Prenner Illui (child genius) at the age of six, when he was able to recite many pages from the Talmudic tractate *Baba Kamma* by heart. Dov studied with his father until his untimely death in 1897. Although only twelve, Dov stood on the top of a crate and brilliantly eulogized his father at his funeral. Afterwards, Dov's family moved to Kovno, where Dov continued his studies under the guidance of Rabbi Isaac Blazer, a leading disciple of Rabbi Israel Salanter. Then he went to the Yeshive of Telshe.

At the age of sixteen, Dov Revel had attained such a mastery of Talmudic law that he was ordained a rabbi. In addition to mastering Talmudic literature, he also studied Jewish history and Hebrew language and literature on his own.

In 1906, Rabbi Dov Revel, using the name of Bernard as a translation of his Hebrew name, arrived in the United States at the age of twenty-one. He immediately entered the Rabbi Isaac Elchanan Theological Seminary where Orthodox scholars, most of whom had received their early training in Europe, continued their studies of Talmud and commentaries.

Rabbi Bernard Leventhal, the leading Orthodox rabbi of Philadelphia, met Rabbi Revel at the Yeshiva and persuaded him to return with him to Philadelphia to serve as his secretary and assistant. He encouraged the young man to perfect his English and to study at Temple University. After one semester, Rabbi Revel took up studies at New York University.

In 1906, Bernard Revel knew no English and had never attended a general college. Three years later he received not a B.A. or regular college degree, but the higher degree of Master of Arts in Philosophy from New York University.

Rabbi Revel continued his education in Philadelphia. He enrolled in Dropsie College, newly organized to impart advanced study in Hebrew and other Jewish subjects. As the first graduate of Dropsie, he obtained his degree of Doctor of Philosophy in 1912.

There had been hopes for many years of building up a strong institution of Torah learning for the Orthodox community of America. In 1915 at the urging of Rabbi Moses Z. Margolis, the dean of the American Orthodox rabbinate, Dr. Revel accepted the position of president of the recently merged Rabbi Isaac Elchanan Theological Seminary and Yeshiva Eitz Chaim. Students could now begin their study at the Yeshiva high school level and continue to study for rabbinic ordination.

The next twenty-five years, under Dr. Revel's leadership, the institution told an amazing story of progress and growth. Dr. Revel's first task was to organize the high school department to fulfill the requirements of the State of New York and to provide all studies given by the public high schools. At the same time, a full program of traditional Jewish studies was emphasized. From the beginning, in spite of the long hours and double program, students at the new Talmudical Academy ranked in the top level in scholastic competitions and admission to colleges.

In 1921, the Teachers' Institute founded by the Mizrachi Organization of America in 1917 to train orthodox teachers and supervisors for the Hebrew schools of the United States and Canada, became an integral part of the Yeshiva, and the growing institution moved to larger quarters on the Lower East Side.

The increased student body and expanded activities of the institution, in a few years, began to outgrow the new quarters. At the same time, a large number of Yeshiva students were simultaneously continuing their general education on the college level, in the late afternoon and evening, under hardships and excessive strain. Their main difficulties helped to emphasize the advantages of establishing, as a part of the Yeshiva, a college of liberal arts and science wherein the students of the Yeshiva, and ultimately other qualified students, might pursue their academic studies in what Dr. Revel termed an "atmosphere harmonizing the age-old truths and ideals of faith and culture with the fruits of modern knowledge."

In late 1923 Dr. Revel announced his plans for the organization of a liberal arts college to enable graduates of the Yeshiva's high school to continue their studies in a college administered by the Yeshiva. The foundation for the transforming of the Yeshiva into a degree-granting institution was laid on March 27, 1924, when its charter was amended by the Regents of the University of the State of New York, to authorize the institution to confer the degree of Doctor of Hebrew Literature. Dreams and means were pooled, and on May 1, 1927, the cornerstone of the present home of the institution, on Amsterdam Avenue, 186th and 187th Streets in uptown Manhattan, was laid. These buildings, which were erected at a cost of $2,500,000 were dedicated on December 9, 1928, in the presence of hosts of Jews from all over the United States.

In September of that year the college opened its doors with a full-time faculty and distinguished associate faculty consisting of eminent Jewish and gentile professors. For the first time in Jewish history, a Yeshiva was housed and equipped in a manner that compared favorably with the facilities generally provided for the better public and private educational institutions. The authority to offer courses leading to the degrees of Bachelor of Arts and Bachelor of Science was granted it.

The student body was required to attend simultaneously either the Rabbi Isaac Theological Seminary preparing students for the rabbinate or the Teachers' Institute, for a full program of Jewish studies, in addition to the college program. Since it was intended that the Jewish education should be in addition to, and not in the place of, a thorough college program of liberal studies, little credit —only two points a semester of the one hundred and twenty-eight required for graduation—was allowed for the Jewish studies, toward the satisfaction of the requirements for the Bachelor's degree.

Bernard
Revel

§216

In September 1932, the first number of *Scripta Mathematica*, a quarterly journal devoted to the philosophy, history and expository treatment of mathematics, appeared. Subsequently, *Scripta Mathematica* was greatly extended and expanded and three other publications were launched: *Horeb*, a semi-annual in Hebrew devoted to original studies and research in Jewish history and literature; *Talpioth*, a Hebrew quarterly devoted to source materials in Jewish law and ethics, their exposition and application; and *Sura*, an annual in Hebrew designed to serve as a bridge between Jewish life in Israel and that in the Diaspora.

As Dr. Revel's twenty-fifth year with the Yeshiva began, the faculty made plans for an elaborate celebration. Originally scheduled for the end of 1940, the meeting was postponed so that the Chief Rabbi Isaac Herzog of Palestine could come.

These plans did not come to fruition. While delivering a lecture to a senior rabbinic class on November 19, 1940, Dr. Revel suffered a stroke. Two weeks later he died at the Mount Sinai Hospital at the age of fifty-five.

In his last written article he found some comfort in the fact that, " . . . before the spiritual sun of Israel has set in Europe, a sanctuary of the eternal soul of Israel has been started on this continent."

Dr. Revel realized his ambition to organize a graduate department in advanced Jewish studies. In line with the authority acquired through the 1924 amendment to its charter, the Yeshiva began to offer graduate work in 1935. In 1937, these courses were embodied in the Yeshiva Graduate School, which in 1941, was renamed the Bernard Revel Graduate School, as a memorial to the institution's first president.

In 1945, the Regents of the University of the State of New York conferred university rank upon Yeshiva College and it became the first American university under Jewish auspices.

In 1950, the same body amended the Yeshiva charter permitting the establishment of a medical and dental school. Today, the Albert Einstein College of Medicine of Yeshiva University, the heart of a $200,000,000 medical city, marks the first medical school under Jewish sponsorship in the history of Diaspora Jewry.

In 1954, a gift of $500,000 made by Max Stern, prominent New York City industrialist, enabled Yeshiva University to open Stern College for Women, the nation's only liberal arts college for women under Jewish auspices.

As Yeshiva University expands, so does the name of its founder, Bernard Revel, become enshrined even deeper in the historical scene of American Judaism.

Yeshiva University stands as his monument—stately, dignified and secure. It is a living testimony to the man who built it and gave it his life.

1939 § ALBERT EINSTEIN: Father of the Atomic Age

Albert Einstein changed the world we live in. It was he who fathered, for better or for worse, the atomic age.

Until Einstein evolved his epic Theory of Relativity, physicists believed that matter (for example, a bar of uranium or a brick) and energy (heat, for instance) were two different things, neither of which could be created or destroyed. But Einstein said that the physicists were wrong.

All matter was actually energy in a different form, he declared. According to his thinking, matter could be transformed into energy (or vice versa) under the formula $E=mc^2$. Spelled out, this stated that Energy equals Mass (mass being the amount of matter) times the Velocity of Light (186,000 miles per second) squared.

To scientists, this theory was radical beyond words. If it was valid, it meant that there was an incredible amount of energy locked up in every form of matter, regardless of how small. It meant that the splitting of a few tiny atoms would liberate power greater than any ever dreamed of by man.

His theory further endeavored to explain the entire relationship of mass, gravity, space and time. It held, in part, that there was mass even in a beam of light and that, in a universe in which space and time were inseparable quantities, a single beam of light could be affected by the tugging of gravity.

At first many of the scientists thought that the German born physicist was wrong. It took an eclipse of the sun before they would admit that Einstein was one of the greatest thinkers of all time.

The eclipse occurred in 1918 and it afforded astronomers a chance to see in the blacked-out sky whether light coming from the stars

ALBERT EINSTEIN

would be deflected by the gravitational pull of the sun, as Einstein predicted it would be.

Physicists on five continents waited impatiently for the results, and the results were precisely what Einstein had anticipated.

In 1932 laboratory experiments also showed that Einstein's $E=mc^2$ formula was valid.

Einstein's revolutionary import did not stop with his Theory of Relativity. In 1950 he brought forth another theory, one which may prove to be more important than his definition of relativity.

"The Unified Field Theory," Einstein termed this, and in it he sought to show that every form of nature—planets, stars, electricity, light, the very particle inside the atom—obeys the same basic natural laws.

Einstein referred to the international reception of his triumphs with dry humor. It is merely, he wrote, another proof of relativity. "Today in Germany I am hailed as a German man of science and in England I am pleasantly represented as a foreign Jew. But if ever my theories are repudiated, the Germans will condemn me as a foreign Jew and the English will dismiss me as German."

He was born on March 14, 1879, in Ulm, a small Württemberg city in Bavarian Germany. The Einstein family was well-to-do; the father, an engineer, owned the town's electro-technical works, but business made it imperative for the Einsteins to move to Milan, Italy, in 1894. Most of Albert's youth, however, was spent in Munich, where he received his early education. It was not until he was fourteen that he showed his mathematical talents. Then he startled his schoolmasters by learning integral calculus and analytical geometry all by himself. At seventeen he studied at the Zurich Polytechnical School in Switzerland, later winning his Ph.D. from the University of Zurich. In 1902 he became a Swiss citizen and obtained a position as an examiner in the patent office in Berne.

In 1905 the *Annalen de Physik* published a thirty page paper by the twenty-six-year old Einstein, "On the Electrodynamics of Moving Bodies," a modestly entitled and seemingly academic document which was destined to alter our whole concept of the properties of matter as well as the structure of the universe. Its impact was not grasped at first, but it became apparent by 1920, when a translation of Einstein's *Relativity, The Special and General Theory* challenged physicists and mathematicians throughout the world.

Although his Special and General Theories of Relativity had wrought more of a revolution in science than the works of any other man, Einstein continued to seek more accurate descriptions of the physical universe. In 1921 his modifications of the prevailing theories of radiant energy—particularly in his extension of Planck's quantum principle that radiant energy is emitted in a broken stream of particles or "quanta"—won for him the coveted Nobel Prize. The results of his investigations included the equation known as "Einstein's Photoelectric Law." An outgrowth of this law was the "electric eye" which made possible television, sound motion pictures and numerous modern inventions.

Einstein had been professor of theoretical physics at the German University in Prague, was a member of the Prussian Academy and had moved to Berlin.

In 1933 Adolph Hitler rose to power in Nazi Germany and internal conditions even for Jews with world reputations made it inadvisable for him to remain in the country. All of his possessions and his bank account were confiscated by the state. He forsook Germany and came to America, where he was given a lifetime professorship at the Institute for Advanced Studies in Princeton, New Jersey. He became an American citizen in 1940.

Although he had always been a fervent pacifist, on October 11, 1939, a month and a day before the Pearl Harbor incident, Einstein sent a letter to President Franklin D. Roosevelt, pointing out that "the

Germans are working on atomic fission and the United States must start research at once or civilization will perish."

The President acted. The United States government's program on atomic research was set in motion and four billion dollars of the American taxpayers' money was risked on the Manhattan Project. An advisory committee on uranium was appointed. Research was carried on simultaneously in many American universities. The most significant development was the first successful atomic "chair reaction pile," achieved on the squash courts of the University of Chicago. Meanwhile the United States atomic power development program at Los Alamos, New Mexico, the most sensational scientific undertaking of modern times, was placed under the direction of Dr. J. Robert Oppenheimer, a forty-one year old Jewish physicist.

At 5:30 A.M. on July 16, 1945, the skies over the desert lands of New Mexico were rent by a terrifying explosion. Its dazzling burst of light was brighter than the noonday sun; its heat melted the desert sands and rocks together. A great volcano of dust and debris churned from the desert and seethed high into the sky.

The group of scientists assigned to the Los Alamos branch, working on Einstein's equation of the conversion of matter into energy and the uranium fission theory evolved by Niels Bohr, the Nobel Prize winning physicist from Denmark, and his Jewish colleague, Lise Meitner, were enabled to make the atom bomb. Their experimental bomb—perhaps the most important single experiment ever attempted by man—was a success. The key to the release of the almost limitless power within the atom had been found. Man had entered into the age of atomic energy.

When the U. S. Army Air Force dropped the atomic bomb on Hiroshima, on August 6, 1945, eighty thousand people died as a result of the application of Einstein's abstruse reasoning. By this time it was agreed that the physicist's theories had caused the greatest revolution in science since Galileo.

Einstein himself was a gifted writer and had published several volumes. His general writings are available in three major collections in English: *The World As I See It* (1934), *Out of My Later Years* (1950) and *Ideas and Opinions* (1954). In them, as in his frequent speeches, he fought hard for peace, for democracy, for Zionism and for tolerance. He declared his faith in a completely logical universe: "I cannot believe," he said, "that God plays dice with the cosmos."

Nearing seventy-five Einstein was honored all over the world. More than five thousand books and pamphlets in every language had been published about him and his work. His presence at a dinner helped raise several million dollars to build the Albert Einstein College of Medicine of Yeshiva University.

After a sudden brief illness, Einstein died at the age of seventy-six. Apparently he had been suffering from hardening of the arteries, which caused an arterial rupture and death occurred on April 18, 1955.

Even in his last days Einstein's thoughts were only of science. For in his will, Einstein left his brain to science, the brain that had revolutionized human thought.

1943 § SELMAN A. WAKSMAN: Discoverer of a Wonder Drug

For twenty-eight years, Dr. Selman Abraham Waksman pored over the test tubes and flasks in his cluttered little laboratory in the Rutgers University College of Agriculture, searching for microorganisms in the soil that would prove beneficial to mankind.

It was the theory of this microbiologist that "there are probably more different kinds of tiny plants and animals in the soil than there are on top of it."

And that there is a continuous warfare in the earth between these countless microorganisms, with each type using its own chemical weapons to prevent the growth and even to kill off the others.

And that scientists could isolate these chemical weapons for which he coined the name "antibiotics" (meaning "against life"), and use them as a means of destroying such types of microorganisms as do injury to man, animals and plants.

Those twenty-eight years were filled with disappointments for Dr. Waksman, but at the end of them, in 1943, he discovered streptomycin, the "wonder drug" that comes close to penicillin in life-saving powers.

The development of the antibiotic program was a difficult assignment. He had to find an antibiotic which would kill man-harming microbes without itself doing harm to man.

As he has said: "We had to look for selective poisons, substances that would destroy certain bacteria, or inhibit their growth, without affecting the cells of the human body."

This meant testing and retesting thousands of microorganisms one

DR. SELMAN A. WAKSMAN

after the other. Some, like actionomycin and streptothricin, produced by microbes of the streptomyces type, which he found in soil taken right out of the Rutgers campus, in New Brunswick, New Jersey, looked promising but proved to be worthless in the treatment of human diseases. Others, like gramicidin, produced by a soil bacillus, which one of his ex-students, René Dubos, found in a mixture of different soils, had disease-killing potentialities but turned out to be injurious to humans.

And continually there were obstacles. In 1941, for example, a university official urged that Waksman, who was earning a very meagre salary, be dismissed as a matter of economy since his work was considered too theoretical. Providentially, Rutgers did not follow his advice.

Then in 1943, a local poultryman brought a sick chicken to the Rutgers College of Agriculture for diagnosis. The poultry pathologist saw something unusual in the chicken's throat, took a culture of it, and sent it to Waksman for his examination.

Interested, Waksman nurtured the culture and ran some experiments with it. He saw that the culture (and one very similar to it which was soon isolated in his laboratory from heavily fertilized soil) produced highly effective antibiotics.

Both organisms, he found, were strains of a group of microbes, the actinomycetes, which he had previously studied extensively. He named the culture *Streptomyces griseus*. It was similar to one he had isolated from the soil in 1915, but, unlike the old one, these were deadly germ-killers. In the test tube, they actually killed many disease-producing bacteria, including one of the toughest of all disease germs, the tuberculosis organism, commonly known as the tubercle bacillus.

But would they do as much in humans?

After successful test-tube experiments carried out by Waksman and his students, streptomycin was tried on experimental animals and then on the most desperately ill patients suffering from tuberculosis at the Mayo Clinic in Rochester, Minnesota. The patients fought a close battle with death, and thanks to treatment with streptomycin, they won. For the first time, mankind had a genuinely effective weapon against "the white plague." It was soon apparent that streptomycin was also effective against virulent forms of pneumonia, meningitis, whooping cough, dysentery, gonorrhea and many infections resistant to or not responding to penicillin and the sulpha drugs.

The isolation of streptomycin proved to be a turning point in the study of antibiotics not only in Waksman's laboratory, but in numerous other university and industrial laboratories throughout the world. The particular significance of streptomycin was its action upon both gram-positive and gram-negative bacteria and the tuberculosis organism. Screening programs designed to isolate new antibiotics were now universally initiated. Waksman and his students and associates subsequently isolated several new compounds produced by other species of *Streptomyces*. Most important were "neomycin," and "streptothricin." These compounds along with streptomycin came to occupy a highly important place in the chemotherapy of human and animal diseases.

Waksman signed over his rights to the earnings of the drugs to the Rutgers Research and Endowment Foundation which used the money to build an Institute of Microbiology. One of the most unique institutions of its kind in the world, it embraces various branches of microbiology and ranges from ecology to molecular biology.

At the present time some twenty companies in the United States and elsewhere in the world are engaged in the manufacture of streptomycin. Merck & Co. was the first one to put it on the market. For every gram (1/28 of an ounce, now valued in bulk at only three cents) sold, Rutgers receives a two and a half per cent royalty. By last count the university's harvest of pennies reached over $15,000,000.

Selman Abraham Waksman, the man who started it all, was born on July 22, 1888, in a small town (Novaia-Priluka) in the Ukraine,

Selman A. Waksman

§223

Russia, not far from the city of Kiev, the son of Jacob Waksman and Fradia London. His father, a weaver by training, wanted him to take up industrial chemistry, but young Waksman was far more interested in biology. After graduating in 1910 from the Fifth *Gymnasium* in Odessa, he left Russia for the United States. He planned first to study bio-chemistry but chose soil microbiology and enrolled in the College of Agriculture at Rutgers. He received his bachelor's degree in 1915 and became a naturalized citizen the same year. He was then appointed research assistant in soil microbiology at the New Jersey Agricultural Experiment Station and continued with his graduate work at Rutgers, obtaining his master's degree in 1916. He was then appointed Research Fellow at the University of California where he received his Ph.D. under the famous biochemist Brailsford Robertson in 1918. This was followed by an invitation to return to Rutgers, where he received an appointment as microbiologist at the Experimental Station and as lecturer in soil microbiology at the university. He was made associate professor in 1925 and full professor in 1930. In 1931 he was invited to organize a division of Marine Bacteriology at the Woods Hole Oceanographic Institution and was appointed a marine bacteriologist at that institution. When Rutgers organized its Department of Microbiology in 1940, he became professor of microbiology and head of the department. In 1949 he was named first director of the multi-million dollar Institute of Microbiology.

In 1948 Rutgers University gave Dr. Waksman a ten per cent share in the royalties accruing from the production of streptomycin. Out of this sum he devoted one-half to the establishment of a Foundation for Microbiology for the purpose of assisting in the development of microbiology in any country or any institution if such support was needed.

Dr. Waksman has published more than 400 scientific papers and has written alone or with others, twenty-five books largely in the fields of microbiology and antibiotics. Among these are the following: *Enzymes, Principles of Soil Microbiology, The Soil and the Microbe, Humus* and several volumes on *The Antinomycetes*. In 1954 he published his autobiography *My Life With the Microbes*, a literary best-seller. Recently he published another popular book, *The Conquest of Tuberculosis*.

For his great scientific achievements, Dr. Waksman has been honored in all parts of the world, everywhere from Spain and Greece to Sweden, Denmark, Holland and Israel. Even the U.S.S.R. Academy of Sciences offered him 15,000 rubles for the right to publish some lectures he delivered in Moscow. He is the recipient of honorary degrees ranging from law to medicine, from twenty universities throughout the globe. To crown it all, in 1952, he was awarded the coveted Nobel Prize in Physiology and Medicine.

In September of 1958, Dr. Waksman, at the age of seventy, retired as director of the Institute of Microbiology but still maintains an office and laboratory there. His plan is to continue working largely with the activities of the microbes in an attempt to seek more effective cures for other diseases.

1943 § LEONARD BERNSTEIN: Music's Spokesman

On November 14, 1943, a virtually unknown young man of twenty-five was suddenly called upon to conduct the great New York Philharmonic Orchestra, substituting for the indisposed Bruno Walter. So extraordinary was his talent and so electrifying his personality that his unscheduled appearance was front page news the next day. Critics and concertgoers alike hailed Leonard Bernstein's "brilliant musicianship," "the authenticity of his interpretations" as well as "the excellent and exciting qualities" of his performance.

The young man went on to repeat his triumph many times. He appeared as guest conductor with the world's major symphony orchestras. Wherever he conducted, here or abroad, he received ovation after ovation for his "absolute fidelity to a composer's score," "flawlessness of detail" and "a genuine luminosity of tone."

In 1953 he made his operatic debut conducting at La Scala Opera House in Milan. He was the first American-born conductor to conduct at La Scala.

The citizens of Israel packed the streets, as for a conquering hero, when Bernstein first came to conduct there in 1957.

It was that way, too, when he went to Israel on July 9, 1967, and conducted the Israel Philharmonic Orchestra in a victory concert on Mt. Scopus in Old Jerusalem.

For almost twenty-five years now, his name has been the mark of soul-stirring music to the people of four continents.

Nevertheless, Bernstein's fame does not rest on his achievements as a conductor alone. In his various orchestral appearances he has frequently doubled as conductor-pianist, and his performance of concerti by Mozart, Beethoven and Ravel have revealed him to be a pianist of unusual sttainment.

The first of Bernstein's compositions to win wide fame was his "Jeremiah" Symphony which won the award of the Music Critics Circle of New York as the "Most Outstanding Orchestral Work by an American composer introduced during the 1943-1944 season." In the same year came the first performance of his "Fancy Free," a ballet which attained an enormous popularity. In October of 1946, the Ballet Theater introduced his ballet "Facsimile," which like "Fancy Free" was choreographed by Jerome Robbins.

Leonard Bernstein

§226

In December of 1944 he made his first foray into the rigors of the Broadway Theater with the youthful gaiety and vivacity of *On the Town*. In the Fall of 1956 his *Candide*, written in collaboration with Lillian Hellman, was introduced to Broadway. *West Side Story* which opened in New York in September of 1957, and in London a little over a year later, was a great success in both cities. The British production won the 1960 London Critic's Award for the best musical of the year. The moving picture production of *West Side Story* was hailed as the "Best Picture of 1961," receiving ten Academy Awards. Bernstein also wrote the incidental music for the Broadway production of Barrie's *Peter Pan*, for Christopher Fry's *The Lark*, and the score for the Oscar-winning film *On the Waterfront*.

Throughout the years of writing musical comedies, Bernstein has continued his serious compositions, and among these works are his "The Age of Anxiety"; the one-act opera *Trouble in Tahiti;* the Serenade for Violin Solo and String Orchestra with Percussion; the Symphony No. 3, "Kaddish"; and the "Chichester Psalms" for chorus and orchestra. His works also include two song cycles, three sets of "Anniversaries" for piano and a group of pieces for brass instruments.

This unusual man who became a vital force in the music of our country was born in Lawrence, Massachusetts on August 25, 1918, and grew up in Boston. Leonard Bernstein was not a child prodigy. He showed no particular interest in music until his tenth year when a relative sent her old upright piano to the Bernsteins to keep for her. Leonard found it a challenge. "I touched it. It made pretty sounds. Right away, I screamed: Ma, give me lessons." A month of lessons convinced him that he was going to be a musician. This decision did not interfere with young Leonard's ordinary activities no more than if he would have decided to become a doctor or a lawyer. At the Boston Latin School he was a favorite athlete. Later he enrolled at Harvard University with the intention of becoming

LEONARD BERNSTEIN

a pianist. Upon graduation from Harvard in 1938 Bernstein felt that piano playing was not exhaustive enough from the point of view of expression. As a student he demonstrated his uncanny ability to memorize entire scores and he had a sense of style. He impressed such notables as Dimitri Mitropoulos and Aaron Copland who suggested that he study conducting. To this end Bernstein spent two years of graduate study at the Curtis Institute in Philadelphia where he studied under Fritz Reiner. During the summers he worked under Serge Koussevitzky, conductor of the Boston Symphony Orchestra, at the Berkshire Music Center in Tanglewood, Massachusetts.

In September of 1942 after a season spent in teaching and composing a "Sonata for Clarinet" (his first published work) and producing a number of operas for the Boston Institute of Modern Art, Bernstein was appointed assistant to Koussevitzky.

The following season found Bernstein appearing in New York as pianist and conductor.

While at Tanglewood he had already caught the eye of Artur Rodzinski, then Musical Director of the New York Philharmonic, who engaged Bernstein as Assistant Conductor of the orchestra for the 1943-1944 season. When he replaced guest conductor Bruno Walter, he began his unswerving march to the pinnacle of musical fame.

From 1951 through 1955 Bernstein was head of the Orchestra and Conducting Department of the Berkshire Music Center and from 1951 to 1956, he was professor of music at Brandeis University.

At frequent intervals he appeared on the Philharmonic podium as guest conductor. With Dimitri Mitropoulos, he was one of the two principal conductors of the Philharmonic in 1957–1958, before he became permanent Musical Director in 1958.

The first American-born and trained Musical Director of the New York Philharmonic, he brought new prestige, popularity and informality to America's oldest symphony orchestra. He enthusiastically began to conduct the kind of music avoided by the Philharmonic and other members of the orchestral Establishment. Oriented to the twentieth century, he offered music of his own time, Stravinsky, Bartok, Hindemith, Shostakovich, Copland—they all figured prominently in his programs in addition to the standard repertory.

Leonard Bernstein made his television debut in 1954 on the "Omnibus" television program, a forerunner of the later CBS series, "Leonard Bernstein and the New York Philharmonic" in which he turned the entire country into his classroom. Because of his many coast-to-coast television appearances, recording and public lectures in which he widened our capacity to respond to the many styles and kinds of great music, he has been called "music's most articulate spokesman." He has an unusual ability for presenting difficult concepts in down-to-earth English and as a remarkably endowed pianist, he can illustrate his lectures with complete authority.

Believing that there is a happy medium between the "music appreciation racket" and purely technical discussion, he wrote his first book, *The Joy of Music*, to stress the point. It immediately appeared on best-seller lists throughout the nation and has sold more than 100,000 copies in this country alone.

Bernstein's genius for intensifying our pleasure in music, in making clear its language, its forms and its intentions also shines through the pages of his book *The Infinite Variety of Music*.

As in his lectures, his discourses range from the glory of Mozart to the ludicrousness of canned "music" that assaults us in planes and elevators, from the classic tradition to the challenges facing today's serious avant-guard composer.

Of his work Virgil Thomson wrote in the "New York Herald Tribune:" "It is as if all the most important questions about music were being answered by a man of knowledge, talent, experience and consecration."

Leonard Bernstein will not return as Music Director of the New

York Philharmonic when his current contract expires in the Spring of 1969. He intends to concentrate on composing.

In 1969 he will become "Laureate Conductor" of the New York Philharmonic, a title especially created for him. By then he will have held the directorship longer than any conductor since the Philharmonic and the New York Symphony were merged in 1928 and Toscanini was made musical director. To date Bernstein has conducted more concerts than anyone in its one hundred and twenty-five year history. His 736th performance was given in 1966.

Bernstein's fervent absorption in music has not shaded his awareness of world problems. As an adherent to the Jewish religion he feels deeply the problems of "a whole people in a world of no security" which moved him to write his "Jeremiah Symphony." While he does not feel obligated to project a specific type of Jewish music, he maintains that when a musician expresses himself sincerely, he creates out of his own integrity and heritage without self-consciousness.

When he was nineteen, a world-famous conductor urged him to change his name for he was warned that a name like "Bernstein" would prove too great an obstacle to success. But Leonard Bernstein refused to search for a place for himself in the world under an assumed name. And the world is infinitely richer for his dedication to his art as a brilliant conductor, a composer of serious works, musical comedies, ballets and modern jazz and for his writing, teaching and lecturing.

1947 § BERNARD BARUCH: Faithful Public Servant

Bernard Baruch was thirty years old at the turn of the century. By then he had made, lost and remade a million dollars in Wall Street speculation. Not content solely with material achievements, he turned to politics, and during the years of the New Freedom was drawn into the circle of the Democratic Party's high command.

A faithful public servant of the American people throughout the regimes of nine presidents from Woodrow Wilson to Lyndon Johnson, his unselfish deeds have made him an American legend. During America's two World Wars and the Korean Conflict, he was the one individual, though not an official of any government agency, called upon to help solve a nation's crisis. Heralded as "adviser to presidents" and in his later years as America's "elder statesman," he was the one individual whose advice was eagerly sought by presidents, important Washington agencies, cabinet officials, congressional leaders and the people at large.

His chance to serve came first, when, as an advocate of economic as well as military preparedness, he was appointed by President Wilson to the advisory commission of the Council of National Defense in 1916. This in turn led to his role as chairman of the War Industries Board, the managing agency of America's industrial mobilization. From his WIB experiences Baruch learned lessons to which he referred on numerous occasions: the need to have ready for times of crisis a total mobilization program, and the feasibility of government economic planning. Twenty-five years and one war later Baruch lent his efforts to the even more staggering demands for total economic mobilization. Then, though invited to head various agencies and appreciating the value of his independent position, he served mainly in unofficial capacity as adviser on industrial problems.

In 1934 when the United States was more interested in regaining its economic equilibrium than in rebuilding its defenses, Baruch—always the apostle of preparedness—warned of war and urged the stockpiling of strategic materials. War is coming, and it will find us desperately short, he said. How right he was history has demonstrated.

In 1937 Baruch urged an apathetic government to prepare an economic mobilization plan for war. We must get our plans ready now or it will cost us thousands of wasted lives and billions of wasted dollars later, he argued. Again as events showed, he was right.

In January of 1941, Baruch came out for an immediate freeze on prices, rents and wages. If we wait, it will mean inflation, he stated. Here, too, he was right.

In 1942 President Roosevelt asked him to investigate the alarming rubber shortage. Within thirty-seven days, Baruch brought in one of the bluntest reports ever submitted to the president. Almost all of his drastic recommendations—restricted annual mileage for cars, a nationwide speed limit of thirty-five miles an hour, gas rationing—were put into effect and the wartime rubber problem was eased.

When the Korean Conflict broke out, President Truman told Congress that merely a few economic controls were needed to speed the rearmament program. Baruch disagreed. He urged Congress to enact

Bernard Baruch

§230

all-out regulation. Congress listened to Baruch and the legislation it passed was along the lines he advocated.

When peace time problems supplemented those of war, President Kennedy summoned Baruch to help work out a way of life for the American people.

Adviser to the mighty and friend to the little man, Bernard Mannes Baruch was born in Camden, South Carolina on August 19, 1870. It was his proud boast that on his mother's side there were seven generations of Americans of Spanish and Portuguese descent behind him, so that he was a lineal descendant of the Sephardim. His father, Dr. Simon Baruch, who had served as a surgeon in the Confederate Army, was a German immigrant, partly of Polish descent.

Bernard Baruch

§231

When Bernard was eleven years old, his father decided to move with his family from Camden to New York City. Soon after his arrival, Dr. Baruch was appointed first chairman of the medical board of the Montefiore Hospital and became one of the prominent medical men of the city. To Dr. Baruch goes the credit for first diagnosing and successfully operating upon a patient with a perforated appendix and for the development of surgical techniques in appendectomy. He was the pioneer exponent of hydrotherapy in the United States. It was due to his efforts that free municipal bathhouses were established first in Chicago, then in New York and later in more than one hundred other cities.

Bernard was sent to the College of the City of New York from which he graduated in 1889 and to which in later years he made many endowments. After graduation he entered the Wall Street brokerage firm of A. A. Hausman and Company as a clerk at three dollars a week. With his modest earnings plus six hundred dollars borrowed from his mother, he began to buy and sell stocks. In 1896 he was made a partner of the firm and for a number of years following was a highly successful member of the New York Stock Exchange. Some of Baruch's business associates, respecting his judgment, persuaded him to investigate business conditions for them in the West; and while on this trip he bought the Liggett and Myers Tobacco Company outright. His judgment in financial matters was such that almost everything he touched turned to gold. At the age of thirty, he became known as America's most fascinating financier and was making and losing fortunes. Another one of his coups consisted of selling a railroad to J. P. Morgan at a profit of ten million dollars.

Before, during, and after World War I, Baruch held nine government posts under Presidents Wilson and Harding, including the chairmanship of the War Industries Board. It was his "know how" in this capacity that enabled America to defeat Kaiser Wilhelm. In 1919 he served as a member of the American Commission to Negotiate Peace, as economic adviser to the American Peace Commission, and also as member of the President's Conference for Capital and Labor. During World War II, whether it was the broad problems of defense, the manpower squeeze, lagging airplane production, or factory reconversion. Presidents Roosevelt and Truman summoned this man of many facets to devise escape from the bewildering tangles.

*Bernard
Baruch*

§232

In 1946, upon reaching the three score and ten mark, for nine long months Bernard Baruch began the most important job of his career. As United States representative on the Atomic Energy Commission of the United Nations, Baruch grappled with the most dreaded and mightiest force man had ever unleashed, atomic power. He formulated the Baruch proposals for international control of atomic energy. In lauding the "elder statesman's" tireless and patriotic endeavors on behalf of atomic control, ex-President Truman asserted that the prevention of atomic war was a tribute to Baruch's patience and skill.

It was precisely because of his profound faith in moral values and basic human decencies that Mr. Baruch chided the nations of the world, including our own, for their lack of moral watchfulness in approaching the Jewish problem, and refusing admission of Jewish refugees to Israel. Despite his hard work, he had kept a watchful eye on what was going on in Europe; and rose to almost prophetic heights when he told an audinece early in 1950 that "politics of a dubious nature had swayed the world from the plainly marked path of duty."

Yet while in the midst of an atomic bomb controversy which itself reflects and epitomizes the moral decline of man, Mr. Baruch had faith to assert that "the moral side of the Palestine and refugee question had been ignored and wiped out," thus presupposing the existence of moral factors and considerations in international and human relations.

The Wall Street wizard who made, lost and remade several fortunes, gave away over $3,000,000 to charity.

In 1944 he created the Baruch Committee on Physical Medicine in honor of his father, Dr. Simon Baruch. The work of the committee, which functioned until 1949, laid the basis for modern concepts of physical medicine and rehabilitation.

Among its activities were the granting of $400,000 to the Columbia

University College of Physicians and Surgeons, $250,000 to the Medical College of Virginia and $250,000 to New York University to establish programs in physical medicine and rehabilitation.

When the committee was organized there were no teaching programs for physical medicine and rehabilitation in our medical schools.

Today, most of our medical schools have departments for physical medicine and rehabilitation and at least seventy of them conduct teaching programs.

Bernard Baruch

In 1948 the specialty was formally recognized by the creation of the American Board of Physical Medicine and Rehabilitation.

§233

Many honors were bestowed upon Bernard Baruch. None were more rewarding than his knowledge that as a result of his personal interest and the work of the Baruch committee, millions of physically handicapped persons not only in the United States but throughout the world have had an opportunity for rehabilitation which has permitted them to become dignified, productive citizens.

On August 19, 1960, in Washington's Lafayette Park, the leafy square across the street from the White House, there was dedicated a "Bernard Baruch Bench of Inspiration." It marked the ninetieth birthday of the parkbench statesman. For many years it had been a common sight to see him conferring there with top officials, bestarred generals, foreign ambassadors and the "Who's Who" of the world. (He had a park bench "office" in New York's Central Park, too.)

On the eve of his 94th birthday, he said he wished he felt as he did at "93 or 92."

He said that at 92 he went bird hunting. But now "I can't keep up with the dogs, I can't keep up with the birds, and I can't keep up with the people."

Bernard Baruch died on June 20, 1965, a few months before he was to have celebrated his 95th birthday. To the end he continued to write letters to newspapers and made his views known on many topics. Baruch felt that the greatest contributing factor to the increased lifespan of the average American today, was "private enterprise."

The subject of several full-length biographies, Bernard Baruch had written *My Own Story* and its sequel, *The Public Years*, which recounts his public services for four decades. Looking back at his experiences, Baruch interweaves his philosophy of government, service and values.

The public record of Baruch's legendary career reveals only two known examples of involvement in Jewish matters. In 1919 he intervened with a Polish statesman on behalf of the suffering Jews of that country and in 1946 he delivered an address at a dinner of the United Jewish Appeal. On occasion he accepted honors from Jewish organizations.

He had been a life-long member of New York's Reform Temple Shaaray Tefila. After his mother passed away Baruch continued to visit that temple every Yom Kippur in respect to her memory.

Bernard Baruch

§234

1947 § ABBA HILLEL SILVER: Champion of Zionism

Since the destruction of the Second Temple in Jerusalem in the year 70 C.E., Jews have always looked in constant hope and prayer for their return to the city and land of their birth.

Modern Zionism was actually begun and practical work for the rebuilding of the Jewish National Homeland started when the first Zionist Congress was called by Theodor Herzl in Basle, Switzerland, almost seventy years ago.

A new type of leadership, closely attuned to the American scene but motivated by classic Zionist concepts was exemplified by Rabbi Abba Hillel Silver of Cleveland, a leading figure in the work of the Central Conference of American Rabbis, and in Jewish affairs for almost half a century.

Rabbi Silver was born in Lithuania, the son of a rabbi. He was a member of the fifth generation in his family to become a rabbi.

He came to this country at the age of eight and grew up on New York's Lower East Side. He studied at the University of Cincinnati and at the Hebrew Union College, being ordained a Reform rabbi in 1915.

His first congregation was in Wheeling, West Virginia. In 1917 he went to Cleveland as spiritual leader of The Temple in that city. In World War I he served as chaplain in the United States Army in France and later received a high decoration for his service from the French government.

Rabbi Silver built his congregation in Cleveland from a small synagogue to one of the outstanding religious institutions in the country with a membership of 2,500 families. He attracted wide attention early in his ministry through his theological writing, his vigorous and powerful oratory and his advocacy of civil rights, the rights of labor and his activities toward ending unemployment. Under President Hoover he was a member of a national committee formed to fight unemployment. Later, he was chairman of the Ohio Committee on Unemployment Insurance and a founder of this state's unemployment insurance movement.

Meanwhile he had become one of America's most impassioned and most effective spokesmen for the rebirth of the Jewish Homeland in Palestine. He was chairman of the American Zionist Emergency Council in 1933-1934 and again from 1945 to 1948. During the latter period he was one of the leading fighters of world Zionism at the new United Nations and one of the most prominent participants in the UN debates that led to the UN adoption of the Palestine Partition Plan in 1947.

When Rabbi Silver arose in the pulpit to speak about Jewish needs and the Zionist cause, he was a dominant and magnetic figure. His deep, booming voice filled large synagogues and small temples, and when he stood erect, he was more than six feet tall and his grey hair flecked with black, glistened as he shook his head for emphasis.

He had a reputation as a brilliant orator and a keen administrator and negotiator, but his main attribute, many said, was the fact that when he spoke people listened.

Time and again—with an almost around-the-clock unswerving per-

ABBA HILLEL SILVER

severance—he championed the cause of Zionism. He lashed out at the British Administration in Palestine for its policies concerning the Jews. He played one of the major roles in getting resolutions favoring the new state of Israel through both houses of Congress.

His efforts on behalf of the Zionist cause reached a climax on May 8, 1947, when as chairman of the American sector of the Jewish Agency for Palestine he presented a case before a committee of inquiry of the United Nations for the establishment of Israel as a nation. But perhaps his greatest moment came on November 29, 1947, when he pleaded for acceptance by the United Nations of the partition plan that would bring about the rebirth of the State of Israel. And when in the late afternoon of that day the partition plan was voted by the United Nations, he broke down and cried in the United Nations waiting room and uttered a prayer of gratitude in Hebrew.

Once independence was proclaimed, former President Harry S. Truman acted swiftly to extend de facto recognition, to exchange diplomatic representatives, to negotiate a $100,000,000 loan, and to support Israel's application for United Nations membership.

On May 14, 1948, with the birth of the Jewish State, new horizons opened up for the Zionist organization and its institutions. No longer a "State on the way," the Zionist organization became a faithful ambassador of the Jewish State to the mass of Jewish people in the Diaspora. The common effort was now concentrated on mass immigration, the rapid absorption of the newcomers, and the upbuilding of the country. Toward this end no community abroad has played as magnificent a role as the Jews of America. Their profound appreciation of Israel's great struggle to create a nation for the oppressed and homeless of seventy lands around the world has expressed itself in the most generous outpouring of free gifts the world has ever known.

Abba Hillel Silver

§236

1948 § DAVID MARCUS: Israel's Secret Warrior

At four o'clock on the afternoon of May 14, 1948, David Ben-Gurion read to a small audience in the Museum of Art in Tel Aviv: "We . . . hereby proclaim the establishment of the Jewish State in Palestine to be called Israel."

After centuries of persecution and wandering, after inhuman suf-

COLONEL DAVID MARCUS

fering and superhuman sacrifice, the ancient hope was fulfilled. A people breathed the air of a free land, a land where it could be itself once more. Dr. Chaim Weizmann, world-famous chemist and early Zionist leader who was instrumental in the issuance of the Balfour Declaration, was named Israel's first president.

It is a strange thing. Many years before the men of the American Revolution proclaimed the doctrine, "Resistance to tyranny is obedience to God." These founding fathers of America found inspiration in the Bible story of the Jews in Ancient Palestine. In our own day, the Jews of Palestine found inspiration for their struggle in the story of the founding of America and the fight necessary to attain its liberty. In Palestine, Jews showed they were willing to give of "their lives, fortunes, and sacred honor" as our own Declaration of Independence puts it.

American Jews who had just put off their uniforms following World War II could not stand idly by. They could not read of the suffering Jews of the displaced persons camps, or of a tyranny whose word and solemn promise could not be trusted from day to day. They had not fought a war for such a solution.

Dov Seligman, of the Bronx, New York, was one of the many young Americans who went from uniform to uniform. Their war was somehow not to be counted finished until the last displaced person was provided with an address. In January 1942, Dov, a two hundred pound six footer, enlisted in the United States Army. In 1944 he was sent to the Pacific Theater as a sergeant in the ground crew of an air transport command unit. In 1946 he was mustered out and promptly transferred to Palestine in a settlement owned and operated by Shomer Hatzair, a Zionist youth organization. Early in 1948, while driving a tractor on the collective settlement, he was ambushed by the Arabs and killed. This announcement followed by two days the disclosure that another American, Moshe Pearlstein, a Brooklyn youth, had been slain by Arabs in the Holy Land while leading a food convoy to a settlement of Hapoel Hamizrachi.

October 10, 1948, was set aside to honor another fallen Brooklyn hero. It was called "Colonel Marcus Day" in memory of Colonel David Marcus, a veteran of World War II who was killed on June 11, 1948, while leading Israeli troops near Jerusalem. In almost incredible confluence of ironic circumstances like Stonewall Jackson of American Civil War fame, Mickey Marcus was accidentally shot down by one of his own sentries.

Marcus devoted to Israel less than the last half year of an action-rich life that was snuffed out so haphazardly at forty-six. His teaching and example continued their impact through the later, brilliant stages of the Independence War and even at Sinai eight years later.

David "Mickey" Marcus was born on Washington's birthday, 1901, in New York's Lower East Side.

A graduate of West Point he was at various times the intercollegiate welter-weight champion, New York Commissioner of Correction under Fiorello La Guardia, Commander of the Ranger's Training School in Hawaii, volunteer paratrooper in Normandy and Pentagon legal adviser to two presidents. His ten military decorations included the Distinguished Service Medal and Commander of the British Empire.

But the crowning point of his career came in the Holy Land, where, although lacking previous identification with Zionism, he blazed a trail of leadership and inspiration from the moment of his arrival on February 2, 1948.

In the few short weeks of March, 1948, Mickey Marcus had written out in long-hand the 400-page Military Manual that became the basis for Officer's Training in Israel—blending the best in the Israeli's wartime British and pre-independence underground experience with American techniques. He injected into the night-fighting Palmach—Israel's Partisan-style raiders—the vital virtues of discipline and chain-of-command obedience. He persuaded the civilian chiefs that shoes and clothing were as important to soldiers as guns, the military chiefs that a brigade was more effective than battalions and a division more mobile than brigades. He preached successfully the doctrines of concentrated attack—the "striking fist"—and of surprise harassment, helping thus to confuse and halt the armored Egyptian advance in the Negev. He had a major hand in planning three offensives against Jordanian-held Latrun, the key to Jerusalem.

A measure of the Israelis' esteem was that in their time of sharpest peril they entrusted to this foreigner the unifying supreme command over all elements on their central front. With it they gave Marcus the effective grade of General. He was the first to hold such rank in Israel's modern army, and the first in Israel since the time of Judah Maccabee, in 167 B.C.E.

Between the memorable battles against the Arab Legion at Latrun, Colonel Marcus constructed the Israeli "Burma Road," the incredible cliff-hurdling highway that decisively shattered the enemy stranglehold on Jerusalem.

A few hours before the first truce, death came to the gallant West Pointer who was described by David Ben-Gurion as "the best man we had."

David "Mickey" Marcus had fallen within a hundred feet of the spot where many centuries before, the immortal warrior-king for whom he was named had danced and sung in praise of the Lord.

The perfect accolade for this hero came from ex-President Truman, who wrote that the life and death of Colonel Marcus "symbolizes all that is best in the unending struggle for liberty."

He is the only American buried in the venerable cemetery at West Point who was killed fighting under a flag other than the Stars and Stripes. His epitath reads, "Colonel David Marcus—a soldier for all humanity."

In 1962 Doubleday and Company published *Cast a Giant Shadow* by Ted Berkman, a biography of Colonel David Marcus, the American war hero who, as Supreme Commander of Haganah, broke the Arab siege and saved Jerusalem.

Mr. Berkman implies, without ever saying it, that even without the crowning fulfillment of the passage through Israel, the life of David Marcus had already "cast a giant shadow."

1949 § HERBERT LEHMAN: Governor, Senator and Philanthropist

Herbert Lehman, a leader in reform democratic circles, was the first of his faith to be elected to the United States Senate by popular vote. Other American Jews who had served in the upper house of Congress before him had been either appointed or elected by state legislatures, a procedure changed by the 17th Amendment to the Constitution which called for election by the people. Four times he was elected governor of the State of New York. In all, Herbert Lehman won more state-wide elections than any other person in New York's history.

He was born on March 28, 1878, in a brownstone house near New York's Central Park, a section in which he lived for the rest of his life.

He was the seventh son of Mayer and Babette (Newgass) Lehman and his father was a prosperous private banker. Mayer Lehman and two brothers, Henry and Emanuel, had left Germany in 1848 and emigrated to Montgomery, Alabama where all were active supporters of the Confederacy.

Their cotton warehouse was burned during the Civil War and in 1858 they moved to New York and the firm of H. Lehman became the banking firm of Lehman Brothers. Lehman Brothers co-founded the New York Cotton Exchange. Among the companies the firm had bought into, along with P. A. B. Widener and John Jacob Astor, was the Electric Vehicle Company, an early automobile manufacturer, and the Rubber Tire Wheel Company of Springfield, Ohio, the first American maker of pneumatic tires. In spite of his background of luxury and affluence, young Lehman was to dedicate much of his time to the widest possible public and humanitarian interests.

The future Governor and Senator attended Dr. Sachs Collegiate Institute in 1891 and after his graduation was sent by his father to the Columbia University School of Mines. One of his professors advised the banker that he had no talent for engineering so that in 1895 Herbert transferred to Williams College. Although he was a rather shy young man, he was chosen president of his class one year. He managed the track team, was acting manager of the football team and was the fact-assembling, rather than oratorical, member of the debating team. He graduated with a B.A. degree in 1899.

After graduation, Lehman went to work as a salesman of cotton goods for the textile firm of J. Spencer Turner and Company. By 1906 he had advanced in this firm to vice president and treasurer. Having proved himself, he was then taken into the family bank as a partner in 1908. During the next twenty years he made a large fortune and was active as a director in many corporations. (Today Lehman partners sit on boards or dozens of United States corporations, guide several billion dollars worth of investment funds, including the assets of the Lehman Corporation, itself a half-billion-dollar concern).

But even before Herbert landed his first job, he had undertaken the other responsibilities which his family felt they owed the community. He went to the Henry Street Settlement and asked Lillian Wald the director, "Give me something to do."

Lehman entered upon philanthropic service supervising a club for boys at the Henry Street Settlement. Expanding his community interests, altogether he was to serve more than twenty-five other philanthropic and educational organizations, displaying special interest in those dealing with child welfare.

He acquired a beginning interest in politics and became a delegate from his assembly district to the 1910 Democratic State Convention. Mr. Lehman was a serious citizen who approached the democratic process of nomination with careful deliberation.

When the United States entered World War I, he was turned down for infantry officer training because he was ten years overage.

He worked in the office of Franklin D. Roosevelt, then Assistant Secretary of the Navy, for several months, then obtained a direct commission as a captain in the army.

When the war ended, he was a colonel, handling procurement and transportation on the general staff.

In the early twenties Lehman joined a democratic club and through his political work met Alfred E. Smith. He was named by Governor Smith as a mediator of industrial disputes in the garment industry. Then he became a member of a commission to revise the banking laws of New York state. So conspicuous was his ability that soon he was prevailed upon to run for public office. He won his first election as lieutenant-governor of New York in 1928 as the running mate of Franklin D. Roosevelt. To Roosevelt, Lehman was "my good right arm," and Lehman regarded F.D.R. as "one of the great men of

HERBERT LEHMAN

modern history." When Roosevelt went to the White House in 1932, Lehman was elected Governor. He was re-elected governor three times and served in that high office for ten years. In all, Herbert Lehman won more state-wide elections than any other person in New York's history. He obtained national recognition as a man of courage, industry and social idealism. Senator Paul Douglas once described Herbert Lehman as "the closest thing to a saint I've met in politics."

His accomplishments as governor included a revitalized workmen's compensation law; creation of labor relations and mediation boards; establishment of unemployment insurance; savings bank insurance; assistance to the aged, blind, crippled and dependent children; a great public housing program, minimum wages legislation and extended expansion of the state's public park system.

Applying business techniques to the management of the state government, he converted a state budget deficit of $106,000,0000 which he found when he took office in 1932 into a surplus of $80,000,000 when he left.

In 1942, he resigned the governorship to become President Roosevelt's Director-General of the United Nations Relief and Rehabilitation Administration. As head of UNRRA he established the agency's successful program of aiding the many millions of displaced persons, refugees and other victims of the enormous devastation of World War II.

In 1949 at seventy-one, Lehman went to Washington as Senator from New York, to open a colorful new phase of his public activities. The new Senator began his services at the opening session of the Eighty-first Congress. He served two terms and became known as "the conscience of the Senate" and as America's greatest champion of civil rights and anti-discrimination. When others quavered before the onslaught of McCarthyism, it was Herbert Lehman who offered the resolution for the removal of the Wisconsin demogogue from his committee chairmanship. On matters close to his heart—immigration to continue the American dream and civil rights to uphold the American constitution—he battled relentlessly against the forces of evil.

In 1956 Lehman announced that he would not seek reelection. While formally retired from politics, he remained an active and powerful influence in the Democratic party in the city and state.

Throughout his lifetime, Herbert Lehman was a contributor and highly successful fund raiser for the Federation of Jewish Philanthropies of New York, the United Jewish Appeal and many other Jewish causes.

In 1914 he helped organize the American Joint Distribution Committee, the major channel for American aid to needy Jews throughout the world.

After he had passed his eightieth birthday, he could still be found in rain and cold carrying on his crusade for social and political betterment in every section of the city.

He died suddenly of a heart attack at his home on December 5, 1963, aged eighty-five. He had no warning before the end came. His bags were packed the same day for a trip to Washington to receive from President Lyndon B. Johnson the Presidential Medal of Freedom, the nation's highest peace time award to a civilian. The citation, given to him posthumously, read: "Citizen and statesman, he used wisdom and compassion as the tools of government and has made politics the highest form of public service."

Former social worker, governor, United States senator, director of United Nations Relief and Rehabilitation, and philanthropist, Herbert Lehman left a legacy of public service that would be difficult to emulate.

Revered by all, the memory of this great man of private heart and public courage will live on to inspire us for generations to come.

Eddie Cantor

§244

In every phase of American life in which they have participated, Jews have exhibited a wealth of talent and ability. To the stage, screen, radio and television, they have contributed an amazing number of gifted entertainers.

Eddie Cantor, America's widely beloved vaudeville comedian and screen star, was the artist who, like Al Jolson, entertained New York on Broadway, all of America over the radio and television, and the entire world by his musical films.

He was the first American actor to receive the degree of doctor of philosophy in recognition of his art. The citation bestowed upon him on June 14, 1951, by Temple University, appropriately read:

> A great American, endowed with high personal ideals and generosity of spirit, whose innate talents as entertainer have made him a national institution . . . His great use of his life is to spend it for something that outlasts life itself, for his humane activities in bringing pleasure to mankind do not end at the footlights or before the cameras.

Born in 1893 on New York's Lower East Side with all the cards stacked against him, Eddie Cantor grew up to be a highly rated screen, stage, and television comedian, philanthropist, model husband and father.

Cantor made his "professional" debut at amateur night in Miner's Bowery Theater at the age of eighteen. He then became a singing waiter in Coney Island. His first real break came in 1912 when he joined Gus Edwards "Kid Kabaret" along with George Jessel and Walter Winchell, who was then a dancer. A good part in his first musical comedy quickly followed, as did an offer from the fabulous Florenz Ziegfeld to appear in the *Midnight Frolics*, and his marriage to Ida. Soon came *Broadway Brevities* in 1920, *Make It Snappy* in 1922, and stardom in *Kid Boots* in 1923. Reaching the top, he made many movies, including such hits as *Whoopee, Kid From Spain, Roman Scandals*, and *Strike Me Pink*. Later he entered radio. Besides entertaining millions, he introduced such stars as Deanna Durbin, Dinah Shore, George Burns, Gracie Allen, and Eddie Fisher.

EDDIE CANTOR

Despite his rise to fame, the banjo-eyed star never forgot the underprivileged youth. In the early 1930's he financed a camp in New York for improverished children. When Hitler came to power, he conducted an intensive tour of England and the United States to raise funds for Youth Aliyah so that refugee children could escape to Israel. He brought in close to a million dollars. When Israel faced an unprecedented economic emergency situation, he led a great drive in behalf of Israel Bonds, giving unstintingly of his time and talent.

With all the joy he has afforded audiences, and all the extraordinary service he has performed for the State of Israel, the underprivileged and oppressed, Eddie Cantor was equally admired for what he did in the struggle against the terrible killer, polio. Not only did he originate the "March of Dimes," but he gave the nation-wide campaign its name. Begun by him in 1936, the March of Dimes became one of the widest spread and best known campaigns against disease.

Donating to numerous charities and working for better intercultural relations, he has spent almost as much time in welfare work during the past quarter of a century as in being an entertainer. For his humanitarian work alone he was cited by the Congress of the United States.

Hollywood itself placed its stamp of approval on a famous and universally beloved human being when it made the motion picture known as *The Eddie Cantor Story.* Often hilarious, often touching, it tells the story of the unconquerable spirit with which Eddie Cantor fought his way up out of the slums to the topmost peak in the entertainment world with his name flashing among the brightest lights of Broadway and from there across the country and around the world.

Eddie Cantor

The banjo-eyed comedian whose clowning, singing, dancing and pattycake hands entertained millions during more than fifty years in show business died on October 10, 1964 at the age of seventy-two.

§246

Earlier that year he had received a medal from President Lyndon Johnson for his service to the United States and to humanity.

As president of the Jewish Theatrical Guild, as philanthropist, as originator of a great humanitarian campaign, as an actor and comedian, Eddie Cantor richly deserved the praise he received from his own people and the love of all Americans.

1955 § JONAS SALK: Conqueror of Polio

American Jews have made notable contributions to medicine in many of its branches. Several have won the Nobel Prize and have made significant medical discoveries.

At the age of forty, Dr. Jonas Salk became world-famous as the discoverer of the anti-poliomyelitis vaccine that bears his name. Dr. Salk's vaccine has now become mankind's most powerful weapon to beat back the forces of this dreadful disease.

It was an odd set of circumstances that led the quiet and modest scientist to one of the world's outstanding discoveries in the continuous struggle against the dread diseases of mankind.

Born in 1914, Jonas Salk attended the public schools of New York City and Townsend Harris High School which was reserved for exceptionally bright students. He entered the College of the City of New York at the early age of fifteen. His intention was to study law, but, as a freshman, he suddenly decided to add science to his curriculum purely to give himself a broader background. At once he saw where his real interest lay. From then on his life was to be all science. He entered New York University's School of Medicine. There, after his first year, he won successive fellowships in chemistry, experimental surgery and bacteriology. He went on to take his degree in medicine and to interne at the Mount Sinai Hospital, but now his full interest was in research.

He began his work on the influenza virus while still a medical student and resumed it once again in 1942 when the National Research Council awarded him a fellowship at the University of Michigan. There he rejoined an old teacher, Dr. Thomas Francis, Jr., and together they developed the influenza vaccines now in use.

In 1947 the University of Pittsburgh's Medical School expanded its work in the field of virus research and Dr. Salk joined its staff as director of its special virus research laboratory. While he began to work on his major task, he became interested in the prevention of poliomyelitis.

For years scientists had sought in vain a means to control this disease. In the course of time and with a March of Dimes grant, Dr. Salk acquired his first prerequisite: a collection of representative strains of all three types of polio virus. A second prerequisite was furnished by the discovery of Dr. John F. Enders, of the Children's Medical Center in Boston, of a simple method of growing the virus in a test tube.

When Dr. Salk finally discovered the vaccine he thought would work, he chose to use himself and his own three young sons as subjects for the first experimental injection. When that worked, further experiments continued on a broader scale with many children. And

JONAS SALK

then in 1954, the National Foundation for Infantile Paralysis put the Salk vaccine to test in the greatest medical experiment ever undertaken. At a cost of $7,500,000, a total of 422,743 children in forty-eight states received the vaccine. Others got "placebo" (blank) shots; still others were merely observed.

Some of those who did not get the vaccine got polio; many were crippled and some died. Of those who got the vaccine up to ninety percent were spared the effects of the disease. Now for the first time in medical history an effective means of preventing the disease had been found. The Salk vaccine was safe, effective and potent.

On April 12, 1955, the official licensing of the Salk vaccine took place.

In that same year the Commonwealth of Pennsylvania established a Chair of Preventive Medicine for Dr. Salk at the University of Pittsburgh. Dr. Salk's title was later changed to Commonwealth Professor of Experimental Medicine.

Today all forms of poliomyelitis, both paralytic and non-paralytic, have virtually vanished from the United States.

The effect of the use of the vaccine was such as to make it clear that Dr. Salk's attention could be turned elsewhere. In 1960 plans were announced for the establishment of the Salk Institute for Biological Studies in San Diego, California, but it was not until 1963 that work began in temporary laboratories there. By the summer of 1966 the new permanent structures to house the Institute which received its major financial support from the March of Dimes were ready and operating. Here Dr. Salk and the institute faculty of foremost scientists from many parts of the world are looking into many disease areas.

There is talk of the possibility that a single vaccine may be developed to protect a child against many common infectious diseases. There is the speculation about the power to isolate and perhaps eliminate certain genetic errors that lead to birth defects. There is also talk of creativity.

As a biologist Dr. Salk believes that science is on the frontier of tremendous new discoveries; a philosopher, he is convinced that humanists and artists and scientists must join to achieve an understanding of man in all his physical, mental and spiritual complexity. Such interchanges might lead, he would hope, to a new and important school of thinkers he would designate as biophilosophers.

Americans Jews have recognized that the equality of all citizens under the American constitution imposes civic duties and responsibilities. They have taken part in municipal, state and national affairs. They have been elected and reelected, often for decades as mayors, aldermen, city counselors and congressmen, as state and federal senators, and as judges of municipal, county, district and state courts. Some have been appointed to high public office.

Arthur J. Goldberg

§249

On July 20, 1965, Arthur J. Goldberg was appointed to the high diplomatic post of United States representative (chief delegate) to the United Nations. Known widely in the past for his skill as a labor-management peacemaker, Goldberg, who was summoned at the request of President Lyndon B. Johnson, brought to the post a record of achievement which won for him an earnest and respectful hearing in the world's highest parliament. He succeeded the late Adlai E. Stevenson to a post President Johnson considered imperative to the attainment of a lasting peace. Ambassador Goldberg had served previously as Secretary of Labor in former President John F. Kennedy's Cabinet and as an Associate Justice of the United States Supreme Court.

At his swearing-in ceremony at the White House on July 26, 1965, he expressed his philosophy best. He was going "to New York to curse no one but in my own way to help keep the candle of peace burning." And he added:

"I have no illusions that peace can be achieved rapidly, but I have every confidence that it is going to be possible to inch forward to it, inch by agonizing inch."

Dynamic, persuasive and, when the occasion demanded truculent, Ambassador Goldberg, one of the nation's most prominent labor lawyers for a quarter of a century has had a voice in every significant labor-management decision.

He played a major role in 1955 in ending the twenty year civil war in American labor and effecting a merger between the American Federation of Labor and the Congress of Industrial Organizations. He drafted the ethics code that became the merged federation's spiritual armor. It was he who proposed to call the organization the AFL-CIO after negotiators had been unable to agree on a name. He

ARTHUR J. GOLDBERG

drew up the no-raiding pact that curbed interunion piracy and spear-headed the mobilization of labor for John F. Kennedy in 1960.

In the million-member United Steelworkers of America, Goldberg often was more president than counsel. His was the dominant union voice when contracts were being concluded. He invented what many analysts consider the most imaginative of all plans for taking the countdown element out of collective bargaining—the establishment in steel of a joint Human Relations Committee to study automation and other explosive problems on a year-round basis without strike deadlines.

As Secretary of Labor, Goldberg came close to converting himself into a one-man peace crusade on the strike front. He plunged into everything from a paralyzing strike of railroad tugs in New York harbor to a threatened walkout of musicians at the Metropolitan Opera. Every opinion poll former President Kennedy took while Goldberg was in his Cabinet showed the Administration's policy of protecting the national interest in labor disputes was the most popular element in its entire program.

Arthur J. Goldberg was born on Chicago's West Side on August 8, 1908, the youngest of the eight children of Joseph and Rebecca Goldberg, poor Jewish immigrants who had come from Russia in the

1890's. His father owned a wagon and a blind horse and made a living carting fruits and vegetables from the Chicago markets to hotels. Arthur was eight years old when his father died and the older children had to go to work to support the younger ones. He was the only one of the Goldberg children to finish high school, but he too started working at the age of twelve. From one of his early jobs, delivering packages for a shoe factory, he received his first lesson in collective bargaining.

While still in high school, Goldberg had attended the trial of Leopold and Loeb and Clarence Darrow's conduct of the defense helped him make up his mind to become a lawyer. Accordingly he entered Northwestern University Law School in the Fall of 1926, working nights at the post office and during vacations as a laborer on a construction job. He received the degree of Bachelor of Law in 1929 and Doctor of Jurisprudence in 1930 graduating summa cum laude. During his senior years he was editor-in-chief of the *Illinois Law Review*.

He practiced law in Chicago from 1929 to 1948 handling many cases for labor unions. In 1948 at the request of Philip Murray, he moved to Washington to become general counsel to the Congress of Industrial Organizations and the United Steelworkers of America, both of which Mr. Murray headed.

During the late 1950's Mr. Goldberg was deeply involved in the Congressional battle over labor reform legislation.

His perception and integrity impressed John F. Kennedy, then a Senator. When Kennedy was elected President he chose Arthur Goldberg to be his Secretary of Labor in 1961.

Mr. Goldberg as Secretary did not confine himself to the mediation of labor disputes. He became one of President Kennedy's closest advisors on a variety of policy questions, many of them far removed from the labor sphere such as foreign affairs, psychological warfare, missiles and the future of arts.

He also directed the beginning of a substantial Federal effort to retrain unemployed workers—the start of the development of a coherent national manpower policy.

It was during the days as Secretary of Labor that Goldberg got to know the then Vice President Johnson well. The two men worked closely on President Kennedy's Committee for Equal Opportunity.

On August 29, 1962 after Justice Felix Frankfurter retired from the Supreme Court, President Kennedy picked Goldberg to fill the vacancy.

The inventiveness of intellect that made him so resourceful a negotiator reflected itself in new approaches to legal history and interpretation.

Many scholars respected him for the thoughtfulness as well as the freshness of his opinions.

His departure for the United Nations position brought a letter from Dean Louis H. Pollak of the Yale Law School asserting that "no man in the history of the Court accomplished so much in so brief a span."

Arthur J. Goldberg

§252

Goldberg's tact, persuasiveness and ingenuity, his ability to arrange a compromise without sacrifice of principle, his activism, enthusiasm and pragmatism—these qualities all became apparent at the United Nations, as in the world of labor, the law and government.

On April 30, 1966, Ambassador Goldberg speaking before the Golden Jubilee Convention of the National Jewish Welfare Board reiterated his sense of belonging to the Jewish people as well as his devotion to their highest ideals. He hailed the "dramatic progress" in the postwar era toward "the breakdown of anti-Semitic barriers" in "virtually every segment of American society," but added a warning that this gain posed the danger of loss of Jewish identity among American Jews.

He cautioned the present American Jewish adult generation against setting itself up as a model "for the succeeding generation." "Our real message to them," he said, "is not our own sterling virtues, nor in our activities but in something far deeper—the Jewish heritage, whose prophetic tradition should be a model and inspiration for the idealist and reformer of tomorrow."

On May 23, 1967, Gamal Abdel Nasser, President of the United Arab Republic imposed a blockade on Israeli shipping through the Gulf of Aquaba to Elath. This is Israel's only port for shipping from the south and east and the main supply route for her vital oil imports. The United States and other countries sought peaceful means of lifting the blockade.

As a defender of truth and the rights of all peoples, the greatness of Ambassador Goldberg's soul was brought out clearly during the United Nations sessions on the Middle East crisis. His voice was that of America as well as that of the United Nations when he defended Israel's rights against the belligerency of the Arab States as supported by the Soviet Union and their friends.

The Defenses of Freedom, Arthur J. Goldberg's first major book in a decade, appeared in 1966. It includes not only his most important addresses and United Nations speeches but his most significant Supreme Court decisions as well. Among the wealth of subjects discussed are: human rights, the rule of law in domestic and international affairs, freedom versus authoritarianism, and freedom of the press. An impassioned yet judicious portrait it is, in effect, the intellectual biography of a brilliant, dedicated and effective public servant.

On April 25, 1968, Ambassador Goldberg announced that he is planning to leave his United Nations post. He will continue to work for peace and look forward to a "tomorrow when strength will walk with justice, peace with progress, and the good life will be for all people."

Arthur J. Goldberg who rose from the slums of Chicago to national and international eminence personifies the continuing opportunity afforded by American democracy to its ablest sons.

Arthur J.
Goldberg

§253